LOST AND FOUND

A Memoir

Ernest Merchant

Publishing Division

Lost and Found
by Ernest Merchant

Copyright © 2017

Published in the United States by
CLASS
Publishing Division
P.O. Box 2884
Pawleys Island, SC 29585
www.ClassAtPawleys.com

ISBN 978-1-941069-70-7

Poetry written (over the years) by Ernest Merchant

Dedicated to my beloved mother,
Lottie Jane Field

Chapters

Chapter One
Black Sheep

For a period of time in my childhood my mother's brother was a sheriff's deputy in our little town of Poland, Maine. When my mother grew exasperated with her children's misbehavior, she took advantage of Uncle Arnold's position to threaten us.

I recall him in full uniform, pistol resting menacingly against his hip, glowering down at me while my mother recounted my juvenile misdeed. I suspected they did not send small children to prison for angering their mothers, and my Uncle Arnold, a benevolent man, appeared to struggle with his role as intimidator and to suppress the smile hovering over his lips while he described to me the horrors of incarceration.

The only significant thing about this memory is it was the first time I was made aware that people were put in cages and forced to live in deplorable conditions as a result of displeasing others.

I was pretty sure I did not ever want to go to jail and, for most of my life, was pretty sure I wouldn't. As with many of the things I thought about myself and how my life would be, I was wrong.

On December 1st, 1998, about mid-afternoon, I was brokering a relatively small drug deal with a local Mexican gangster called Shadow. I sat on my bed with a three ounce bag of crystal meth on my lap and my pistol within reach. Shadow sat across from me in a wrought iron chair and lit the glass pipe to sample my wares. As he inhaled deeply and passed the pipe to me, the house seemed to implode.

Windows crashed in and the doors burst open simultaneously as a dozen police officers swarmed in, dressed in SWAT team riot gear, assault rifles readied for a shootout, yelling, "Police, everybody down!"

It was just like in the movies. It didn't feel real to me and my brain was so addled from long-term drug abuse that it took me a few seconds to realize it was very real and to fully comprehend what was happening to me. Before I could move to hide the drugs and the gun, they crashed through my bedroom door.

Guns pointed at my head, I was instructed to roll over, face down on the bed, and put my hands behind my back to be cuffed. I did as I was told.

I didn't even consider flight or resistance. I felt a surprising calm relief envelop me. It was all over. I was saved. I was saved from myself and the drugs that were killing me, saved from a bullet in the head from the wrong crack head or greedy gangster, saved from a knife in the neck from a tweaked out pimp or one of his desperate whores who had been hanging around my house. Saved from the mounting bills, sleepless nights, bad dope deals, self-starvation, the pity and embarrassment in my friends' faces, and the awful sound of fear and worry in my sweet mother's voice on that rare occasion I had the balls to pick up the phone when she called.

I knew I was going to prison this time and I was scared, but almost eager to get on with it and be removed from a life I couldn't handle anymore and wasn't worth saving. It was the only answer for me by then. I couldn't and wouldn't stop the drugs on my own. I just wanted to get to my cell in the Orange County Jail where I could pull a scratchy gray wool blanket over my head one more time and shut out the world.

The booking process is agonizingly long and humiliating. Finger prints and photos, questions and orders, piercings removed, tattoos photographed for gang related identification, medical and psychiatric evaluations completed, stripped and showered and dressed in my hideous orange jumpsuit, I was sent to the J mod section for homosexual prisoners one more time to ponder my future, sleep, and endure yet another bout of painful withdrawals.

I recognized many of the guards and inmates, and they me. I guess I made those arrogant cops absolutely right when they bid me farewell on my last release with a "see you next time." My fourth visit to jail in two years practically qualified me as a habitual offender now. I didn't really give a shit what they thought, or about anything else at the moment. I grabbed a bed roll and waited for the hollow clang of the cell door opening, directing me to my temporary home. A few inmates stood at their doors, curious of who was joining their community. It was night by the time I lay on my bunk. After a brief greeting for my new cellmate, I was finally allowed to curl in a ball and check out of the world again.

I was assigned a public defender at my first hearing. I had no more money for private attorneys, and it would have been a waste to fight it anyway. Bail was denied. The judge that sentenced me seemed to do so reluctantly. He knew from my records that I was not a career criminal. He knew that prior to the last few years I was a successful and law-abiding citizen who had spiraled downward with addiction. But he also knew that the courts had already given me several opportunities to address my addictions and turn my life around, and it appeared I was unwilling or unable. I had given him no choice but to send me to prison, and he gravely wished me good luck as he handed down my sentence.

Possession of a firearm by a convicted felon in the state of California is a guaranteed prison term, and the only question left was how long I would spend there. I made the public defender's job very easy by pleading guilty to all charges in exchange for a three-year sentence to a California state prison and a subsequent three-year parole term. Given my recent history and my stubborn refusal to change my behavior, I was grateful I was given only three of the seventeen potential years suspended over me. I accepted their offer eagerly and settled in for the wait to "catch the chain."

"Catching the chain" is the term used for the transportation process from county jail to state prison. In transport, the inmates, now wearing red jumpsuits (red is a much better color for me than orange, so I had at least one positive thing to look forward to), were chained at the ankles, cuffed at the wrists, and all chained together at the waist like a team of oxen being led to slaughter.

I used my time waiting for the chain to write my loved ones and question the other inmates on what I might expect once I arrived at state prison. This time I wasn't going into a cushy rehab, and I wasn't going home any time soon. This time I wasn't going to have a home to go back to. This time I would not be in protective custody in the county jail, locked down twenty-three hours a day and separated from the most dangerous inmates. This time I would live, work, and walk the prison yard with thousands of hardened convicts and nothing to protect me beyond my own wiles and wit.

I was naturally nervous of the unknown, but I wasn't scared to go to prison. It couldn't possibly be any worse than the life I was leaving behind, and my sentence was long enough to put some real distance between me and the mess I had made of my life. To some degree I was wrong on both counts.

I can't remember how many days passed before an officer's voice came over the intercom and said, "Roll it up, Merchant, you're catching the chain."

I was about to enter the twilight zone of raw human experience: a men-only world of anger and violence, power, passion, and fear, a world of guilty secrets and false bravado, of broken boys and soulless men, of unreasonable hope and unattainable desires, of justice fairly met and a legal system gone awry, of blood and shit and pain and tears, of men without the gentility of women to calm their savage beast and satisfy their hungers and lust for dominance and power. A world where the color of your skin makes decisions for you and can mean life or death, a world of drugs and sex and a ruthless code of honor few could manage to uphold in the free world, a world where the line between the good guys and the bad guys is blurred and constantly changing without warning, a world where men kill each other over a pack of cigarettes but are willing to die for the honor of a fellow convict.

And sometimes, too, a place of humor and camaraderie, of boyish games and silly pranks, of good-natured competition and friendships bound by many years of mutual hardship, suffering, and loss.

And, sometimes, even a place of love. Love between men who have forgotten the scent of a woman and have abandoned the memories of freedom and family. Men who have turned to each other for either brief, clandestine moments of guilty ecstasy or, more often, unashamed public declarations of commitment and love so dedicated and powerful they rival many marriages ordained outside those walls. Men who have captured and held close the last vestiges of their humanity in the arms of a trusted friend and lover. For them there is no gay or straight, no men or women. There is only what is left when everything else is taken away.

The bus ride to the prison was an initiation of humiliation and discomfort. Chained together in enforced silence, threatened with grievous bodily injury for even speaking, cramped together like sardines in a can, sweating silently, we set out for the long journey from purgatory to hell.

I believe they make the bus ride so brutally uncomfortable that you are actually grateful to finally arrive at their prison and more docile in that gratitude.

The bus makes a few stops along the way to pick up prisoners in other counties. Though absolute silence is enforced through threat and intimidation by the guards, they couldn't silence the thoughts of the men as we contemplated our destination. The air was thick with thought.

For some it is all too familiar. For others, the sheer terror on their faces exposed their inexperienced imaginations.

I wasn't frightened of the other men. Men don't scare me. I decided long ago that I was just about as strong as any other man and sometimes equally as weak. I have always been an object of curiosity and sometimes disdain in the world of men. The attention I received on the bus ride was just a small taste of what was to come. It was an entirely different atmosphere from the county jail already.

On that bus, chained to a stranger, I came to the unavoidable realization that I was officially a loser. For several years I held on to the illusion that I was merely a reluctant visitor in the ghetto underworld of drugs, crime and convicts. I was just a thrill seeker. I wasn't one of them. I saw myself as a sort of prince held captive by the enemy and forced by unfortunate circumstances to live among the peasants and criminals. Surely someone would notice this horrible mistake of justice, rescue me, and send me back to my lovely tree-lined neighborhood in Orange County.

I would sit by my pool sipping mimosas, enthralling my haughty friends with all the sordid details of my social experiments among the underclasses. I would throw a lavish party announcing my return and be welcomed back to my rightful place among the privileged. I would put on a thousand dollar outfit, redecorate my house, and attend the latest theater production all the critics raved about, or fly to Cancun and get a tan on a white sand beach after my dreadful ordeal.

But that is a life for winners. I wasn't a winner anymore. I was a loser and I felt like one. I felt angry and cheated. But most of all I felt determined: determined this was not how it was all going to end for me. I had not come so far from our little house in Maine and selling my teenage ass on the street for a meal and a pack of Marlboros to let it end at thirty-eight years old, chained like a dog, thrown into a cage and treated like shit by a bunch of tin-badge, overpaid, wannabe cops with a whole lot of power and very little intellect or compassion. No way was I going to go out this way, and I was determined everyone know it.

The guards could tell how I felt about them, and they were rankled by my obvious lack of respect for their self-appointed importance and attitudes of superiority. They expected me to be humble and were taken aback by the way I carried myself with confidence, reasonability, and dignity. It's fair to say that, even when I did not feel confident, I strove to appear otherwise.

I recognized that the officers were only doing their job, and I also recognized those that took their job a little too seriously. I was ever vigilant of the exact guidelines of their job description, and did not hesitate to remind one should he feel an impulse to step outside said guidelines and violate what few rights I had left as a human being and an inmate.

I was determined to find my way back to the other side of those chains and walls and the mess I made of my life. I was determined to be brave and smart and strong. To stay clean, find the positives in this experience, and walk out of there changed for the better.

I prayed to the Gods, or God, or whatever powers that be, to let me survive this excursion into hell, and vowed I would turn it all around. I would stay clean, pay my debt to the legal system, and rebuild a life, and a man, I could be proud of again.

Before my final destination I was taken to a part of the prison called a reception center. That sounded very nice to me. One could almost imagine a warm reception where one was welcomed and greeted with flowered leis, a fruity drink with a little umbrella in it, and a sumptuous buffet for the weary traveler. Alas, instead of flowers and cocktails we were greeted with verbal insults, guns and pepper spray. We had arrived at Wasco State Prison, deep in the California desert.

Nearly all of California's prisons are in remote areas of the state. The politicians and prison guards union push for more prisons and convince the voters they are not safe without them, but nobody wants one too close to their expensive neighborhood. The desert and poor agricultural communities welcome the jobs and revenue the prisons provide, and the rest of the state doesn't have to be reminded that they incarcerate more people in their state than any European country. The added benefits of remote locations include the impossibility of escapes. Anyone crafty enough to escape would most assuredly die trying to find their way out of the desert and back to civilization.

It was winter and the high desert can be a bitter cold in winter. As each of us exited the bus, our shackles were removed, and we were ordered to strip.

I was mortified. No man wants to be stripped naked in the cold. We tend to suffer some embarrassing physical side effects in the cold. I was amused to notice many men grab their dicks and give them a few yanks in an attempt to stretch them out in prideful defiance of the brisk temperature. I confess to being one of them. No man wants to appear to have the smallest dick in the room. It's a man thing. I at least refused to be one of those that attempted to cover themselves in shame. My pride would not allow public shame.

I believe the process to be only the beginning of the psychological warfare waged against the inmates by the prison staff. Standing in line at the mouth of the concrete and steel monster, naked, exposed, humiliated, and vulnerable, there is no question who is in control.

Herded like mute cattle into the building where dozens of both male and female correctional officers and non-uniformed staff perform their coldly robotic duties, I perused the hundreds of naked men around me. We were every size, shape, color and age. I was surprised and somewhat saddened to see very young boys and very old men among us. They seemed too vulnerable to be among the rich testosterone-driven power of those in full-fledged manhood. They looked like sparrows among birds of prey.

Prior to prison, my exposure to other prisoners was limited to the protective custody unit of the county jail, where everyone was separated into likeminded groups, and I was unaware of the spectrum of humanity caught in the wide net of our legal system.

Our reception continued with a long series of questions concerning physical and mental health to determine each inmate's housing assignment within the prison. The prisons foremost concern is not an inmate's comfort or safety, but its own liability risks. They are frequently sued by inmates or their families for neglect or abuse and go to great lengths to appear the consummate professionals.

It was certainly a unique experience for me to stand naked in a public place before a strange woman and answer questions concerning my mental disposition. It was tempting to ask her how she would feel if our positions were reversed, but it was pretty clear the staff was not interested in banter or conversation, so I left it alone.

The reception process ends with the infamous cavity search. I find it amusing when I share my prison experience with free people that this is one of the inevitable subjects that arise. The other is prison rape. I suppose these two experiences rank high on the fear scale in people's imaginations. There's enough time now between me and those experiences to have compiled a half dozen standard jokes I use to diffuse the obvious discomfort I sense when broaching these subjects with free people. Neither rape nor a cavity search rank high among the worst things I witnessed in the next two years.

The cavity search only takes about sixty seconds, but it's a long sixty seconds.

We inmates joked about the guy who has the job of cavity searches. What does he talk about when he goes home at night? I wondered if he felt like a politician, looking at other assholes all day.

Still naked, we passed through a metal detector. Why would you have to pass through a metal detector if you're naked? Is it possible for someone to actually hide a gun, knife, or bomb in their anal cavity? I would like to know, with the tens of thousands of men and women that pass through, how many and what kind of interesting artifacts have been discovered in butt holes and vaginas to justify this humiliating procedure. I might even like to meet a few of these anatomically unique people out of sheer curiosity and a grudging respect for their tenacity.

With the officer holding a flashlight, you are ordered

to open your mouth, stick out your tongue, and lift it. You next run your fingers through your hair (if you have any), lift your arms, show the palms of your hands and the soles of your feet, lift your testicles, and, finally, turn your back, bend over, spread your cheeks, and cough. Apparently one has little control over the sphincter when coughing and whatever they might be looking for is expected to fly out and land at their feet. I personally did not witness anything interesting make an exit during my ordeal or during any of the other dozens of cavity searches I endured during my incarceration. I did notice the officer had the forethought to wear protective goggles and stand at a safe distance, which seemed reasonable.

As usual, my tattooed body brought me more attention than even an exhibitionist could tolerate, given the circumstances.

There are some crazy tattoos on convicts, but they are prison tattoos. I can easily spot a prison tat, as opposed to street art, after having been there. Many are crudely done; few have any color other than black and blue, and most are gang- or prison-related in theme. Mine are obviously street work. Colorful and finely crafted custom art, they were nearly all done by a single artist in Southern California, and much envied by the convicts that either never had the opportunity or the money to get professional street tattoos. Both the officers and inmates alike openly admired the ink art on my body. My body art gained me a little respect right away. There's a lot of money and a high tolerance for pain obvious in my tattoos, and both inspire a degree of respect among convicts.

I'm not easily shocked or offended. My years in the LA punk scene exposed me to some wild body art, but some of the convicts really grabbed my attention with their ink. Full body coverage, including the face, head, hands and penis, of violent and grotesque imagery, make it hard to imagine them ever having a normal life outside of prison. I was particularly intrigued with the man who had the word "Fuck" on one eyelid and "You" on the other. I felt he sent a very clear message of an anti-social attitude, and I had no desire to befriend him.

Finally, we were given boxer shorts, the hated orange jumpsuit, socks and cotton slippers, and were allowed to dress. Each of us was given a plastic bag containing a toothbrush, a disposable razor, a comb, a roll of toilet paper, and a booklet titled "California Department of Corrections Title 15 Rules and Regulations."

Once you were in possession of Title 15, ignorance of the rules is an unacceptable excuse for breaking them. I found this to be true as soon as I started breaking them.

It had been a long, torturous day, but I was wired with tension as they led us single file into the belly of the beast. All color other than orange and the drab olive green of the officer's uniforms ceased to exist. Acres of gray concrete and steel surrounded and swallowed me, and the outside world was gone.

There were roughly seven thousand men at Wasco. There are six buildings and three yards.

Our escorting officer held a clip board and deposited each of us at the barred and locked gate of the building we were assigned to. The corridors echoed with the jingling of the officer's keys and the whispering shuffle of our cloth slippers. No other sound penetrated the concrete walls.

When the barred gate closed behind me, a solid steel door opened and the silence abruptly ended, replaced with the voices and activity of a thousand inmates and officers going about their daily lives in one huge rectangular stone warehouse, lined on three sides and two stories high with tiny cells.

Many of the inmates stopped and stared openly as I

handed my new prison ID to an officer seated in his glass office, positioned to view the entire building. My cell had already been assigned before I entered the building. The officer gave me my cell number and pointed me in the right direction. I remained silent during the entire assignment process, other than providing brief answers in response to his direct questions, and went directly to my second tier cell to view my new home.

The newer prisons have done away with the old barred cells we see in the movies. They now have solid steel doors with a small window that allows staff to observe from outside and remain safe from inmate aggression. The cells look the same as at county jail, except smaller. An 8x10 cell holds two bunks, two metal lockers, a combination sink and toilet, and a small steel table with two attached stools. Everything is gray. A sliver of window lets in a shaft of light and looks out on more concrete, steel and razor wire. You may have two feet of available space for two men to move around in. Nothing is soft, warm or inviting. It is a cold, hard womb designed for the gestation of bitterness and deprivation.

The idea some in the free world have of prisoners living a life of comfort and reward on your hard-earned tax dollars is an urban myth. Every time I hear someone complain that inmates are not punished enough, that they watch cable television, eat three delicious meals a day, and get good quality, free medical care, I am simultaneously amused and outraged by their propaganda-driven ignorance. I suppose if you think a two-inch thick mattress on an unyielding slab of steel, food that is unrecognizable let alone edible, freezing in the winter and suffocating in the summer, and smelling someone else's shit from an open toilet two feet away from where you sleep is comfortable. Or waiting up to two weeks to see a nurse just to get a Tylenol, seeing feeble old men struggle to get up a flight of stairs, or watching men die of cancer, hepatitis, and

AIDS from neglect, is good medical care. I suppose if you think living under intimidation and the constant threat of violence, witnessing suicide and murder, humiliation and despair, insanity, loneliness, and hopelessness on a daily basis, is living in the lap of luxury, perhaps you might be living on the wrong side of the bars yourself.

If you have never watched the hopeful faces of hundreds of men fall, day after day, during mail call, as they stand with their faces pressed against the small glass windows of their cells, waiting for just a single card or letter from someone letting them know they are not forgotten nor unforgiven, that they are still a part of the human race. As the officer passes them by, the faces fall away from the window one by one, only to appear again at the same time the next day. There are those who don't get off their bunks anymore during mail call. They know there are no more love letters from wives and girlfriends, no more pictures of the children they left behind. Often their parents die without ever being able to say goodbye. When someone does get a letter or photos from home, he is held in higher esteem for just a moment. The other men want to hear and see every detail of the letter and pictures and vicariously feel the outside world through someone not forgotten.

If you have never seen a man up before the sun on visiting day, dressed and meticulously groomed, as excited as a child on his way to Disney World, sit all day waiting for the promised visit that didn't come, then you know nothing of punishment. Most would rather be beaten daily than forgotten or abandoned. Cuts and bruises heal. Losses are forever.

My cell was empty when I entered, but there were signs I had a cellmate. I knew the first man in gets the bottom bunk. That rule applies to all cell living. I preferred the top bunk anyway.

Before I could climb up and rest from a long stressful day, men started filing past my cell to have a look at me. The guards had already spread the word there was a new "girl" in the building, and that's good for an afternoon of entertainment. All the men who are shopping for a cell-wife start their mating rituals with offerings of favors and material goods, peppering conversation with sexual innuendo and questions of false interest, hoping to have you on your knees by nightfall.

Reception can be a dangerous place. County jail, and your eventual placement in a prison, is determined by levels of security and the danger potential of the inmate. At reception, every level of inmate, except death penalty cases, is thrown together for sorting. A level one first term inmate like me could easily be celled with a dangerous level four career gangster. When my cellmate, commonly called a "cellie," returned from the yard, it didn't take me long to figure out that was exactly what had happened to me.

Al was a hardcore convict. About fifty years old, 6 foot 4 inches tall and muscular, salt and pepper hair, covered with prison ink from neck to ankles, he was an imposing figure. The men who had gathered around the cell door flirting with me quickly dispersed upon his arrival. He didn't greet me with a smile or enthusiasm, but with a nod and a grunt, before stripping to his boxers and flopping down on the bottom bunk. I lay on my bunk waiting for him to speak first and drifted off to sleep.

I woke several times in the night. I stared at the ceiling, listening to Al snoring lightly, and thought about my life and what I had done to it. Regret flooded my spirit, and depression descended on me like a thousand pound weight. All I could think of was the life I had left behind, the time that stretched in front of me, and all the things I would have done differently had I the chance. How had I fucked everything up so badly? The determination I had to survive, only a few hours before, disintegrated in the tiny gray cell. I cried silently in the night and missed the comforting sound of my mother's voice. There are no phones at reception, and I wondered if I would ever hear it again. I realized I had no idea what lay ahead for me. I was a five-hour drive away from my home and all my friends. My family was over three thousand miles away in the little town I grew up in, deep in the Maine country-side. I thought of everything that led me to that little cell – a childhood of torment and humiliation at the hands of bigots and bullies, the years as a homeless teen wandering the country, doing things I didn't want to do in order to survive, searching for something, someplace, someone, that felt right and good, my discovery and engagement of the gay culture of the mid-'70s, my hard won rise to success and privilege, and the scourge of AIDS on the people that became my family in the '80s. I thought of my loves and heartbreaks and the years of wild abandon that culminated in the downward spiral of drug addiction, crime and prison.

It was cold in the cell. I stayed in my clothes, under my single scratchy wool blanket, and wrapped a towel around my head to block out light and sound.

It was a lot to think about, but I had a lot of time to think.

Black Sheep

Hey black sheep, how far will you roam,
away from the normal nest?
Hey black sheep, how uncomfortable is home
when you're different from all the rest?
Hey little lamb, does your life feel lonely
When you feel like the only one?
Because as you wander life's fields
more black sheep are revealed
that have spent their lives too on the run.

E.M.

Chapter Two
Phantoms

There are no pictures of me as a baby. None before my kindergarten picture at five years old. In that one is a big-eyed blond boy in a crew cut and a bow tie who I don't remember being at all. There are few pictures and fewer stories of me as a child, as if I barely existed. I was lost in the crowd of my mother's children in her memory and in my own. I asked my mother once what time of day I was born and she looked exasperated and said, "God! I don't know, honey. I had so many of you I forgot all that." I resented that answer at the time. It made my birth seem inconsequential.

I suppose that's fair. I was the sixth of eight children born in roughly ten years. I imagine it all ran together into one ten-year pregnancy in her memory. Still, I thought my own mother would remember the details of giving birth, regardless of how many times she did it.

Apparently, it was obvious to everyone else that I was different from my five brothers and most all the other boys around me when I was quite young. I didn't feel any different until it started being pointed out to me. I didn't like to play rough, and I didn't like to get dirty. I hated sports, and preferred the company of girls. I clung to my mother, and detested and was terrified of my father, who I thought was an obnoxious, drunken savage. But I didn't know I wasn't supposed to be what came natural to me.

As soon as it became obvious I was not like the other boys, the whispering began. "It must be because of what happened to him," they said. We will get to that, the thing that happened to me. The incident that dogged what was left of my childhood. What I did not need was to be singled out for pity or ridicule. But that's what happened anyway, and I believe it set the stage for my own confused self-image for years to come.

It was certainly hard enough to try to grow up in the tiny rural town of Poland, Maine with an uneducated, impoverished, single mother who struggled and worried to keep clothes on our backs, food in our bellies, and the lights on in our little four-room shanty with no indoor plumbing. With only her meager factory worker's pay in 1962 to sustain us, my mother divorced the drunken, abusive savage that was my namesake and set out to raise eight kids by herself.

My namesake: out of six boys, I was the one burdened with my father's name and therefore the awesome and absurd responsibility of somehow living up to his idea of its value. I'm quite sure he was the only one convinced his name actually had any value, as most associated it with bullshit and brutality. My father brought no honor or dignity to his family name. I suspect few of his predecessors did, either. My paternal family history was not one of good character, and he did nothing to improve it.

My father was a good-looking man. He was an intelligent man with a silver tongue and a quick mind, but he was not a good person, and his was a life of tortured contradictions and unfettered rage. Ma said once, when I asked her what made him so attractive to so many women, "He could talk a girl's panties off before she ever knew what hit her."

I found the image as repulsive as I found him. My father's idea of manhood was that he could "Out fuck, out fight, and out drink any man under the table." Those are his words, not mine.

Later in life I took a mean-spirited pleasure in the irony that a man like my father should be cursed with the very son chosen to carry his name turning out to be gay and far less than the ideal image of manhood he demanded in his sons. I found it a fit punishment for his hypocrisy that I should be as far from his ideal as possible, though I didn't plan it that way.

If I wanted to attempt to defend my father's indefensible life, I could point out that he did not have a fair start, either. His own childhood was not easy as the son of an alcoholic whore of a mother and an absent, small-time gangster and bootlegger for a father.

After his parents' divorce, his mother remarried a man with fists the size of canned hams, and it has been said that he used them liberally on my father. To say my paternal grandparents were colorful is a gentle understatement, and my father's brief childhood was fraught with vice, abuse, and abandonment. Unfortunately, my father never had what it takes to rise above his childhood, and carried on through his life perpetuating the very cruelties he claimed were at fault for his weaknesses and defects of character.

His mother's second husband brought a daughter into the marriage, and my father's younger sister made three. It wasn't until I was grown that I heard the stories of how those two abused each other's children. I don't know if they ever tried to right their wrongs with their kids. But I know that you can never give back a stolen childhood. I know my grandmother was jealous of her stepdaughter, and dressed her in rags and made her life hell, and I heard stories of the brutal beatings my father took from his stepfather before he was thrown into the street to fend for himself at fourteen years old. I suspect my father's sister suffered the same lecherous abuse my step grandfather attempted with many women who crossed his path, but it is only a suspicion, not confirmed. It was less than a year before she died that my mother revealed to me that my step-grandfather had raped her when she was eight months pregnant with one of my siblings, and a former sister-in-law claims to have been sexually assaulted by him also. Ma told me she never allowed my sisters to stay there because she feared he would harm them. She put distance between her children and former in-laws when we were growing up. She knew what kind of people they were and did not trust them.

My mother was a kind woman. Kind even to those that were not kind to her, and her in-laws were not kind to her. I recall her telling me of an incident where she complained to her mother-in-law that my father was beating her and drinking all their money, and my grandmother slapped her face and told her never to complain to her about her son, and it was her own fault for getting pregnant. So she kept her secrets and her fear close to keep the peace, and I was a grown man before she told me the ugly truths about my paternal grandparents. I don't know why she decided to tell me these things at the end of her life, except maybe to reassure me for the last time that life is not really fair, and that bad things happen to good people, that people are not always who you think they are, and that you just have to get through it, like she did.

When my grandmother aged past her whoredom and remarried, they opted for a country life and moved my father, his sister and stepsister a quarter mile down the road from an old farmhouse occupied by a simple and sweet farming family who probably had no idea what kind of trouble had just arrived on their old dirt road. Or that their new neighbors would forever change their lives and youngest daughter's future.

Their youngest child was a naive, sweet girl named Lottie Jane. Lottie Jane was my mother. She was twelve when my father moved down the road, and he was fourteen. My Gram said he was already "hell on wheels."

My maternal grandparents were polar opposites of their new neighbors. I can only imagine the look on my Grandmother Fannie's face the first time she encountered the tattooed, foul-mouthed, chain-smoking, bleach-blonde woman they called "the Blonde Bomber," more formally known as Maisie.

Ma's mother Fannie was a perfect rendition of the Norman Rockwell granny with the curly silver hair, wire-framed glasses, flower-print dresses, no makeup or jewelry save her wedding band. She never drove a car, flew in an airplane or wore a pair of high-heeled shoes. She never drank, smoked or cussed, and I'm absolutely sure my Grandpa was the only man she had ever lain with. She smelled of talcum powder and lavender, was soft-spoken and kind-hearted. And I am confident that anyone who knew her would agree that she was entirely without flaws in her character.

I remember them as always being old, so the stories of all my grandparents as young people fascinated me. They smiled at the memories of their family life before my father came along and made their lives so hard. Ma was born during the great depression, and they were poor, but her memories of childhood were happy.

Naturally, many of the young girls in town were enamored with the blond-haired, blue-eyed bad boy that moved to town, and I suppose their mothers were equally wary of him. My mother had the advantage of geographic proximity, and the friendship of my father's two younger sisters.

She also had the disadvantage of growing up in an environment that prohibited the kind of discussions mothers have with their daughters now about how to avoid unwanted pregnancies. Ma told me she had no idea what was happening to her when she got her first period, and Gram was too embarrassed to talk about it. At fourteen she believed a girl could get pregnant by French kissing. I'm not sure she was joking when she said she wasn't absolutely sure how a girl got pregnant until she had been so gotten, at seventeen and unmarried, by my father, the town's resident juvenile delinquent.

Such a scandal it must have been! Add that to the fact that at nineteen, my father had already been married and divorced, fathered two children while in the military, and fathered an illegitimate daughter with another young woman who refused his proposal of marriage. He went on to father fourteen children and stepfather six more among six women in the course his life. He was fifty-five when he fathered his last known offspring with his nineteen-year-old wife. Unsurprisingly, he is ending his life virtually alone, and I have spent only a little time resenting the irony that he outlived my mother, and take solace in the assurance that her life was a life of quality, lived with love and remembered fondly and respectfully, while his continues with the same loneliness and deprivation that he heaped so mercilessly upon those he should have cherished, and he will quickly be forgotten and thought of only as an example of a wasted life.

Suffice it to say that my father could not bear the sight of me. It was inevitable that my presence offended his masculinity to the extent that the very sight of my face or sound of my voice provoked his criticism and rage. My obvious terror in his presence did not elicit one iota of compassion, but quite the opposite. He enjoyed terrorizing those he loved. He was a bully. As with all bullies, my perceived weakness only emboldened him to further torment and humiliate me in his self-appointed duty to "make a real man out of me." I suspect he only repeated what was done to him as a boy. It was what he knew.

My poor sweet mother, having suffered years of his brutality, tried to balance the power he had as the father of her children, her fear of his vicious reprisals when contradicted, and her protective instinct for her babies.

My father does not merit a starring role in my story. He is merely the first villainous male I remember, and one who set the bar high for any in the future.

My mother, Lottie, was a woman worth remembering, worth talking and writing about, a woman of strength and dignity, passion and humor, kindness and, above all else, love. If my mother loved you, she would always love you, no matter what you did.

She was the baby of four – two brothers and a sister – and what many may have considered the naive, full-figured, farmer's daughter, often the main character in all the old traveling salesman's jokes. She was a buxom, blue-eyed brunette. Not beautiful, but pretty, and made almost beautiful by a shy but saucily mischievous demeanor.

I reach out for the memories of my mother's love, strength, loyalty, and humor when I am lonesome, afraid, or lack confidence in myself. Though at this writing she has been deceased nine months, she continues to be our family's favorite topic of conversation. I am confident that the stories of the humble but extraordinary woman who birthed a bloodline that will survive centuries will do justice to her memory. In death, her life is becoming nearly mythic.

She was only twenty-five when I was born, and I am sixth in line. Her eighth child was born right after she turned twenty-eight. Eight kids in ten years. It's exhausting to even think about. She used to say it took her that long to figure out what was causing it. Then she would giggle and say, "I never was too smart, ya know."

She was altogether so honestly human, and without guile or pretense. She was a natural woman, and yet sometimes she seemed like a little girl with the weight of a thousand women whose dreams were shattered by no-good men sitting on her little shoulders.

She smoked nearly all her life, but rarely took a drink. Alcohol was the force that fueled my father's rage, plagued her second marriage and several of her children's lives, and she hated it and what it did to people. I recall her saying more than once, "They should wipe that shit right off the goddamn planet. It doesn't do anybody any good."

If you find a contradiction in my description of my mother as a woman raising her children alone while she and my stepfather were together forty-two years (seventeen unmarried and twenty-five more as man and wife), it is because my mother's children were her responsibility, and he did not participate in the support or influence of our development or discipline. He had three daughters of his own whom he did not see often, but when they grew older they joined our family, and loved my mother as their own. Everett was not a bad man, but he was absent as an active father to us, and to his own daughters as well.

My stepfather was in his late twenties when they met. Still a young man with a lot of wild oats to sow, he spent a large part of his working life as a long-haul trucker, and a lot of his free time on a bar stool. He tended to visit rather than live with us, and it was probably best that way for the both of them. She had been hurt by every man she'd met before him and had zero trust in men as husbands or fathers. She was jealous and suspicious of him, as all of her relationships before my stepfather provided more than ample reason for her mistrust.

I wasn't aware, until far into adulthood, that the incident that resulted in "what happened to Ernie" and, simultaneously my year-older sister Tina, at the hands of a trusted lover was a catalyst for how she conducted her relationships, and would endow her with guilt and suspicion for the rest of her life.

When I was old enough to hear them (and she was too old to keep her secrets any longer), she told me the stories of the humiliation, deprivation and abuse that were the chronicle of her marriage to my father, the rape by her father-in-law, a brief love affair that resulted in one of my younger brothers being fathered by another man, the lascivious advances of the married men in our small town, the trusted lover who shattered her heart and family by sexually abusing two of her children, and, finally, the quiet, brooding, hard-drinking country boy who became my stepfather.

She worked in the shoe factories all her life, making only seventy-two cents per hour when she divorced Dad, and some years picking apples in the orchards to make a little extra money when the factory work was slow. She worked hard and was known and respected for her work ethic. She struggled to get by and care for her loved ones. She embodied the finest qualities of her own mother, but was considerably more hard-edged than my saintly Gram. Life had dealt her enough blows that she grew tough to fight back. She had a very clear breaking point when pushed, and didn't take too much shit before letting someone have it.

Lottie Jane was not the saint her mother was. The School of Hard Knocks made that impossible. But she was a woman of substance, a woman of solid character and humility. She could be trusted. She was a comforting blend of discipline and free-spirited naked emotion, and you always knew where you stood with her. She was soft-hearted and compassionate. She felt bad for people who had it hard (and few had it any worse than she did), she wept at sad movies and stories of other peoples tragedies, and often pointed out to us how lucky we were compared to those less fortunate. I remember wrinkling my nose at our dumpy existence and wondered who the hell was less fortunate than us?

Growing up in that run-down little house with no indoor plumbing was embarrassing to me. It had only four small rooms: a kitchen, a living room and two bedrooms. Each room had a single window. The bedroom for us kids was never sheet-rocked, had a single bare bulb hanging from the ceiling, and roughhewn wood floors peeking through the worn linoleum. The house had only one small closet and no doors inside. Cloth curtains hung in the doorways for privacy. Ma bathed us in a washtub in the kitchen with water carried from a brook on our property, and she washed our hands and faces with a wet cloth every morning before school. I remember a hole in the kitchen floor where the wood had rotted, and you could smell the damp dirt cellar if you put your face close to it. Ma kept it covered with a throw rug. I remember side-stepping that hole in fear of falling through to a black grave of dirt. Our furniture and most of our clothes were the cast-offs of the more fortunate. We kids rarely invited other kids to our house in fear that they would ask to use the bathroom, and we would have to direct them to the outhouse. Our little house was in a beautiful spot in the country, accessed by a road that was dirt when I was boy, but is paved now. A small brook ran down one side of the property. It provided fresh water, small brook trout, and countless hours of entertainment for us kids. Wild strawberries, blueberries, raspberries and blackberries were at our back door seasonally, and the front windows faced an empty field perfect for ballgames when it wasn't buried in snow. Though now the empty field has houses and yards, and the dirt road is paved and busy, there are still deep woods in the back where berries can be found and the brook still babbles, though it seems so much smaller now than it was when I was a child.

I was ashamed of being poor. I exasperated my mother with unreasonable demands, completely unaware of how she struggled to cover just the necessities. My father never paid a penny of child support for any of his children. She was on her own. His wives either feared his retaliation or were so grateful to be rid of him that they never sought to force him to help raise his children. Ma was grateful just to get by.

I lived in a fantasy world of books and TV shows like the Brady Bunch and the Partridge Family, where everyone wore the latest fashions, had their own rooms and possessions, and had two parents whose sole purpose in life appeared to be the happiness and comfort of their children. I dreamed of a life where everything was pretty and everyone was nice. Ma insisted I was a sweet and quiet child until puberty hit and all hell broke loose.

I remember my childhood only in bits and pieces, like flashbacks, but can't actually see or feel it as a whole experience. I wonder sometimes if everyone is that way or just me. I'm not sure how old I was, maybe seven or eight, when people started noticing I was not like most of the boys around me, but I do know they started calling me "faggot" long before I understood what it meant.

I did cling to my mother, and recall her often pushing me out the door and telling me I should go play with the boys. I didn't like the boys. They were too rough. They were too physical. Their idea of fun usually involved getting dirty or bloody, and neither of those options appealed to me.

Ma even made a half-hearted attempt to introduce me, unwillingly, to the world of boys by forcing me to play little league baseball. I was a dismal failure. I hated every minute of it and was not good at hitting or catching a ball.

It was confirmed by the other players with their groans and taunts when it was my turn at bat. I was pissed at her for that humiliation, but I realize now she thought it was the right thing to do, her duty as both mother and father.

Other kids made fun of me. I remember her exclamation of dismay when asking my older brother, "Why does everyone pick on him, there's nothing wrong with him." I love that she said that and felt that way, but it was only a few years later, when I started to change and give her trouble, that she changed her mantra to "What the hell is wrong with you?"

Now that I am fifty years old, and out of the closet thirty-five years, I can look back at how it all unfolded, and so much of it makes sense. How difficult it must have been for her to have a child she did not understand, a child different from her others and her friends' children, and how she thought each one of us reflected back her capability as a mother.

The world we live in today is very different for young gays. They have openly gay icons to admire and emulate. Movie and music stars, sports figures and even politicians have come out and provided positive images of successful, confident, and happy gay people to encourage and identify with. People actually talk openly about it. My generation didn't have that. Our youth was spent in fear, loneliness and isolation. And those that came before us for a thousand years had it infinitely worse.

Nevertheless, being gay in rural Maine with seven non-gay brothers and sisters to be constantly compared to and competed with was, at the very least, a test of character and strength that I did not intentionally aspire to, and to this day would not wish on anyone except my few enemies.

Unfortunately, "What happened to Ernie" was to be not only the end of my innocence at six years old but also the way I was defined by the people around me, and possibly how I came to define myself. Years later, in the various forms of therapy and rehabs that I found myself, I learned much about the shaping of personalities and social structure that develops around the child designated with victim status.

So, I am the molested child.

The series of events following this brief period of my childhood are emblazoned on my psyche and perhaps inevitably woven into the fabric of who I've come to be. How could it not, if we are in fact personalities made up of the sum of our experiences?

I am completely confident that I have fully processed and put to closure these events in a way that would please any psychologist, but can't help but wonder what I might have been like had it not happened. Maybe I would be no different at all. It is a futile endeavor to dwell on what might have been, though I still do it more often than I like to admit.

I am loath to share the perverse details of an adult sexually engaging a child, but to some degree it's necessary. Not only to expiate the demons of shame visited among molested children, but hopefully to impart the impact of what amounts to a life-changing incident for me as a child and my family as a fellowship.

During a period of six years, between my father and stepfather, my mother, for the first and only time in her life, seized an opportunity to, by her own description, "have a little fun."

She spoke of those days with a twinge of guilt and regret, and I wished she didn't. She had every right to have some fun. She was still young and pretty, had eight kids and worked full time in the factory. In my opinion, she was entitled to it. She had survived some very hard years married to my father.

I was too young to remember my father living with us. I was only two when they divorced. But I heard many tales from my older siblings of the poverty, beatings, and humiliation he heaped upon my mother, and witnessed it firsthand as he repeated it on the three wives that followed her.

I know he drank away what little money they had, and if she tried to keep any from him he beat it out of her.

I know when there were still only five kids, they lived in a chicken coop, in the winter, on my grandparents' property, and Ma said she stuffed newspaper in the cracks of the walls to keep the snow out and piled all her kids in one bed to keep warm.

I know she went straight from the shoe factory to the hospital to have six of her eight babies, subsequently turned us over to a sitter, and went right back to work or there would be no money to feed us.

I know that once my Gram looked out the window one winter night, awakened by the sound of gunshots and screaming, to witness her youngest child running barefoot and pregnant in a nightgown through the snow, while the vicious drunk who made vows to honor, love, and cherish her shot at her feet and called her filthy names.

They lived in the chicken coop because my Grandpa never allowed my father in his house, and warned his daughter if she married him he would never take her in. He stubbornly stood by his threat, and my grandmother was helpless to do anything but watch her daughter's miserable life and slip her a few dollars in secret for food for her children without Grandpa's knowledge.

I know that I only came to understand when I fell in love with someone bad for me that she loved him. She loved some part of him I never saw. Perhaps the mother in her loved the broken child in him. Maybe he was exciting to her. Maybe she believed he would change if she loved him enough. Maybe she was simply afraid to be alone.

I heard people say that my father could be a good man if he would only stop drinking. I never believed that. I believe if you take the alcohol away from a drunken asshole, all you have left is an asshole. Alcohol is a symptom, not a cause, and that man was mean pure to the core of his black and bitter heart.

I asked Ma why she had so many kids with him, knowing what a rotten husband and father he was. She answered that she loved having kids, and we brought her life purpose and comfort, and she knew that no matter what he did, she would always have us and never be alone. She also said he kept a pistol under his pillow and threatened to shoot her if he caught her practicing birth control. I like the first answer better, but the second is probably closer to the truth.

I know that my youngest brother was conceived after their divorce, and my father already had another woman pregnant with twins. Ma described her last pregnancy as a moment of weakness when she was lonely. Several other family members have described her last pregnancy as the result of my father forcing himself upon her during a visit to his kids. Their version is more likely. Ma was not a woman prone to weakness, and my father was the type to force himself on a woman.

I have photos of my father and his third wife Sally. She was a tall, lanky redhead, widowed, with three kids, and pregnant with a set of twins by my father. I spoke to her recently about her marriage to my father. She is the only one of his five wives still alive or available. She was kind enough to illuminate those years for me.

I contacted Sally for two reasons. The first was an effort to understand why so many women found my father attractive enough to marry. She parroted my mother's words when she explained he could be a great guy when he wasn't drinking, but he had so many problems that the good times were few and far between. The second was to clarify a story of Sally being "accidentally" shot in a gun cleaning accident. She confirmed my suspicion that the shooting was no accident. My father had been at a party where someone angered him, and he came home to get his gun and return to the party to shoot his antagonist. When Sally tried to stop him, he threatened to shoot her. My father often threatened to shoot people, so I guess she didn't take him too seriously, until he pointed the gun at her and shot her in the thigh. He didn't spend a single day in jail for that crime, or for all the others he inflicted on his wives over the years. There wasn't much law out there in the Maine countryside forty-five years ago, and though I suspect it wasn't legal to shoot your wife, not many people would have dared to interfere in domestic issues. In the world I grew up in, women were possessions, not partners.

It's hard to believe Sally remained married to him for two years after being shot, but she explained he could be very convincing in his apologies and regret, accompanied with promises of change he could never keep. Ultimately, she took her children and stole away to Florida to escape him and his madness. She lives there today, and so do the half-brother and sister I have not seen in forty years.

When my mother took those few years of freedom for herself, to be young and have some fun, no one could fault her for it, and she certainly deserved it. But her uncanny ability to attract the wrong men was intact when she met and fell in love with Roger. He was my mother's lover for only six months.

I remember very little about Roger other than his physical appearance, and he was not spoken of in my presence after he was gone from our home. I know he was French-Canadian, divorced, and liked photography. I know he was romantic, and took her out a lot and made her laugh.

He was nice to her kids, and she was hopeful about the relationship. She believed it almost impossible to meet a man interested in a woman with eight kids. I'm not sure how long they dated before he came to stay with us, but I know he was only there a few months before he wreaked havoc on our family. My sister Tina, always my closest ally and childhood friend, insists he violated her before me, gave her pocket change and swore her to secrecy. She was seven years old. I was six.

He devised reasons to keep one of us home with him and send our siblings to school when Ma was working. My sister never told me what was happening, and I didn't tell her, until the day he kept us both home together. I remember it like a dream, vague but persistent, and for many years to come I experienced triggers that flashed me back to that particular morning. The smell of stale alcohol on a man in the morning repulses me. Rough, calloused hands and the feel of chest hair tickling my nose all take me back to his sickness. I knew what he was doing was wrong, his entire demeanor was different than usual, but I didn't know why it was wrong.

The morning my sister was present is vivid, except I cannot see her in my recall, though I know she was there. I know it was morning, because I was ordered to bring his coffee to the bedroom. When I entered the room with the hot coffee, he pulled back the covers and sat nude on the edge of the bed. I remember feeling embarrassed by his nudity. Nudity was not a big issue with a large family in a small house, but Ma encouraged general modesty and children seeing adults naked was not common or acceptable, and I knew it.

In my preteens, my father married for the fourth time. His fourth wife Mary Jane and her family owned and lived in a nudist colony. When we had the rare weekend in my father's custody, it was in the company of nudists. It is quite different from random unexpected nudity when everyone is equally unclothed in an entirely non-sexual environment, though for a preteen it was still uncomfortable.

I find it unnecessarily vulgar to provide the details of Roger's sexual abuse, but I will assure you that he did not sodomize nor physically injure me. I do not remember any physical pain. I do remember foreign physical sensations that were not altogether unpleasant and later feeling guilty that some of the things he did felt good. I don't know whether guilt or fear held him back, or if he was satisfied with just that much contact with children. To the best of my knowledge, he never confessed his thoughts or intent or, indeed, confessed to his crimes at all.

Roger gave soft-spoken instructions, and I recall his touch as gentle, as if he appreciated my fragility.

Ten years later, as a teen runaway living on the streets, I experienced the brutality of violent sexual assault, and again in my thirties while in a drug-induced stupor, so I am all too familiar with the difference between molestation and rape.

I don't remember what I felt at the time, or if I felt anything at all. I do recall the handful of quarters used to buy my silence. Those quarters were the most money my six-year-old hands had ever held. When searched for and found, they were the proof of his guilt and facilitated his downfall. At no point did anyone ask me what happened, or speak of it in front of me. Decades later, my mother and I discussed it all, and I saw how distressing it was for her to remember. It actually made her sick to her stomach, and I spared her further suffering when she began to retch at the few details I reluctantly shared.

Tina told my older sister Rose about what happened, and Rose told my grandmother. She in turn made my mother aware, and the stashed quarters were found to validate his guilt. My mother never questioned his guilt, and said later he had been acting strangely, and she guessed that was the reason after it all came to light.

We have all heard of mothers who turn a blind eye to abuse, usually in fear of losing a partner, but my mother immediately took the appropriate measures to protect her children and we did not suffer the additional insult and trauma of being ignored or dismissed as liars. In 1966, it was nearly unheard of to prosecute sex abuse in domestic cases. The best she could do was to remove him from our home. The shocking violence that occurred after his departure was at least, if not more, psychologically damaging than the abuse itself. I can't speak for my sister, but I believe it for myself.

I don't know where we were returning from when we arrived home that day. If I let it, it plays in slow motion in my head like a movie I watched but was too sleepy to keep my eyes open and see clearly.

We had an old green station wagon, and I was in the back seat. I can still hear the gravel driveway crunching under the tires as we arrived home. My mother abruptly stopped the car with an exclamation of dismay and horror. There was a dead animal in the driveway. She instructed us to stay in the car as she exited to investigate. Someone went with her, one of my older brothers. We were all so young that none of my siblings seem to remember the details I've asked for all these years later in an attempt to piece it together in my own memory. Against Ma's orders, I climbed out and stood against the wheel well of the car as the scene unfolded.

Ma's voice went from curious to fearful to hysterical as his path of destruction revealed itself. The windows of the house were broken, and more destruction waited inside. The outside was littered with the carcasses of all our animals – most he had bought for us – each with a bullet in its head. I have no idea how many, but it was dozens, at least. We had goats and rabbits, chickens and a horse. And they were all gone after that day.

I remember leaning against the car tire and picking at tiny rocks stuck in the tread. I remember feeling ashamed and somehow responsible. I knew who had done this, and I knew why. I had let him do those things to me, and I had kept his secret. It was a very bad thing I was involved in and everyone was upset, and it felt like it was my fault.

I remember nothing of the aftermath. I do not recall the removal of the dead animals or the repair of the house. It was all very quiet in my six-year-old world.

My last memory of that day is prying the tiny rocks from the tire tread. I suppose it was a trauma. I don't remember feeling traumatized, but I've been told most people do not recognize trauma when it's occurring. There was no point at which, afterward, someone sat me down to ask me what had happened, or to assure me I had done nothing to bring this on myself and my family. It was handled all wrong. I know that now. It wasn't my mother's fault. There were no resources for her to consult, and I'm sure she just wanted it to all go away.

No one told me that I was just a little boy dragged into the dirty world of adults and was not responsible for the things they did. No one told me that something bad had happened to me, but I was not bad because of it. Nobody ever said they were sorry. There was only silence, and the whispers that stopped when I entered a room. It seemed like the air around me changed, and a vacuum was created where the voices were all distant and muffled, and I could not feel the life around me. I retreated into the silence, shy and ashamed, and my beloved sister Tina, my only friend and fellow victim, was the only one I felt close to.

I don't think I was ever a real little boy again.

I've studied the few photos of me before the incident, and some after, to see if I could see visible signs of change. In the earlier photos I am always smiling. In the latter the smiles are gone.

I suppose it was elementary that when I began to show signs of what was later homosexuality, but at the time described as "acting like a girl," that it was an easy conclusion for the people around me to blame my unusually feminine behavior on the sexual abuse.

Knowing what I know now, I refute that conclusion. I believe I was born gay, and no one will ever convince me otherwise. I've even recognized that Roger's attention felt wrong because he was an adult, not because he was male. Perhaps he sensed something different in me that encouraged him to choose me among the other boys. Perhaps he saw a vulnerability or willingness that signaled an easier prey. I have read that men like him know instinctively which children are easiest prey: the shy, quiet children, the children more desperate for love and attention, those of us outside the sphere of notice.

I was a boy who tried to stay out of everyone's way. Being noticed was dangerous, and I was not good at defending myself. Beatings from bullies and taunts from my own siblings and father were enough to drive me to dark corners with a book, where I got lost in a story not my own. I played with dolls with my sister, and I liked to make pretty things with crafting and art projects, and I eagerly helped my mother with housework to avoid being forced outside to the brutal fate of my brothers' cruelties and away from the protective eye of my mother.

It's odd now to look at family photos and recognize that I really did stand apart, but didn't realize it at the time. The photos show seven bedraggled, poor country kids, making faces and slouching, and the eighth a slight, pristine, tow-headed, hair-parted-neatly, clothing-matched-meticulously and pressed, hands clasped in front, smile frozen in place, little catalog model. Looking closely, I can see the smile does not reach my eyes. I was not a happy child. I felt alien and dispossessed among my own people.

I recall a guest in our house notice me and rudely say to my mother "Where did that one come from?" I knew exactly what she meant.

After the carnage left behind by Roger, Ma didn't date or go out at all until a friend introduced her to the man who is my stepfather of forty-two years and was her husband until her death.

People always imagined our big country family as being something out of the TV show like the Waltons. It was far from that. We were hungry all the time. Hungry for enough food, for attention and affection, hungry for all the things we saw the other kids at school and on television had that we didn't. Being a poor family is not a sweet and wholesome TV show that has a happy ending once a week.

I had no special place in the family. Not the oldest nor the youngest, not the best looking or the best ball player; just another face in the crowd of Lottie's kids. I was a very good student and brought home good grades, but that was not significant in my family. I suppose we were all expected to go into the factories anyway, and good grades wouldn't change that. There was no money for higher education, and the concept was outside of our social and economic status. Books and words and school work came easy for me. That was about all that came easy for me. I desperately wanted to belong somewhere, to be a part of something, to break through the bubble I lived in and feel the world around me. The people around me would much rather I had been a good ball-player, or fighter, or fisherman, than have those useless good grades.

I had a handful of friends. My sister Tina and I were inseparable, and we made friends with some other kids our age, but I always felt like it was a package deal, and

I didn't have anyone who just liked me. My sister Tina was a pretty girl, and boys were nice to me to get to her because she wouldn't even talk to a boy who picked on me, and she defended me like a mother bear. She was held back in the second grade and I caught up to her, so we went all through school together. Her name is Ernestine, mine Ernest, and we looked so much alike everyone thought we were twins. We enjoyed our special bond as siblings and friends, and sometimes lied to others that we were twins because it made us feel unique in a world where almost no one was.

We were typical kids in most ways – getting into trouble, having crushes, fighting with each other and our siblings, and trying to find or establish our identities. We had older brothers who were getting into all kinds of fun and trouble, and we were eager to be a part of it. There was a teen center in town in the basement of the library. You had to be thirteen to join. At eleven and twelve, we were chomping at the bit to be members. We had already stolen a few beers and cigarettes and found our way to the cornfields, the hiding place for the country kids to meet and make out and share their stolen booty.

It warms my heart to remember those times when Tina and I walked those country roads to look for something to alleviate our boredom. Sometimes we lost track of time, and it got dark before we got home, so we would hold hands and run with our eyes closed because we were afraid of the dark. Perhaps that is a metaphor for our lives. Holding hands and running in the dark, scared of the dark woods around us and scared of being left behind.

Lloyd, Rose, Norman, Bucky, Tina, Ernie, Harold, and John, the eight of us, from oldest to youngest, but it was only Tina and I, joined not only in the bond of brother and sister but also in real friendship and the as yet unrealized knowledge of our mutual damage.

My mother was very proud of all of her kids, and often said so. All my brothers and sisters are good people with warm hearts and solid ethics. They all stayed in Maine, married and had children, and now many of their children have children. At her death, my mother's direct descendants numbered over fifty. I was the only one who broke the chain of family tradition to follow a treacherous road leading away from home and into the world outside of small-town Maine.

As often happens, I became difficult as puberty arrived.

Tina and I were eager to gain the freedom and privilege our older siblings enjoyed, and, aside from my sister, I continued to feel estranged from the world around me and looked for someone to identify with. Though I had excellent grades, I wasn't comfortable with the school "brains." They were most often from the better families in town, and my shame at our poverty shied me away from them. Obviously, I wasn't a jock. Those boys were my tormentors, and I avoided them at all cost. We didn't belong to a church, and I was never a Boy Scout.

I wanted to be a "cool" kid. There was a group of fringe kids – the outsiders, rebels, some leftovers from the hippie era who I admired for their individuality, their daring to be different, their seeming oblivion to the constraints of tradition and social obligation. They wore long hair and loud clothes and smoked pot and skipped school. They were glamorous to me. There didn't seem to be a lot of rigorous rules to belong with them, and the other kids seemed to almost envy them.

By then, I realized something was different about the way I felt. The girls who had always been my friends and safe harbor started to look at me as a potential boyfriend, and that made me uncomfortable. As my own sexuality awakened, I realized my fantasies and crushes were all directed at other boys. My very first crush, that I can recall, was my sixth-grade English teacher. I did very well in his class, and he complimented me often. Perhaps my crush was more a result of positive feedback from an adult male, as I had little to none of that prior to him. I basked in his praise and attention and worked extra hard in his class to please him.

Looking back I wonder if my attraction had anything to do with his physical resemblance to the man that molested me. It has always slightly disturbed me that I find myself attracted to stocky, dark-eyed, dark-haired men, and wondered if perhaps Roger left an imprint on my six-year-old brain of what all my future potential sexual partners should look like.

Around the age of twelve, not only did I start to notice boys, but some particular boys – and men – started noticing me.

I was a feminine boy, tow-headed and slight of frame, easily the smallest boy in my class and prone to choose clothing I thought was pretty and provocative, rather than masculine. I did nothing to attempt to blend in with other boys. Only much later, when I was a grown man, did I delve into the intricacies of the human psyche, particularly the common behavior patterns of the molested child, and I learned that I was attempting to be sexually provocative by my choice of clothing.

I chuckle when I think of the look on my mother's face when I pointed out the clothes I wanted from the Spiegel catalogs she bought most of our clothes from. She bought our school clothes from catalogs on credit, and spent the whole year paying the debt off, only to do it all over again for the next school year. Every year was the same for us boys. Dungarees, plaid shirts, Fruit of the Loom underwear, tee shirts and socks – three of each for each boy – a pair of school shoes, and, when winter arrived, a winter coat, boots, hat and mittens. Those clothes were to come off after school, and last year's clothes or hand-me-downs were for play. Every few months we boys were taken to the barber and given fifty-cent crew cuts.

No one complained. It was just the way it had always been. Ma's response to any resistance was always "when you get a job and buy your own, you can do what you want."

My brother Norm was four years older than I, and very handsome. When he was sixteen, and I twelve, he had a job and bought his own cool clothes, grew his hair long, and got a car. He was my idol. He was a rebel, and all the girls liked him, he knew all the new music, smoked and drank, stayed out late, and, I suspected, used drugs. I did not realize what a troubled young man he was. I just thought he was cool and wanted to be like him and wanted him to like me.

He was the oldest at home and had way too much responsibility for us other kids, and he resented it. Norm was expected to be the man of the house when he was still a boy. He treated us all like his slaves and, like my father, seemed to have a particular distaste for me. He bullied and brutalized me, and I came to fear being in his presence. He was a volcano of emotion and rage, always on the brink of eruption, and he fought with Ma constantly when she tried to restrain him.

I overheard Ma ask him once why he was so mean to me, and he told her that I embarrassed him. He was ashamed of me and my peculiar ways and the way that other boys made fun of me, and it made him mad. I don't ever remember being so crushed and heartbroken as I was at that moment when I realized my idol was ashamed of my being his brother. The bubble around me got bigger. I was an alien among my own people, and I felt my own anger finding its way to the surface of what was once my mother's quiet and timid little boy. I had taken beatings, abuse and humiliation all of my short life and the time had come when I started fighting back. I was a good kid, and it wasn't working out for me.

Up until this time I had always clung to my mother, and it seemed more and more she was always pushing me away. I know now she thought it was unhealthy for me to be so dependent on her, and in her way was encouraging me to find a place outside her protection and be a part of the world she knew I had to face in the near future. Finally she pushed me away one too many times, and it was many years before I found my way back to a safe and loving relationship with her.

As happens with most teens at some point, she became the enemy. It might have been the look on her face and distasteful tone in her voice the first time I tried to pick my own clothes.

I imagine now that poor country girl didn't know what to think when her twelve-year-old boy started picking out the clothes you would see on Rod Stewart and Elton John at the time. That style was a long way from coming to small-town Maine, but it was what I wanted, and I wouldn't budge. I wanted tight bell bottoms and bold polyester shirts with wide lapels and platform shoes. I wanted to stand out, and bless her heart if she didn't know that that was the last thing I needed to do. I wanted to look like a rock singer or a movie star. I had begun to look at the drab country life around me with disdain. Everybody looked the same to me, all the beer-drinking factory workers in dirty clothes, living on the edge of, if not over, poverty. This was not the life I wanted. There was nobody here who looked like what I felt inside. I felt like the people I saw on television. They had money and nice houses and looked happy and glamorous. That was who I felt I was supposed to be. And so began the rapid deterioration of the tenuous thread that held me to my own people and heritage.

The battle that ensued after my style of dress (she

relented on my birthday and bought me what I asked for) was over my hair. I was still wearing the much-hated crew cut, and all the cool guys had longer hair. Men were starting to go to beauty salons instead of barbers to have their hair styled, and that's what I wanted. That request was received with yet another of those looks she gave like she smelled something bad, and was followed by a resounding "No!"

Prior to this recent hormone surge of mine, I likely would have accepted this answer with little more than a roll of the eyes and a small gasp of exasperation, and then only if I was out of slapping range. But the new, glamorous, disdainful, preteen me, emboldened by recently won battles over clothing, was not to be dissuaded from my course. Mind you, she had three other teens at home and her patience was worn pretty thin by the time I started getting uppity or, in her words, "too big for my britches." So I chose an avenue other than whining and pleading, which I had grown to believe were beneath my dignity, and graduated to direct defiance.

The haircut incident was carefully planned. I retreated from the argument, and she assumed she had won.

It bears mentioning that this was the same woman who, only a few years earlier, when I was sent home from school with head lice, doused my clipped head with kerosene, wrapped it in a towel, and sat dangerously close by smoking a cigarette, while my parasites suffocated and I fearfully imagined myself exploding into a human torch any minute. When I complained about her smoking near my flammable head, she said, "Oh shut up! I would have to actually stick my cigarette on your head for anything to happen." I still say I detected a slightly wicked gleam of threat in her eye. Nevertheless, I found her lack of prudence disconcerting, and her sudden concern with my cranial decor a bit out of character. I don't think she really cared as much about how I wore my hair at that point as she did about being the boss of me.

When haircut time rolled around, she dropped us four youngest boys at the barbershop, quarters in hand. Norm was no longer getting haircuts, or I probably would not have been able to execute my plan without interference, as he had the position of second-in-command. When I sat in the chair, I told the barber my mother said to just give me a trim, because I was letting my hair grow. He did as I asked, and I left feeling deviously smug.

When I entered the house, she took one look and said, "You did not get a haircut." I said, "Yes I did. I got a trim, and I like it." She was instantly furious. I stood my ground and prepared for battle. I was twelve. I had been hit by my mother plenty of times, we all had, but never when I didn't have it coming. And she had to be provoked. She said, "You are getting your hair cut short." I narrowed my eyes, crossed my arms, looked her square in the face and said, "I am not, and you can't make me."

I don't remember who else was in the room, but it went silent. As with most siblings, we tended to enjoy watching someone else get in trouble, and my brothers and sisters were not about to miss this show.

I thought that I had won another battle when she left the room, and I puffed up like a winning prize fighter. When she came stomping back out with scissors in her hand, I was quickly deflated and seized with mad fear of this crazed harridan holding a deadly weapon.

When Ma was a young woman, she had to have all her upper teeth removed. Gram told me it was because she suffered malnutrition during all her pregnancies and didn't eat right. She wore cheap and ill-fitting dentures, and when she yelled you could see them moving, and they made a light clacking noise. As a spiteful teen, I would sometimes mimic that clacking noise behind her back to amuse others, and she never figured out what I was doing or she would have surely slapped the hell out of me for my rudeness.

So there she stood, scissors in hand, teeth clacking, and yelled, "No goddamned twelve-year-old boy is going to talk that way to his own mother. I'll cut your hair myself, and you'll wish a barber did it!"

This was around the time that the old shanty house had been torn down, and Ma had bought a three-bedroom, one-bath mobile home to replace it. We finally had an indoor bathroom with a tub and shower, a washer and dryer and even a little fake fireplace with a tinfoil wheel that turned and sort of looked like flames. Yup, we were officially trailer-trash, but at least we had a bathroom. Who knows how long we would have stayed in that run-down little house if the state social services had not decided to implement new standards of living for people receiving government assistance. Our little house did not meet their requirements and was condemned. My mother was informed that if she did not find a suitable home for her children, not only would she lose the government assistance, but she would be declared an unfit mother, and we would become wards of the state. (The state did not offer any financial help to improve our accommodations. They only offered the negative consequences.)

The trailer had four metal steps from the front door to the ground. During the winter in Maine, those steps could be treacherous with layers of ice.

When she started coming toward me with those scissors in hand and a nearly gleeful look in her eyes, I said the unthinkable. Backing away, I shouted, "Stay away from me, you fucking bitch!" No sooner was it out of my mouth than I knew I was going straight to hell for talking to my mother that way, and would most definitely get my ass beaten. But there was no taking it back, and the only thing to do at that point was run. And she was right behind me. They should have put me in Little League that day, because I would have been the fastest boy on the team.

I went out that front door, grabbed the porch rail, and landed flat on my feet in the driveway. Unfortunately, Ma tried to take the steps at a run and hit solid ice. Both feet flew out from under her and, airborne for a few seconds, she landed with a squeal and a grunt on her butt and bounced. With her mouth open in a yell, her denture flew straight out and skidded across the ice. As she tried to scramble for her teeth and kept slipping on the ice, I started to laugh and couldn't stop myself. I have always thought it was funny to see people fall down. I can't help it.

She saw me laughing at her and said, "When I get my hands on you, I'm going to have to kill you!" I still think that at that moment she really did want to kill me.

Well, obviously, she didn't kill me, and, amazingly, she didn't make me get my hair cut either. She got tired of fighting with us and probably gave in more than she should have. I'm sure I was punished for my foul mouth, but it wasn't significant enough for me to remember.

After an episode like that, she would be so worn out she would go to her bedroom and cry. Sometimes she'd get so frustrated she would threaten to call the state to come get us, or even worse, send us to live with our father. We would feel bad about making her cry, and knock at her door and say, "Don't cry, Ma, we're sorry," and she would say, "Don't talk to me! You're ungrateful brats."

Hearing my mother cry was the worst punishment I can remember. Right to the end of her life, I would rather have been branded with a hot iron than hear my mother cry.

The clothes and haircut were just the beginning of the changes coming over me. I was way too young to do all the things I wanted to do, but I didn't think so at the time. We never do. I often tell young people today, "Don't be in such a hurry to grow up, it's not that great." I think immaturity sees only the concept of freedom, and none of the realities and responsibilities. At twelve, I had already decided that a lot of people were having a lot more fun than I was, and I didn't want to wait any longer to get mine. I became a class clown to get attention and try to make the other kids like me. My teachers were concerned about the change in my behavior, but my grades remained good. I was often admonished for talking too much. I still am.

When Ma would see those comments on my report card she would tell me, "You need to shut up!"

My mother never missed a day of work and always worried about having enough money. It would be hell to pay if she had to leave work to come to that school. She'd say, "If I have to leave work and come down to that school because you can't shut your mouth, I'll beat ya!"

In our small town, you went from kindergarten through eighth grade in one school and were bussed to the city of Auburn for high school. Our little town has its own high school now. The teachers could still hit you back then, too. And if you were unruly enough, you were sent to the principal's office for a formal paddling. Those bastards paddled me all the way out of that school and into the ninth grade city school.

I started smoking and drinking as soon as I could get my hands on it. I smoked my first joint and engaged in my first consensual sex act at twelve years old. I look at a twelve-year-old today, and I am absolutely horrified to think of those babies doing anything but homework and hopscotch. I know I was unreasonably young to be doing the things I was doing, but I never felt young. I did have my innocence taken away at six years of age and figured I was damaged goods anyway. I felt damaged, and I felt that people treated me like I was tainted by what had happened to me. I heard all the whispers. If you want a child to listen to you, all you have to do is whisper, and there was plenty of whispering going on about me.

I noticed that certain men had started noticing me. I'm sure it was my obvious femininity rather than physical attractiveness that caught their attention. And I was more often being mistaken for a girl. It seemed every time I would walk the roads, a car carrying a single man would stop to offer a ride. At first I wouldn't get in. I sensed their secrets and was not comfortable with my own, and somehow knew I was not ready for what they were offering. I had men follow me in stores, and some boys my own age, or slightly older, were different to me when other boys weren't around. They were gentler when they didn't feel threatened by the judgment of others, and they seemed curious about me.

I suppose I was a curiosity. An enigmatic little creature, holding his secrets close, caught in the limbo of prepubescence. A disconcerting asexual with a tiny frame, fair, hairless skin and long, cornsilk blond hair, with a voice that had not yet deepened. I remember being mortified at being mistaken for one of my sisters when answering the phone. Add some bell bottoms, and platform shoes (not helping my already feminine stride) and the result was gender confusion. Even I can laugh at myself today at what a flamboyant picture I presented.

But still, there were boys and men who knew I was a boy and still seemed drawn to me.

My first was a boy named Michael. He lived up the road with three brothers, and Michael was the first of a long line of bad boys in my life. He went on to have a terrible life of drugs and jails and illness and divorces, and still lives in Maine, they say. His home life was full of violence, abuse and sexual issues. It was easy for him to get cigarettes and alcohol from his house, and we would pitch a tent in the backyard and tell our moms we were camping out. Michael was fourteen when I was twelve. I was most impressed to have a friend that was an actual teen, though his poor learning skills had us in the same grade at school. On this particular occasion, Michael had outdone his thievery by procuring a mother lode of his stepfather's pornography. I had seen my older brother's Playboy, and saw plenty of bodies at the nudist colony my dad lived in, but I had never seen anything like this. These were newspapers with triple x and quadruple x scenes of every possible sex act and combination thereof. I was repulsed and titillated at the same time.

It was only a few years later, when I truly comprehended the things that went on in that house, that my heart went out to those boys, and especially Michael. He was often battered and bruised, and I remember being horrified when he showed me the burned fingertips he received as punishment for a petty theft. His stepfather had burned his fingers on the kitchen stove. He stole things, he set fires, he ran away from home, and he fought constantly. He was what everyone thought of as a really bad kid.

As we lay on our stomachs drinking a beer, puffing a cigarette, and thumbing through this porn, Michael kept pointing out various photos and saying "I've done that." It did not occur to me at the time to wonder who he had done all those things with, but I have a pretty good idea now. There are many secrets in the impoverished homes of rural America, then and now, that you would not have seen on "The Waltons" or any other television show. Just on our dirt road there was twenty-seven kids in three houses. Alcoholism and some degree of abuse occurred daily in all three.

Whenever we complained about our unfair lot in life, Ma would always say, "Well, at least you're not some of those poor kids up the hill." And she was right. Ma took better care of her kids alone than both those families did with two parents in the home. We didn't have much, and

Ma was looked down on by some for allowing my stepfather to live with us before they were married, but after my father was gone and the incident with Roger, there was no abuse in our home: plenty of yelling and sometimes a slapping, but not abuse or neglect. I think she wanted to, but was just too damn worn out to beat us, even when we had it coming.

As Michael and I perused the stolen porn, I felt myself flush with heat and an unfamiliar but not unpleasant feeling coursed through my body. Even then my eye ignored the female images and was drawn to the men. Michael told me that his older cousin had taught him how to do many of the things in the photos and offered to show them to me. Some of the things he pointed out I flat out refused as unimaginably disgusting, and he did not pursue it. He was more persuasive than aggressive, and gave me the impression I was missing out on something good. There my resistance dissolved, and I submitted eagerly to the world of consensual sex. And not then or since have I ever felt a shred of guilt or shame over what I chose to do with my own body. Not to say that I was not fearful of being caught and humiliated, as I knew other people thought it wrong, but sex with another male did not feel wrong or unnatural to me.

A dear friend who happens to be a psychologist told me once that I was one of the very rare men she had known in her career who had absolutely no sexual hang ups, either gay or not.

And she's right. I don't, and I never did. I was simply born this way, and never questioned or doubted it. I never felt like there was something wrong with me, and never felt I had to fight it. I had plenty of problems because I was gay, but they were other people's problems, not mine. I never understood why it was anyone else's business, and I still don't. I've always said, "Even if I go to Hell like the

Christians claim I will, I'm not taking anyone else with me, so why should they care?"

At certain points in my life, as I explored my own psyche, I did realize the issues of being a molested child were woven into the fabric of a cloak I could never shrug off. I still did not struggle with my sexual identity. I knew I was gay, I accepted it, and everyone else was just going to have to get over it.

I have always thought fondly of Michael. He was the first to show me I was not alone in the world, that there were others like me. We were two troubled boys whispering and giggling and sharing a secret. As I lay on my back smoking a shared cigarette with him, and the rain beat on the canvas tent, he leaned over and kissed me softly on the lips and said, "You know, you're kind of pretty for a boy." He was the first boy to ever kiss me, and it felt as natural as my own skin.

All your life you will only have one first, and mine was Michael.

Somewhere in that timeline, I started to figure out something about people. They like to feel good, and if you can make them feel good, they will like you. I thought also that if you made them feel good, they would love you and not hurt you either. But that part isn't true. Nobody escapes getting hurt. I noticed there were two kinds of people who made everyone feel good: someone sexy and someone funny. I had a quick wit and a sharp tongue and an inherent sense of style, and when the bubble burst and I came out ... it was in full force!

I've always said, "I did not just come out of the closet: I blew the fucking door off!" I wanted to be sexy and I wanted to be funny. I wanted to be wild! I wanted to be noticed. I wanted to be wanted!

I had just found out there were boys who liked boys like me, and the girls thought me adorable, like a pet. And if

I made them laugh, they were laughing with me, not at me. The adults around me did not find me at all amusing, but I didn't care because they were the enemy anyway, and it was my pleasure to annoy them.

I believe my first school suspension came around this time, for setting off firecrackers pilfered from an older brother in the school halls. There was no one at home during the day, and my mother thought it suitable punishment for me to spend my suspended days at my father's house to insure I did not enjoy my time off from school or get in further trouble. Prior to this apex of criminal behavior, my father made no secret of the fact that he was displeased with this particular son and of course blamed my mother. I avoided encounters with him whenever possible, as I knew how he felt about me, and I knew I could do no right in his eyes. Ma had always stood between us as a buffer and stepped in when he went too far, thus validating his claim that she babied me too much and made me this way. I knew I was relatively safe when Ma was present, though I rarely got away without at least a good shaking, slapping or verbal threats of what he would do to me should I continue disappointing him. But now she had thrown me to the wolves. I was stunned and terrified. How could she? Didn't she know what would happen to me in his hands?

I begged her not to send me there, but she claimed there was no choice, and I truly believe she had decided drastic measures had to be taken. I was officially "out of hand," and something had to be done. We boys were occasionally required to stand before the presence of his highness, our father, the lord and master of all white trash. He would give Ma his story of how he had a right to "his boys" and pretend he wanted to spend time with us, and then put us to work the entire time we were there while he sat and drank with his buddies and poked fun at us, especially me. And he had a damn pig farm! Can you imagine a prissy gay boy on a pig farm? It was disgusting, filthy and smelly, and they were so mean to the poor pigs.

We fed animals, cleaned stalls, bailed hay and shoveled shit until we could hardly stand, and I never remember his doing a lick of work beyond sitting on a tractor, lifting a can of beer and impatiently criticizing everyone else's work ethic.

Every spring, when the piglets were born, they had to be caught and separated by sex. Apparently testosterone spoils the taste of the meat. The males had to be castrated, except the chosen few left intact for breeding, and the females were raised for slaughter. Catching those baby pigs was a dangerous game. A mother pig knows her piglet's squeal from a mile away, and she'll come running to save her baby. A pig can run pretty damn fast, and you better outrun her, because three hundred pounds of pissed-off pig with razor sharp teeth is not what you want to fight.

Once you're to safety, you hold the piglet on its back, and someone slits its little scrotum down the center with a razor blade and then pops out the testicles. He then pours a handful of salt on the wound to cauterize it and stop the bleeding. When you let the little fellow go, he runs squealing to his mama, dragging his hindquarters in the cool mud to soothe the pain. I felt so bad for those little pigs, but there was no room for mercy or a weak stomach on a farm.

Now those pig testicles looked like bloody purple grapes, and don't you know that at some point someone had to dare someone else to eat one? These were farm boys with a pretty immature sense of humor, and this sort of daring was common among the males I grew up with. There was no question that I would accept the dare, and I stood ready to bolt should someone decide to force me.

Then my father loudly dared anyone to do it for ten dollars. That was a lot to us back then, and my brother Norm knew he could party for days on ten bucks, so he accepted the challenge. An argument ensued over whether it could be swallowed whole or had to be chewed, and it was agreed that he just had to get it down and keep it down. So he stepped up, picked out a particularly tasty looking testicle, poured salt on it and swallowed it whole. Everyone laughed and cheered him on while I looked on quietly from the sidelines and thought, "These are not my people. This is not my family. I am in Hell, and I blame my mother!"

My father's friends then teased him mercilessly that his boy had been more of a man than he by successfully completing the dare. So my dad had no choice but to save face and follow suit. He puked before it was halfway down his throat, and Norm was crowned king for the day.

During the days of the pig farm and the nudist colony, my father was married to his fourth wife, Mary Jane. She was a nice woman. She was another corn-fed country girl, a bit chubby, with a long blond braid down her back, a plain face, and two little blond girls from a previous marriage. Mary Jane had a third daughter with my father, and they named her Mary Elizabeth. Dad wouldn't even go see her in the hospital because he was mad that she wasn't a boy-child. He acted as though Mary Jane had a girl just to spite him. I don't understand why he wanted another boy: he had a gang of them already and didn't pay any attention to us.

Mary Jane's family owned a nudist colony called The Hilltop Sun Club. It was a pretty spot deep in the woods of Maine, with a man-made lake and little cabins all around it. It was a family environment for nudists and sun worshippers. Singles were not allowed as members to discourage the swinger types. Of course, it was only active a few months in the summer. It's a bit too cold in Maine most of the year to be running around naked.

Mary Jane's family lived on lots surrounding the colony, and she and Dad lived in a falling-down shack with an outhouse and a wood burning stove for heat. Mary was a real farm girl and could outwork any man I knew. She rode a horse, chopped wood, and could kill and gut a chicken in minutes without flinching. She was a good solid woman who didn't drink or smoke and went to church twice a week, and she had a very hard life with him – another sweet and simple girl taken in by his good looks and charm, only to have her dreams beaten out of her. He treated her like an animal, and no one interfered. They never did, as everyone feared his temper, and his guns and knives.

So I was sent to stay for a week of punishment with the nudists, the guns, and the pig farm.

I worked hard and played with my little sisters and made myself very small, hoping he would not notice me. Mary Jane taught me to saddle and ride a horse, and I remember her as a gentle but firm teacher. What an incredible feeling it was the first time I was allowed to take that horse on my own. Her name was Flingo, and she was a beautiful Appaloosa. To sit up so high on this powerful creature, looking down at the world, and to run her down the dirt roads with the wind blowing my hair, I felt so big and so free. It is truly the only fond memory I have of my father's house.

The days were not bad with Mary Jane and the girls, as Dad was at work at the Tool and Die, or drinking with his buddies at the pig farm. As evening neared the atmosphere grew tense, as the beast was due to return to his lair. All his life he drove with a beer between his legs and was on his way to drunk before he came through the door. You just prayed he didn't stop at the liquor store on the way home for the "hard stuff," or it was going to be a bad night.

I slept on the couch in the tiny living room, and my few possessions were in a paper bag.

On one particular evening, near the end of my sentence, Mary Jane and the girls had gone to bed, and Dad was sitting up drinking. I remember him saying to me, "You know, you don't have it so bad. Your mother is a good woman. My mother was a whore, and she didn't love me. I would come home from school, and my mother was getting fucked by three sailors on the living room floor. I had no one that took care of me. I had no childhood."

I was horrified to hear such things about my grandmother, and uncomfortable with my father sharing intimate feelings with me. I had enough experience with him to know that this was not going to be a good night. When he drank, he often went from good time Charlie to self-pity to rage. I have a brother who drinks like that and, once upon a time, so did I.

I remember him weeping briefly as he spoke of his mother, and he reached out to me for comfort. I was paralyzed by this display of weakness on his part and completely unfamiliar with physical affection from my father, or anyone else for that matter. Seeing my hesitation, he raised his eyes to mine and his self-pity turned to rage.

He ordered me to stand and come to him. I was trapped and had no choice. I stood with my head down. He looked at me bitterly, grabbed my wrist painfully and said, "Do you love your Dad?"

I knew what I was supposed to say, but I had only this one chance to hurt him and couldn't pass it up. I looked him in the eye and said "No." It was the truth, and he knew it.

If I had been older and able to articulate my feelings and thoughts, I might have asked him in response, "How can you ask me such a thing? I don't even know you, and what I do know is only the pain and fear and shame you have heaped on me since I was old enough to disappoint you. I should be asking you if you love me, but I know the answer already, because you do not know how to love."

But I was only a boy, and he was not a man you could reason with, so I told him the truth.

He was twisting my wrist so painfully I thought it would break. I did not let a single sound escape to satisfy his hunger to inflict pain on someone. I held my breath and stood my ground until he balled up his fist and drove it into my stomach. I crumpled to the floor gasping for breath. It is the first time I remember having the wind knocked out of me. It's a frightening feeling.

Mary Jane appeared in the door. She must have been listening. She said softly to him "Ernest, stop." He turned viciously and said to her, "Woman, don't you ever tell me what to do with my own son, or I'll beat your ass to the ground." Mary Jane stood silent.

He told me to get up. I got to my feet and he punched me again and I landed on the couch. I did not utter a sound, save my gasping breath. Again he said, "Get up and face me." I did. And again he knocked me down. Mary Jane was in tears and shouted, "For God sakes Ernie, stay down." But I couldn't. What little bit of pride and dignity I had left would not allow it. How I hated him! He really is the first person I ever hated with real passion. Whatever he wanted from me, I was determined to deny him. I was willing to die before I gave him the satisfaction of giving in. I don't know how many times he knocked me down. Eventually he tired or I just couldn't get back up, but it was over, and I curled up on the couch and cried myself to sleep. I was only a boy, and no match for a grown man's rage.

No mention was made the next day, but Mary Jane

was especially kind to me, and when I went home I did not tell my mother what had happened. I got the punishment she sent me for, and it did nothing to solve our problems. They were about to get much worse.

My father did not know it, but he had won our war of wills. He had beaten what was left of a sensitive and timid little boy out of me, and any hope that I had ever held that I might have a father who loved me was gone. He taught me what it meant to hate. And I blamed my mother for sending me there. All hell was about to break loose, and no one was going to stop me.

Phantoms

There are phantoms in my house
of the years gone by and by,
ghosts of gentle carefree boys
with no futures in their eyes.

There are phantoms in my house
of all I loved and lost,
in youthful recollections
our paths still sometimes cross.

There are phantoms in my house
But not ones that terrorize or rave,
Just ones that sing sad songs of painless slumber
from the comfort of youth's grave.

E.M.

Chapter Three
Adrift

At this point in my life I stopped caring about school and grades. I started hanging with the fringe kids and looking for parties. The underage country kids had places they gathered and partied, and my older brothers knew all of them. At thirteen, I could finally go to the teen center on the weekends, and there were all kinds of trouble to get into there.

I smoked my first joint at twelve years old. I had tried various pills to speed you up or slow you down, and I believe I tried hash at least once. I was learning there were a myriad of drugs out there I hadn't tried yet, and I was eager to try them all. I wanted to be the baddest of the bad. I could barely contain my rage. I had vengeance in my heart for my parents and the world of adults, for the teachers and the schools, the rules and religions. I was burning inside with quiet hate and disgust for all the people who controlled my life and freedom. I wanted to tear a gaping hole in the world that matched the one I carried inside me.

Tina and I had befriended a brother and sister our same age, and we paired up as boyfriends and girlfriends. We had sleepovers at their house, and of course, the girls shared a room and so did the boys. Tina and I laughed about it years later when she told me he never tried to kiss her. His sister probably wondered why I didn't try to kiss her either. It was because we were kissing each other. We went through the public motions with each other's sister as our cover, and at every opportunity to be alone we explored our secret desires with all the awkward fumbling and encumbered passion of two preteens on the threshold of their sexuality. We never spoke of homosexuality, of being gay, or of men loving men. We hardly spoke at all. We vented our loneliness and frustrations with our changing bodies, and each time seemed the last until we met again.

It did not occur to us that this was the doorway to a lifestyle. We believed at the time we would be like everyone else and grow to marry and have children. This was just a boy thing, a situation of opportunity and convenience. We met many times in our young manhood, and even once as adults; and it was always the same. We would find a place to be alone – a hayloft, a tent or an abandoned house – and we fed on each other with a hunger reserved only for the most taboo of carnal desires. He lived beside an old cemetery, and I remember a tryst among the dead. It was in the fall, and I remember the bed of freshly fallen leaves crackling beneath us, and the chilled air heating up with our raging young bodies. I remember the paleness of our skin in the moonlight, and the pounding of our hearts in the near silence of our rapture. I remember it because it was beautiful in its innocent lust and loneliness, and because I remember so little beauty from those painful years of pubescence.

He was not my first love. We were friends, but I did not feel passion for him, and as our couplings became fewer and farther between, I did not mourn the loss. I had come to understand by then that boys did these things with their bodies, but I was still too young to know about love. Or to even imagine that men fell in love with each other.

Nowhere around me did I witness any positive images of gay people. "Queer" was a word commonly used to degrade or insult another male, and occasionally one heard stories of particular men being exposed, or even arrested, for being "queer." I remember my mother reading a newspaper story aloud about two young men being beaten and thrown off a bridge to their deaths. Their murderers were quoted as saying they did it because the men were carrying purses. She was disgusted with the murderers, compassionate toward their victims, and bewildered why anyone would kill someone for carrying a purse. I don't believe she made the connection that the victims were gay. She was quite naive to alternative lifestyles. I heard mention of a "queer bar" in the nearby city of Lewiston named The Blue Swan that was, not surprisingly, close to the very bridge those boys were thrown from.

There was a woman in our town, an alcoholic who lived in a trailer deep in the woods, who I thought was a man. She lived with another woman, and Ma referred to them as "lizzies." There was also a hermaphrodite in our town, and he/she was looked upon with revulsion and some pity as he/she was born that way. There were a handful of other boys in school referred to as "sissies," but I didn't associate that label with being queer until a few years later.

Anything remotely outside the norm was addressed and observed with disgust and condemnation, and these abominations were to be avoided, lest one risk guilt by association in the public eye.

The isolation of the gay child is incomparable, and incomprehensible to most. It is proven by the disproportionate number of suicides among gay teens. The lack of support from family and peers, condemnation from religious and political institutions, ridicule and harassment at a time when puberty itself is attacking the body and mind, often culminate in such extreme distress and depression we too often do not survive to adulthood. A broadly accepted ideology that one chooses homosexuality is laughable to the absurd. At no point do I recall being given or making a choice, any more than my non-gay siblings were given a choice not to be.

Surely I would have chosen the easier, softer way. I would have chosen to be a part of the world around me, to have pursued the American dream of marriage and children, a home with the white picket fence and social acceptance. Surely I would have chosen support over ridicule, kindness over cruelty, and to live in the light over the dark corners of shame and fear that was the homosexual underground. But those were not the cards dealt to me. And I had to learn to play my hand quite a bit more carefully than the other players, if I hoped to stay in the game of life.

I started to develop a decidedly androgynous appearance and was often mistaken for a girl at thirteen. Yet another of my personal grooming choices that caused a minor uproar was my eyebrows. The Merchant men, and a few of the women, are cursed with an enormous eyebrow, commonly referred to as a "unibrow" – one continuous thick brow that meets in the middle and threatens to creep down the bridge of the nose. If we did not possess the high hairline that is another Merchant trait, they might have met there too. I despised my unibrow, and as I hit puberty and my white hair began to darken to a deeper blond, the hated brow darkened even more to become a hideous, furry caterpillar living on my forehead. Of course this was a serious offense to my fastidious nature, and something had to be done.

After many years of torture with tweezers and waxing,

they have ceased to grow back, and I am often complimented on the shape of my brow, but at that time the only option for hair removal was the razor. Initially, my goal was just to do some undetectable pruning when I locked myself in the bathroom and picked up the old double-sided razor my mother used to shave her legs. The very first swipe of the razor between the eyes was successful. They did not join anymore. The next one, on the top of the brow, was a bad move, and a large chunk of brow was missing. For just a moment, I stared dumbfounded at what I'd done before being seized with panic. Well, I had no choice now but to try and make them even. I'm sure you can guess the end result: a disaster!

I frantically tried to comb my bangs down to cover them before exiting the bathroom and, head lowered, attempted to pass my mother unnoticed. I was almost out the door when she said, "Stop!" I stopped. She said, "Look at me." I looked at her.

She said, "Jesus Christ! What have you done to yourself now?" I was already on the verge of tears with what I knew to be an impending onslaught of teasing and criticism from my siblings and peers, so I drew myself up in an attempt to salvage my dignity and answered back, "I fixed my eyebrows, and I like it!"

I did not like it. I had made a horrible mess, but my pride would not allow me to admit it.

She was obviously exasperated with me, yet again, and yelled, "Goddamnit, boys are not supposed to do those things! What the hell is wrong with you?"

I didn't want to cry anymore. I wanted to yell, too. So I said, "Well, THIS boy does, and there is nothing wrong with me!"

The eyebrows grew back, and I learned how to groom them properly. I honestly don't recall suffering too much teasing about them, and I'm sure my father never noticed, or he would have turned it into yet another excuse for tormenting me.

My brother Norm had started hanging around with our older half-sister, Melody. Mel was a result of an affair of my father's between his first wife and my mother. Her mother, Colleen, was a beautiful, raven-haired woman who spent most of her life roaming the bars of a ghetto called Lisbon Street in Lewiston, Maine. She seemed an odd, detached woman to me during the brief time I knew her, and I have heard it told that Melody's childhood was one of extreme neglect. We were cursed with the same father, but I had a mother who took good care of us. Melody did not. She started getting into trouble very young, and was in reform school at fourteen.

I do not recall meeting Melody before I was about thirteen. When I first saw her, she was model-thin, with wild, blonde, curly hair and huge blue eyes. She wore a white pantsuit, and got out of a red Corvette with the handsomest black-haired, blue-eyed man I had ever seen: her husband, Mike.

Melody was always nice to me, and called me "little brother." She knew from the moment she saw me exactly what I was all about, and it was just fine by her. She had been through so much in her life and held no judgment. She was the first person to tell me straight out that I was gay, and she took me to my first gay bar. This was a bit later, but I felt that she supported me from the beginning and didn't treat me like I was a freak. Unfortunately, Melody associated with a lot of the criminal class, and my fascination with the underworld had begun.

By the time I was fourteen, I was being suspended from school on a regular basis. I smoked in school, skipped entire days, disrupted class, and disrespected the teachers. I had suddenly become a very angry young man, but really it was not so sudden. I was just finally letting it show. The battles with my mother had become more frequent and intense. By fifteen, I had tried about every drug available except heroin, and that was only because I was afraid of needles.

I managed to find my way into the city streets of Lewiston more often by staying with my married siblings. I walked the streets looking for the fabled Blue Swan, the gay bar I had heard about. It was well hidden, and I did not find it until I was taken there by Melody.

Often, as I walked the streets, single men stopped to offer me rides. I recognized that same look in their eyes I'd seen a few years earlier in the men who offered me rides, but this time I felt I was ready. Sometimes I got in their car. Not always, but sometimes. They always said the same thing, "Where you going?" And I always answered the same way, "Anyplace but here." I'm pretty sure I stole that line from a movie. I liked the careless, worldly sound if it.

So, in parked cars, cheap motels and a few alleys, I found my way into the seedy underbelly of the gay world in the early 1970s. I had my experiences with boys to give me a little confidence, and the art of seduction seemed to come naturally. After all, I knew they wanted me, or they wouldn't have stopped. But these were not boyhood friends, these were men, and only as an adult did I realize they had no business picking up fourteen-year-old boys for sex.

I had passed out of the school I had attended for nine years and was now being bussed to the city for ninth grade. Most of the country kids I knew went too, but they were lost in the crowd of all the unfamiliar faces of the city. These kids did not know my brothers or my family, and had no qualms about tormenting me, including physical abuse. There were few more dangerous than the big lugs commonly referred to as "jocks." They had little more going for them than their size and ability to catch a ball, but they were the lords of the manor, and the most common source of bullying.

We did not have a physical education course in elementary school because the little school had no gymnasium. The only class I ever flunked, and even then it was an "incomplete" rather than a flunking grade, was physical education. Because after only a few humiliating attendances, I flatly refused to go. They might as well have painted a bulls-eye on my back for how quickly and easily I was targeted for ridicule. Once those boys discovered they could bully me without retribution, I hardly had a moment's peace. The teachers did nothing. It was just boys being boys, I guess, and like most American educational institutions, it didn't matter how stupid or rude a boy was if he held an important position on a sports team. I have always been disgusted with the heroic status these boys are given in high school.

I raced through the hallways from classroom to classroom, hoping to avoid confrontations, but it was as if I wore a neon sign that said, "Kick me." Most of the abuse was made to appear accidental. Boys tripped me, slammed into me, knocked my books to the floor, and pressed heated cigarette lighters into my arm in passing. I was stuffed into lockers, hit in the head with balls and food items, and addressed with a colorful array of cruel names. In school, I felt the same as I did in my father's presence; that I was always in danger of being hurt.

Tina and I were no longer in all the same classes in high school, and I did not have the safety of her companionship as I did all through elementary school. I had never felt more alone and unprotected as I did in those crowded hallways. My formal education was coming to an end.

I went to school less and less often. I got off the bus on campus and walked away to wander the streets of the city during school hours, and returned home on schedule so that often my mother never knew I didn't attend. I slipped through the cracks of the school system, and no one seemed to notice or care that I was gone. Eventually, yet another suspension led to what was to be the last time I stayed at my father's house.

I know my mother was at her wit's end as to what to do with me. I was running wild and fought her at every move. I didn't like her at all, and she didn't like me back. I am ashamed now to remember how I treated her. Regardless of what I was going through, she did not deserve to be treated so disrespectfully. I was just so mad all the time. I was miserable, and someone had to pay for it.

This last time I was forced to go to my father's house, I showed up considerably less timid and far angrier than I had been the previous visit. I was ready to fight back, but still not strong enough to win.

My father was a hypocrite. He held everyone to a much higher standard than he expected of himself. He demanded you be clean and neat, but he looked like a dirty hermit. He rarely shaved or bathed, and smelled like booze and pig shit. He demanded respect, but respected no one. He insisted on good manners, but behaved like a savage. He demanded the truth, but lied so often he believed his own lies. He lied, cheated, stole, womanized, drank, smoked, and took drugs. He was a sexist, a racist, a bigot, and an uneducated, ignorant waste of good air. He did not get better with age.

I had no love for him, and even less respect. I had hated him for most of my life, and the only reason I don't hate him now is I don't care enough to.

On that last night in my father's house, I tried to be as invisible as possible, but, unfortunately, I was to be the star of his show one last time. He had his redneck friends over, and they were drinking vodka and chasing it with beers. They were getting loud as the vodka kicked in, and Mary Jane and the girls had already retreated to the safety of the bedrooms. I sat on the couch quietly watching the TV when he raised his voice and said, "Boy, come in here!"

I was seized with panic, and considered pretending I didn't hear him, hoping he would forget me. I did not respond quickly enough, and as I got up he said, "Boy, I said get your fuckin' ass in here!" I moved to the door of the kitchen where he sat with three of his friends, all pretty much social replicas of him, and I could tell from the looks on their faces that I was not summoned to join in on their fun. Because my mother had sent me to him as a result of my being suspended from school, it was made clear that my visit was not an opportunity for father-and-son bonding, but rather an opportunity at justifiable and unrestricted punishment, and he had every intention of fulfilling his obligation, and amusing himself along the way.

Perhaps I was sullen and insolent. Most fourteen-year-olds are, and it was not easy to disguise my distaste for him. I raised my head and looked at him and said, "I'm here." What my tone said was, "What the fuck do you want?"

I don't know what I expected. I knew it wouldn't be good, but I was taken aback when he said, "My friends and I are wondering if you're a fruitcake?" I was stunned to silence with humiliation, and I noticed his friends avert their eyes in discomfort. I lowered my head and said nothing. His eyes glittered with childish malice and he said, "Well, you act like a fruitcake and you look like one, so you must be one."

I was nauseous with hatred and humiliation, so I quietly responded with a lie. "No, I'm not," hoping that would satisfy him and I would be allowed to retreat to safety.

You couldn't win with my father. If you stood up to him, you were disrespectful, and if you submitted, you were a coward. He looked me over with vicious, bloodshot eyes and said, "You need to cut that fuckin' hair. You look like a girl." I suppose I should have simply agreed and said,

"Of course, Father, I will see to it immediately." But, alas, I was not then so silver-tongued or diplomatic as I am today. So I drew up all five feet of me and defiantly stated, "My mother said I could wear long hair."

He flew out of his chair and put me in a choke hold before I could take a step away, and said, menacingly, "You're in my house now, and I make the rules."

His friends were uncomfortable and embarrassed, and one of them did say softly, "Ernest, come on." He either didn't hear him or pretended not to. I struggled for release but he pinned me against the counter where a large hunting knife lay sheathed. There were always guns and knives lying casually about in my father's house. He grabbed the knife, and unsheathed it with one hand, grabbed a large chunk of my hard-won golden locks and sheared it close to the scalp.

I was mortified at this public spectacle of my humiliation, and at that point wished he had cut my throat. He sheared two more large chunks when Mary Jane entered the room and moved to stop him. He kept the knife in his hand and whirled and punched Mary Jane square between the breasts with all his strength. She flew backward into the next room, and her fall was broken by the wood stove.

This was the point where his friends intervened to restrain him, and I seized the opportunity to make an escape out the front door and to the road home. My face was wet with tears of rage and humiliation. I didn't even realize I was crying until the cold air hit my wet face. I walked in the direction of home, which was a forty-five minute drive down wooded roads, and it was already getting dark out. I'm not sure how long I'd walked when Mary Jane pulled up in the car and told me to get in. I continued to walk, and said, "I'm not going back there." And she said, "No you're not. I'm taking you home."

I don't remember us speaking as she drove me home,

and she did not make excuses for him as I had heard her do many times before. She did not get out of the car when we arrived at my mother's house, but waited silently as I exited. It was not her fault, but I hated her too for being connected to him. Anyone who could love him was my enemy, too. My mother had come out the door, and I could tell she had been called and told what happened. I walked past her and into the house while she spoke briefly with Mary Jane at the car window.

When she returned, I sat sulking on the living room couch. She looked at me and said, "You okay?" I refused to even acknowledge her. She was responsible for sending me there. She looked sad and angry, and said, "Your hair will grow back, Honey. Don't worry: I'll never let you go there again." And I didn't.

That was only one of many of the defining moments that occurred over the year or so that preceded my exit from the home I had known all my fourteen years, to the streets and the adventures that have culminated in this writing. The chronology may not be perfect, but the people, places, and events are all real.

This was a time of great emotional upheaval in my young life, and an incessant desire to escape overwhelmed me most of the time. I just knew there was so much more out there, possibly even a place where I fit in, and I was impatient to find it. There is little worse than wanting to run and having no place to run to. I was to experience that feeling many times over in the next thirty-five years. There was still a small part of me that hoped someone would give me a reason to stay, but that didn't come. I suppose it was my destiny to find my life elsewhere.

I had a sweet moment in my fifteenth year: my first love. He was a member of the enemy camp – a jock, tall, muscular and handsome, but not terribly bright. He was older than I, but in my same classes because of his poor grades, and was an admired athlete. He was one of those boys I avoided, but he didn't seem to pay much attention to me anyway. I know that before I saw him in high school, I had encountered him with some other boys on a ball field when they stopped me from walking by.

Someone called out "faggot" (but it wasn't him), then all of them approached me and formed an impenetrable wall blocking my path.

Being called faggot was common to me by now, but no less alarming. It wasn't the word that bothered me as much as the violence that usually succeeded it. He appeared to be the alpha male of the group. I don't remember the volley of words, but I'm sure I did nothing to help diffuse their aggression with my sharp tongue. They were so predictable; boys like them only owned a handful of words. It ended with his hitting me only once and pushing me to the ground. I thought I caught a faint look of guilt or pity on his face as he mumbled something and walked away. I was sure his heart was not into bullying me, but it was required of him among his peers, and I suppose he wanted to be liked as much as anyone else. I picked myself up and walked on, another day in paradise.

He was in my English class in tenth grade.

He approached me leaving class one day and said, "You're pretty smart." I waited for the punch line, or just a punch, but neither came. He looked sad to me. He looked at the ground and said softly, "Hey man, sorry about that time...."

No one had ever said they were sorry for hitting me before. I felt awkward and shy with him. I didn't know what to say except, "It's okay, I wasn't hurt." He seemed genuinely contrite, and I had no choice but to forgive him. I don't know how it escalated into a friendship. We started to hang out together here and there, and then more often. We walked the roads together, and eventually had sleepovers.

A miracle had happened, and the other boys did not harass me much now that I was accepted by one of their own. He was twice my size, and very tough and brave. I had a terrible crush on him. I thought I did well at hiding my desire for him, and he could easily have beaten me to a pulp if I had ever been inappropriate. I believe he took some ribbing for befriending me, and I suspect his parents were not all that fond of our friendship, but they knew my family and were kind to me.

He was very physically playful and easily overpowered me, but did not ever hurt me by being too rough. I believed that he genuinely cared for me, and I know that I felt real love for the first time, and feared losing it.

As teenage boys will do, we often joked and teased about sex, lied about what we had done, and about the many things we would do when given the chance. I started to feel tension at times when we were alone together, and though we had separate beds at his house, we often fell asleep in the same one.

I began to suspect that he was curious, or interested in going further, and I welcomed but did not initiate it. His friendship meant everything to me, and I loved him. I envied his masculinity and fearlessness. He was everything I wasn't, and he became a model I measured other men by in my search for love and companionship until so many years passed that I couldn't remember what it felt like to love him anymore.

One night we shared a bed. He feigned sleep, and accidentally brushed against me. I held my breath in desire and indecision. I let my hand fall against his and inched closer, but not enough that I couldn't recover if I had mistaken his intentions. He rolled to his side, facing me and I felt something hot brush my hip. I rolled to my side, my back to him, and gently pressed against him, inviting him closer.

It was my way to submit, to be overpowered, and dominated. There is little responsibility in submission, no real commitment, no expected level of achievement, and little chance of failure. I took a submissive role naturally and comfortably, and offered myself to him.

When he wrapped his muscular body around my small frame it fit like a glove, and felt so natural to me, I never felt it was wrong. I felt right for the first time in my young life. For the first time, I felt the painful passion of real love and heard the siren song of desire call my name. He was not just a fumbling boy or a stranger in a car. I loved and admired him. I felt safe with him. I wanted to be perfect and beautiful for him. For just that one night, I was all those things. This is what it meant to be gay. I was there.

When we woke the next morning, he could not look at me, and my heart filled with dread. He didn't touch me and barely spoke except to say, "I have to go home." I said, "I'll walk with you." On the walk home, he asked me never to tell anyone, that it would kill his dad. He said to me, "You have five brothers. I am the only son. I can't be that way."

I told him I would tell no one, and my heart ached, because I realized he would not, or could not, love me as I loved him. I left him there on the road and walked home alone, knowing we would no longer be friends. We couldn't go back to how it was before, and we couldn't continue through the new door that had opened. Yet another male had wanted only a piece of me and had cast the rest aside. Had it been left at that it would have been easier to recover from my first broken heart. But there were too many questions as to why our friendship had abruptly ended, and his fear of exposure led him to throw me to the wolves to save himself.

It spread like wildfire that the town queer had at-

tempted to sexually assault the unsuspecting and innocent jock. No one wanted to consider his participation,
or questioned why I still had my front teeth after committing such a brazen and unsolicited molestation. There
was no question I was guilty in the kangaroo court of
small town public opinion, and I was tried, convicted,
and sentenced without representation. I was a pariah in
school. Before, there was only a suspicion, now there was
concrete evidence I was a faggot, and my only protection had betrayed me and turned me over to the teenaged morality police. Being tolerated would have been
a luxury. But nothing they could do to me hurt more than
seeing him in a hallway and having him look away, or
passing him among a group of his friends and hearing his
malicious laughter rise above the others.

This was not simple, childish teasing. This was assassina-
tion. This was real heartbreak. The gossip was not contained to the high school either. It found its way to the
factory my mother worked in. The adults showed no more
compassion than their offspring, which of course is where
most children learn their cruelties. I did not attempt to defend myself against the accusation, and was not given
the opportunity. I didn't want to hurt him, and I had no
valuable reputation to defend.

Sometime later, he wrote me a letter apologizing for
what he did to hurt me. I kept the letter in a box and forgot it. Years later, my mother found the box and letter in
a closet, and after reading it, she discerned the truth of
what had happened. I was in California when she called
me and said, "Why didn't you say something? Why didn't
you defend yourself? You took all the blame. It makes me
so mad what you went through over all that. And that
bitch of a mother of his told everyone it was all your fault.
I would like to show her this letter just to see the look on
her face."

I was glad that someone finally knew the truth of what

happened that night. But I had long moved on to a new life far away from their judgment. I said, "Ma, it wouldn't have done any good to hurt him. I knew my life was over there, and he had to stay. People believed what they wanted to, and I loved him." But at the time, she demanded to know what had happened, and I remained stubbornly silent. I didn't know a heart could break like that, and I didn't care about anything anymore. She did not see my heartbreak, only her own embarrassment at the gossip about one of her kids. This was yet another problem she was too worn out to deal with. She was angry with me for causing trouble, for being different; and I was angry with her for making it worse for me.

I refused to go to school anymore. About two months into the tenth grade, I quit. I couldn't face the taunting anymore. I couldn't face him anymore. Only once did I try to explain to my mother what was going on with me. I sat her down, I looked at her and said "Ma, you know what everyone says about me?" She said, "Oh, just don't listen to it." I said, "No, Ma, it's true." She said, "What do you mean?" I responded with, "You know they call me queer, (I didn't know the word gay yet)? Well, it's true. I am queer."

I hoped she would then say that it was alright and that she loved me and would help me get through this, but that's not how it happened. She said, "Don't say that. You're too young to know anything like that. It's sick and wrong, and you can't be like that and live here."

I had come out. I had spoken the words out loud of what I'd known for a long time, and most had suspected and accused me of. But I had broken a golden rule. I'd drawn something ugly into the open and forced the truth on her. Now we had to deal with it. I recall something being said about taking me to the mental health department, and I ended it with, "There is nothing wrong with me, it's just how I am and it isn't going to change." I had failed to gain her support. I could not go back to school. I felt friendless, unloved and angry!

I went into the bathroom and found several bottles of pills. I didn't know what they were, but I ate them. I just felt hopeless and really wanted to die. I didn't want to do life anymore; barely fifteen and ready to give up. I got very sick, but obviously did not die. I'm not sure how the discovery of my botched suicide unfolded as I was in a fog for a few days after. But I distinctly recall my mother saying, "This can't go on, it's either reform school or your father's. I just don't know what else to do with you. Why would you do such a thing?"

I decided if she couldn't figure out why I was so unhappy, then it was time for me to go.

As if my mother didn't have enough to handle, her mother died. I was there when the phone call came and rarely, before or since, have I witnessed such grief. She wailed in agony and disbelief. Her legs buckled and she lay on the kitchen floor weeping like a child. Until my own mother's recent death, I doubt I appreciated the singularly painful experience of losing your mother. I knew the last thing she needed to deal with was me and my problems.

I quit school, and pushed my mother over the edge. There was no way I would live with my father, and though reform school sounded vaguely intriguing (considering it was all boys), it was a jail, and I wanted to be free of the constraints and rules imposed on me. I spent more time in the city with Melody at an apartment in the ghetto with various other hippie and biker types, and couldn't think of anyplace else to go. It was a big, third-floor walk-up in an old house converted into apartments that leaned to one side and was painted a pale green. There were always people coming and going, and I'm not sure who actually lived there aside from Mel and her cousin Sherry. There was plenty of booze and pot around, but I don't remember any hard drugs. If there were, Melody kept it away from me. I wandered the bars with Mel, and, because I was with her, I was allowed in despite my age. I lied about my age regularly anyway, and few questioned it. Back then the drinking age in Maine was eighteen.

It was during this time that I got my first tattoo, experienced my first arrest, and visited my first gay bar.

I am heavily tattooed now, and I do not regret them. They are a map of my life, and they satisfy my desire to create and control my own image. Perhaps my paternal grandmother's tattoos started my fascination with them, but I know my reason for my first was entirely different from the rest. I was running with a rough crowd and wanted to belong. I wanted to look like the city instead of the country. I wanted to appear more masculine and cool.

My first tattoo was a crudely done zodiac symbol on my right arm. Some biker did it at the kitchen table in Mel's apartment while we drank Southern Comfort, and I tried not to throw up.

I threw up.

Melody had a pair of lesbian friends who visited the apartment and were openly gay. I hadn't ever met an openly gay person until then. One night she and the gay girls took me to The Blue Swan. It was a private club in the basement of an old factory. There was no street sign indicating its whereabouts, and you had to knock to get in. You didn't park your car near The Blue Swan or it would surely be damaged when you returned. The club was a small, narrow room with a tiny dance floor at the far end. It was dark, crowded, smoky and loud, just like all the other bars I'd been in, but the couples were all the same sex. They were laughing and dancing, kissing and hugging each other, seeming like they didn't have a care in the world.

One night when I was in there some drunken good ole boys came in with boxing gloves on their hands and hate in their eyes. I'm not sure how they got past the locked front door. The old queen who owned the place was ready for them when they approached the bar, with a shotgun and a smile. They left without spilling any blood that night, but the experience left me with the certain knowledge of the unreasonable hatred of our kind. I was scared to death that first time. I didn't automatically feel like I belonged just because they were gay. It was all so foreign to me, but at least I had a starting point. It was still a dangerous world and would be for several years to come.

Another night, I drank way too much and was stopped on the street by a cop. I was too drunk to remember what happened, but the end result was waking up freezing and hung-over in a cold, damp cell in the basement of the Androscoggin County Jail that looked like a medieval dungeon. They released me to Melody without charges, and she told me I had just decided to approach and ver- bally attack a cop, until he cuffed me and took me to jail. I remember her being quite annoyed with my stupidity, and I was embarrassed that I had made an ass of myself.

Apparently, most of the people living in the apartment were supporting themselves to some degree with crime. Selling drugs, stealing, and con games were sources of income, and "stickin' it to the man" was justified by our oppression and outlaw status. Other than pilfering ciga- rettes from my mother's purse and the occasional beer from my stepfather, I had only stolen once in my life. I was nine years old and shoplifted candy and trinkets from our local country store. After she caught me, my mother made me return the stolen goods, and gave me a lec- ture I remember to this day.

Two old ladies, the Baily sisters, owned and operated the store that had been a family business for genera- tions. My mother had known them all her life. She told me my Gram went to grade school with those ladies, I had shamed her in front of them, and that she had been poor her whole life and had never taken anything that didn't belong to her. She said she was sorry we were poor and didn't have all the things other kids had, but she did her best, and stealing was not the answer. She said when you're poor, sometimes all you have is your good name, and her family had always had a good name, and she was not going to be the one to raise a thief. She got by on very little, and she expected us to do the same. Dishonesty was never acceptable in any form for any reason.

My now second attempt at a life of crime was no more successful than my first at nine years old.

A burglary was being planned, and I was invited to participate. I couldn't appear a coward if I was to enhance my newfound persona as an outlaw. There were three of us involved, and Mel and I were two of them. A house was chosen. I don't know why that particular house, but when our driver dropped us in front, I was horrified to realize this house was down the road from my grandmother's, and I knew the people who lived there.

People didn't lock their doors back then, so it was not necessary to break in. We walked right in the kitchen door and commenced to ransack the house. In the short time we were in there I found nothing worth stealing, and suspected I had not found my ticket to financial stability quite yet. We were only inside a few minutes when the dark house was lit by headlights in the driveway. Seized with panic, we fled out the back door and into the snow-covered woods.

Our driver was supposed to meet us out front, but he fled in our ride upon return of the homeowners, and later said he drove up and down the road looking for us until he spotted police cars and abandoned us to our fate.

Realizing their home had been burglarized, the homeowners called the police. Our footprints in the snow revealed our escape into the woods. We spent several hours in hiding before emerging a few miles away onto the open road, hoping our driver would spot and rescue us. We were a long way from the city, and had a long, cold walk ahead of us. We had not walked far when our rescue arrived in the form of a police car.

There was no place to run, and no point in trying. Guns were pointed at us, and we were put in handcuffs. I remember thinking there was no actual evidence linking us to the crime until an officer searched Melody and pulled a set of wedding rings out of her jacket pocket. They were inscribed with the names and wedding date of the home owners. I could have shot her myself at that moment for not throwing those rings into the woods when she realized our caper was not going as planned.

Perhaps it was best that I was caught in my very first crime, or I might have been encouraged to make a career out of it. I was ashamed of what I had done, and was embarrassed publicly one more time in the community I was raised in. When my mother was called, she was horrified and embarrassed by what I had done. She had known that family many years, and I had sullied her name with them. She refused to do anything to help me out of my situation, and informed the police that I no longer lived at home and was not her responsibility. I was released the next day, and a short time later returned for a hearing where, as a juvenile and first-time offender, I was found guilty and placed on informal probation. Melody was released on bail and, due to an extensive criminal history, was still facing a potential jail term. She often spoke of going to California, and now, with a jail term hanging over her head, it seemed like a good time to get the hell out of Maine.

Her cousin Sherry and her boyfriend had already left Maine and were living in Topeka, Kansas. We set Topeka as a halfway stop on our way to California. We had no car and very little money. But we had a destination, and thought we had a place to live when we reached California. The only way to get where we were going was to hitchhike. All my possessions fit in a duffel bag. I didn't tell anyone I was going, and Mel had a pending court case, so she wasn't spreading the news either. We just hit the road, stuck out our thumbs, and left Maine behind us.

It was not a great adventure, and we were not wandering, as I did later on. We had a place to get to and not much money with which to get there. Hitchhiking with a woman is always easier because of the truckers on the highways. And some thought we were both women, as by then my hair had recovered from my father's buckknife barbering, and my traveling outfit consisted of denim cut-offs, moccasins and a ponytail.

The trip from Maine to Topeka took less than a week by thumb and was uneventful. We rode with a series of forgettable men who flirted with Melody and ignored me. I seized every opportunity to curl up on a back seat and sleep away days of boring travel.

When we arrived in Topeka, I found pretty much the same situation we'd left in Maine; a group of castaways living in an old run-down house, scrounging for money and doing drugs. I thought it was just a pit-stop on the way to the land of sunshine and movie stars, but it looked like we were going to stay awhile. I was scared of being in an unfamiliar place so far from home, but happy to be free of the oppression of family and their expectations, and the social shame of my recent misdeeds. We slept on mattresses on the floor, pooled our resources for food, and cooked outside on a fire pit because we couldn't afford gas for the stove. It was communal living at its most primitive.

Somehow, I got a job as a waiter in a truck stop named Ruby's Diner. I don't know if I was even sixteen yet, but I lied about my age regularly, and no one questioned it. Ruby's was something right out of a movie set, the stereotyped truck stop with plenty of beer-bellied, loud-mouthed rednecks and big-haired, gum-chewing floozies with names like Mitzi and Lulu. You had all your regulars, and those occasional tourists stopping at the first place they spotted along the dust bowl highway that was Kansas in the 1970s.

Waiters were a rarity in those days, especially in truck stops, and those truckers teased me mercilessly. The ladies I worked with kept an ear open and tongue-lashed them if they went too far. I believe my youth and vulnerability triggered their mothering instincts. I waited tables, washed dishes, swept floors, filled ketchup bottles and hosed the highway dust off the windows. People always seemed curious about the little blond boy with the deep Maine accent, and asked a lot of questions I didn't want to answer. Where was I from? Where was my family? Did my Mama know where I was? Where was I going?

I don't know why I had the fear someone would send me back. I wasn't a real runaway because no one was looking for me, and I had no place to go. I just believed at some point I would be apprehended, handcuffed and told, "Kid, you're going back to where you came from."

We pooled our money at the house I was staying in. After a few of my paychecks disappeared, and I was one of the few bringing anything in, I quickly lost my admiration for the concept of communal living. There was a lot more partying going on there than there was working.

I hated Kansas, I hated where I was living, hated where I was working, and I didn't want to be there. Kansas seemed a lot like Maine, but without all the hills and trees. Same shit in a different place. I didn't know how long Mel planned on staying, but I was ready to go soon after we got there. The charm of the diner wore off quickly, as one more time I grew tired of the predictably ignorant insults concerning my lack of masculinity. The truckers tagged me "Missy," and it stuck. Ruby said, "Pay 'em no mind, they don't mean no harm," and I imagine she had taken a lot of shit from a lot of truckers in her time, but I had hoped I was leaving all that behind me when I left Maine.

One thing I learned quickly, from coast to coast and north to south: there are assholes wherever you go. The good, the bad, and the ugly, and most of the time you can't tell them apart until it's too late. My life was not full of misery from birth to present, and I had plenty of laughs and sweet memories in my childhood. But eight solid years of my teens, from twelve to twenty, were a daily struggle, and I can only guess that the fortitude that ran through my mother's veins was passed on to me, because it was one obstacle or another keeping me from getting a foothold on solid ground. After a few months in Topeka, Mel was tired of it too, and we stuck out our thumbs again and headed for California.

Melody had a cousin on her mother's side who lived in Redondo Beach, California, a quaint seaside community in LA County. He said we could stay with him for a while. Unfortunately, when we arrived, we discovered he lived with his mother, and she was not as welcoming. We had no car, almost no money, no job prospects, and no place to live.

But California was beautiful. The weather was perfect, there were palm trees and the ocean, and the air was electrified with dreams and promises. I was excited just to be there.

I might have been sixteen by then. The days all run together when you have no reason to mark them: no calendars or watches, no workdays and weekends, no place you have to be. I don't even remember what month it was, because California has no discernible seasons.

There was an old truck with no wheels and a mattress in the bed in the alley behind Mel's cousin's house. This was my home for a while. Mel was allowed to stay in the house, and she would bring some food out to me when she could. During the day, I wandered the streets, sometimes with Mel, but most often without. I weaved in and out of businesses asking for a job, blissfully ignorant of my prospects. I had no identification cards, no address, no contact phone and no job skills, but was hopeful someone would come along and offer me a life I couldn't refuse.

I picked and ate the abundant fruit from all the fruit trees hanging over people's fences, and discovered the dumpsters behind the fast food restaurants and grocery stores as sources of free food. I sat on the beach and watched all the people who had a life in that beautiful place. I dreamed to the sounds of crashing waves and screaming gulls, and felt like it was where I could make a home. I had more traveling to do before that could happen. I couldn't live in an alley, and they didn't want me there. Melody had some support from her cousin and wanted to stay, so I decided it was time to hit the road again. I don't know that I had a whole twenty dollars in my pocket, but I knew how to survive by then. I headed for Hollywood.

Adrift

He was a prince who fell from grace,
a lord without his land,
an astronaut gone lost in space,
a gambler's losing hand.
He was a wheel that ceased to turn,
a well that had run dry,
a smoldering fire too weak to burn,
a corpse that wouldn't die.
He was a ship now set adrift
on life's unruly sea,
to find a bridge that closed the rift
from who he was and came to be.

E.M.

Chapter 4
The Spider and the Butterfly

These were not easy years ahead, but this is not some over-dramatized documentary on street kids meant to pull the heartstrings. It was just a time in my life, and I did what I had to do in order to do what I wanted to do.

I suppose I could have gone home. I could have followed my mother's rules and finished school or worked in a factory. I wanted to experience things I couldn't back home. I wanted to be free of judgments and family responsibility. I was hungry to feel something profound and powerful. I wanted crazy, sexy fun.

The streets of Hollywood were crowded with sound and color. Fashion was moving out of hippie and into disco, and even the first sightings of what became punk. The store windows were full of things I'd never seen, and there was music in the streets. There were hundreds of other kids by themselves or in packs, and I watched them and mimicked their bravado. People slept on benches and curled up in doorways to be off the sidewalks as night fell, and the pulse of the streets was charged with the smell of sex, drugs and danger in the air. Some kids showed me a few abandoned buildings where we gathered to do drugs or sleep when I couldn't hustle a guy into buying a room for the night.

The streets weren't prowled by gangs like they are now, and danger was in the individual, safety was in a group. From the time I was very young, I knew there were men who wanted young boys. I didn't hold it against them and might not have survived without them. There were specific areas of the city where men shopped their specific vices, and the pimps were busy with their women and left the boys to themselves. Sometimes we boys paired up, usually for companionship, rarely for sex. And we were transients. Transients know camaraderie, but not love. Love was for someone standing still.

There were still many things I had not done yet, and I was often taken aback by the requests of men with money in their hands and lust in their eyes. I said "no" to men I thought unattractive or creepy, and quickly forgot their faces. But there are still a handful of faces that I remember to this day, handsome, soft-spoken men, scared or shy about what they were doing, and often wearing wedding bands. They were desperate and frenzied in their lovemaking. I saw their secret lives, their need, their fear of getting caught, and recognized it from my recent childhood, and I felt power over them and gratitude that I had escaped their fate. These are the men who would feed me and buy me a room for a night so I could shower and sleep in a bed. These are the men who tried to kiss me and ask me questions about myself and pretend they would not leave soon to go home to their wives and kids. These were the men who bought their fantasies from strangers in small fragments and carried them home to the cold beds of their suburban neighborhoods. These are the men who would return over and over until someone was destroyed for his indiscretion.

I've always had a sweet spot in my memory for a tall, dark-haired man, graying at the temples, with huge sad eyes and smelling of Old Spice and guilt. He lay beside me in a cheap motel, damp with sweat, twirling a lock of my long hair around his finger. He said softly, "I have a son your age." I wondered if he looked at me and pictured his own boy having sex with a stranger for $15 and a drive-thru burger and fries.

I hated when they tried to talk to me. It made it all too real. It made me feel human and vulnerable, and it made me want someone of my own, for every day, not just a night. I just wanted them to teach me how to be better at what I was doing, so I could get where I wanted to be faster. I absolutely did not want them to make me care about them, or anything else beyond the act I was being paid for.

I didn't stay but a few weeks before I headed east. I didn't want to go back to Maine, but it was all I knew, and I was hungry and tired. My trip across the country was more of the same: truckers and single men, but fewer, as I didn't have a woman with me this time to lure the men. But every one of them wanted sex, and many had drugs. I've always thought it ironic that people are willing to give you $20 worth of drugs to have someone to get high with, but wouldn't buy you a $2 hamburger when you're starving, unless you give them something in return.

I took my time heading east, knowing I was headed home, and hoping someone would come along and give me a reason not to. I met a few interesting characters along the way who picked me up for someone to talk to, I guess, but eventually the subject would turn to sex or the hand would creep across the seat. I got tired of the ritual, the phony sincerity, and the innuendo all leading up to the same thing.

I made it to Connecticut where my uncle Frankie lived. I liked my Uncle Frankie and Aunt Ginger. He was my mother's brother. Uncle Frankie wouldn't let me go back out on the road again, and bought me a bus ticket to Maine.

No sooner did I step off that bus in Maine than the familiar cloud of oppression settled over me. I was not happy to be back. I had done nothing meaningful since I left Maine, and felt like a dog with his tail between his legs, returning home hungry and subdued after a spontaneous run for freedom. I learned quickly there's no freedom in poverty.

I did not return to my mother's house except to visit. I couldn't do that to either of us. We were still worlds apart in our thinking. I never lived at home again after I left at fifteen. Much later, Ma would often say that she respected my independence and the fact that I made my own way no matter what. I stayed in the city with my sister Rose until I found a job and a little apartment, my first place of my very own. If I remember correctly, those two rooms and a bath were $18 a week in rent. I was sixteen years old.

I paid that rent doing the one thing I swore I wouldn't do: I went to work in the shoe factory. That part of Maine was full of shoe and textile factories, and families worked there for generations. Three of my older siblings were making shoes, and I got a job at the factory my mother had been in for more than twenty years. My job was right beside her on the conveyor line. It was nightmarishly repetitive and boring assembly work. The conveyor stopped for fifteen minutes in the morning, half an hour for lunch, and another fifteen minutes in the afternoon, and you absolutely could not leave your post for a moment without holding up the entire line of production. People shouted and laughed down the line, and I was amazed that some appeared to actually like their jobs.

It pained me to watch my mother work like that. I watched her work in the suffocating heat of summer with sweat running down her face. She had varicose veins in her legs from standing on those concrete floors during her pregnancies, and for the first time, I realized all she had done for her kids all these years, and I was ashamed of all the trouble I caused her.

One day she was sick, and it was swelteringly hot in the factory. She asked the foreman several times if he would cover her job while she went to the bathroom. Each time he was too busy. I watched her go pale and shaky but keep up with the line. One more time she asked the foreman for a small break, and he shouted at her, "Lottie, if you can't keep up, there's plenty of people that will take your job!"

As I watched her shrink in resignation, my rage was so swift and bitter, my shame for her enslavement so complete, and my fury at this son-of-a-bitch half her age talking to my mother that way, that before I could stop myself, I threw a shoe in his direction. He stopped and turned. Everyone, especially Ma, looked horrified as I shouted, "You piece-of-shit motherfucker, you ever talk to my mother like that again and I'll kill you."

Ma said, "Oh my God, Honey, you'll lose your job. You shouldn't have done that! I'll be okay."

I looked at her and said, "I don't want this job. I hate this place, and this will not be my life, Ma!"

I was fired at the end of the day. It's the one and only time I was ever fired in my life, and it was worth it. I still hate that arrogant, ignorant man for the way he spoke to my mother. She could have run that whole factory better than he could.

I went into one more factory for a brief stint after that. It was a slipper factory. I sat at a sewing machine stitching the fur trim on vinyl slippers. The fake fur came in huge rolls and I just sat there stitching and snipping, stitching and snipping. I was coated with fur at the day's end, and coughing up pink and blue fur balls like a psychedelic house cat.

I was partying a lot, and spending my nights at The Blue Swan. I wasn't a timid boy anymore, and my time on the streets had made me tougher. I knew I was not there to stay and, knowing that, made me care less. I wove in and out of meaningless encounters, and didn't even think about love. I was just doing time until I could find my way out again.

I left the slipper factory and found a job as a shoe clerk in a department store. It was clean, I could dress nice, and the people I worked with were a cut above the factory people. Selling shoes is a lot easier than making them.

One day, I was stocking shelves in the shoe department when I noticed a handsome, stocky, dark-haired man watching me. I asked him if I could help him find something, and his response was, "Yeah, your phone number. I seem to have lost it." Today I might find that line a tad smarmy, but I was young, and he had a dazzling smile.

He asked, "You are gay, aren't you?" I assured him I was, and pulled out a pen to give him my number when he said, "Just so you know, I'm married, but my wife knows I'm bisexual and is cool with it."

I should have walked away right then, but this was a new game to me. I was curious how it all worked, and he was very attractive, so I gave him my number. He called that night and asked me out for a drink. He did not know I was only sixteen and didn't ask. He was thirty-one, his wife twenty-eight, and they had a four-year-old son and a two-year-old daughter.

Today, my conscience does not permit me to date married men, but things were different in the late 1970s. It was the sexual revolution post-'60s pre-AIDS era, and people were exploring sexuality more openly. I figured if he had a wife and she knew about it, it was between them. Little did I know, but was quick to learn, that he had more elaborate plans for us than a simple affair with a young man.

Our first evening together, he informed me that not only did his wife know, but would like to participate, and she was looking forward to meeting me. I had not been with a woman before, and had never wanted to. I'd had juvenile "girlfriends," and more than a few make-out and petting sessions with girls, but they made me kind of nervous, and I just didn't feel the same excitement as with another male. But he excited me, and the idea of doing something different and taboo did too.

The first time I met her was a bit awkward, but I was taken with her beauty. She had waist-length black hair and large green eyes. She was very slender and small-breasted, which I find more attractive in women.

I have not used their names and don't intend to. They are alive and well, though no longer married, and it serves no purpose to embarrass others for their youthful indiscretions.

I embarked on a ménage a trois with this beautiful young couple for several months, and until it ended, I explored and enjoyed all the pleasures and complications of love and sex possible outside the traditional boundaries of monogamy. We laughed a lot and had fun together, but I was too young and selfish to see the pressure on their marriage building to a crisis. I wondered later if the games they played were an attempt to save a crumbling marriage through sexual adventure.

I have always observed monogamy in my relationships, and believe if one must play sex games, it is wise not to do it with someone you love. You should be able to walk away with a clear conscience, like I did with them.

I knew people talked about us, and I didn't care. Some were envious of our sexual sophistication, imagining the private life of the beautiful dark-haired couple and their young blond pet. I thought it all quite daring and outrageous and reveled in my new image as the sexually sophisticated young man breaking all the rules and shocking all the squares. I was ready to really give them something to talk about.

Sex has so much power in our world, and I put all I had into being sexually provocative. Laughter was a close second. Take nothing seriously. Laugh at others and laugh at yourself. Be crazy, be sexy, be funny, and the world is yours. And inside I told myself, above all be smart. Let them all think what they want, but know what you want and go after it. Stay in control.

The gossip again reached the factory, and my mother casually inquired of my shenanigans, but I remained aloof and mysterious as to the nature of my relationships.

My dear mother always loved to ask questions, but hated the answers. When I grew older and we became friends, she amused me by asking questions of a sordid nature and then pretended to be offended. She would say, "Oh my God, that is just terrible!" And after a pause, "And then what happened?"

My first sexual experience with a woman was not terrible. I was not repulsed, nor was I enthralled. It was the experience itself, not the people involved, which excited me. Of course a man to whom I was very attracted was always present, and it seemed it was something he and I did together, and she was the third party. I was quite fond of her personality, and that made it more comfortable to play their games.

I personally have always believed that sexuality is rarely black or white, but more shades of gray. I believe we are more inclined to emotionally attach ourselves to a particular gender and, regardless of what I may have experienced, I have never doubted my identity as primarily gay.

I spent a lot of time with them, but kept my own apartment. We were cautious not to expose or confuse their young children.

Ultimately, the novelty wore off, and I began to notice

tension between them, and I tried to put some distance between us.

She told me often that she cared for me, and sometimes shared her concerns about her marriage. He began to complain about her to me and showed up at my apartment to sleep with me alone. Their marriage was falling apart, and I wanted no part of it. I stopped visiting their home completely, and my last experience with him ended badly.

He knocked on my door late in the night and demanded to be let in. I had neighbors across the hall and hurried to quiet him. He was obviously drunk and upset, as she had thrown him out. He professed his love for me, and asked if we could be together. I explained that I was just turning seventeen, I liked his wife and did not want to betray her, I was planning to leave Maine again, and I did not love him. He was never mine to love, and it was not part of the deal.

I told him all of this, and he became very angry. He looked at me and said, "But you broke up my marriage." I became equally angry at such a preposterous accusation and looked him straight in the eye and said, "Oh, no! You broke up your marriage, not me. You brought me home and into your bed and your life. I am single and free. Now go home to your wife."

He wept, but not for me. I know that. He wept for the mess he had made of his life and from his fear of being alone.

He stood on the sidewalk under my window and cursed me until a neighbor threatened to call the law. It was time for me to get out of there again, and they gave me a perfect excuse.

I did not see either of them again until many years later, on a visit to Maine. I saw him in a restaurant with a woman who was not his wife when I knew him. He did not see me. He was no longer beautiful.

I met a guy in The Blue Swan named Skip who had recently moved to Boston. We slept together a few nights, and he gave me his number and told me to come see him if I was ever in Boston. He wasn't anyone special, but he was handsome and fun and I needed a place to stay. He was just a place to run to for me. I stayed with Skip for a month until he came home with another guy and told me I had to go. I wasn't surprised and didn't care. I was just passing through anyway, and he had a weak chin. I've never liked a weak chin on a man.

I knew another couple who were moving to California and already had jobs and a place to live. They invited me to stay with them. One more time I made California my destination, and took my time getting there. I left Boston, hitchhiked to New York, and did some time on the streets hustling for drugs, money, and a place to sleep. Most of the time I slept in parks and public restrooms. Sleeping outside was considerably more dangerous, so if I could find an unlocked public restroom I could lock myself in a stall and curl up next to a toilet and be safe from predators for a few hours.

Occasionally a guy would buy me a room for the night, and leave when he got what he wanted. Those nights were good because I could lock the door and sleep easy. I could never sleep with a stranger in the room. You never knew what they might do. When I left California the first time to hitchhike alone, Melody gave me a pearl-handled switchblade for protection. So far I'd never had to use it, but was never without it. I kept it in the front pocket of my backpack, which was always between my feet when I got in a car, or slipped into my sock when the backpack had to be out of reach.

Those times when I had a room to myself were bliss. I didn't have to be on guard all of the time, and could shower, relax, watch some TV and sleep soundly. There were areas in New York with lots of gay bars, and the streets were teeming with men looking for boys. I can't recall the names of the streets, and probably wouldn't recognize them now. It was getting colder in the fall of 1977, and I was more often looking for a warm place to sleep than anything else.

My last night in New York began with my hanging out on the street with a few other boys, smoking cigarettes and flirting with men driving by. A big maroon Cadillac pulled up to the curb and a handsome thirty-something man with reddish-blond hair leaned out of the window and smiled at me. He said something about me going for a ride with him, but he had a funny accent and I couldn't make out all he said. There was no mention of money. There almost never was. It was just understood. I asked, "Where to?" And he said, "Dinner and a room?"

That was good enough for me. I went around and got in the car.

Once I closed the door and took a look at him, I realized two things immediately. He was wearing a skirt and white knee socks, and he was enormous. He was not fat. He was about two hundred and eighty pounds of rock-solid muscle, and the skirt he was wearing was actually a kilt. The funny accent was Scottish. I had seen Scots on TV dressed like this and playing bagpipes, but not on the streets of New York in real life. He explained that he had just come from a festival for Scots, and didn't dress this way all of the time. I found him charming and unusual, and I relaxed right away.

We made all of the usual small talk and he asked all of the usual questions. Where was I from? Why was I on the street, etc.? By now I hardly listened to the questions. I knew they didn't care about the answers. It was all a prelude to the same end.

We drove through a burger joint and got bags of food and then stopped at a liquor store. He came out with a bottle and a pack of cigarettes for me. We drove a little while and came to a nice motel. It was better than what I was used to, and he left me in the car while he checked in. He was very relaxed and comfortable and smiled a lot. There was no ring, or imprint of one, on his finger and he didn't have the nervous guilt I had come to recognize in the married ones.

He drove to our room, grabbed an overnight bag out of the backseat, and opened my door like a gentleman. The room was more a suite, with a small kitchen area and sitting room. I can still remember every detail of that room down to the print on the bedspread. It was an orange and blue flower print. They were hibiscus flowers. I cannot see a hibiscus flower without remembering that night.

He said, jovially, "I got us a king-size bed because I'm a king-size man." And he was. He stood at least six foot, six inches tall and had legs like tree trunks. I thought he was beautiful, and his way of speaking was cheerful and amusing.

We ate, and he poured us drinks and turned on the television. I had done a lot of drugs, but was not a big drinker. Alcohol always made me scared of losing control. He encouraged me to drink more, and placed a little white pill against my lips. "Here, take this, you seem a little nervous," he said. "It won't hurt you and it will help you relax." I hesitated for only a moment and swallowed the pill. It wasn't the first time I had swallowed a pill I knew nothing about.

He sat on the bed and leaned back against the headboard and said, "Did you know that Scotsmen don't wear anything under their kilts?"

Until then I did not know that. He then patted the bed next to him, beckoning me closer. I wasn't at all scared of him – he seemed quite nice – but I felt dizzy from the alcohol and unsteady on my feet.

I began to undress, and he said, "No. Let me do that."

I crawled up the length of the bed and lay beside him.

The room was spinning, and I had a twinge of fear that it was the pill I had taken, and briefly wondered if it would kill me. I could hardly feel my body and knew this was not the alcohol I was feeling, but something far more powerful.

His name was Robert. I said, "Robert, what did you give me? Am I going to be okay?" Laughing, he said, "Yes, my little Laddy. You'll be just fine." I heard the sound of fabric tearing and realized he was roughly ripping my clothes off. I had no strength or mind to resist and was being tossed around like a rag doll. I heard him mumble "tiny lad" several times, and he kept up an indecipherable chatter, either to himself or to me, and I felt my tender skin burning with abrasions from his beard stubble. I remember him slapping my face intermittently and asking, "You still with me, Boy?"

I don't know how long it went on, maybe minutes, maybe hours. Time was lost in the drugs and the pain.

Over the years, I'd drawn personal boundaries concerning things I would not do with a stranger, and I was still not well-practiced at some of things males did with each other. I was suffocating from the weight of him and felt my limbs painfully twisted. I was no more than one hundred and twenty pounds at seventeen, and so weakened by alcohol and drugs I couldn't have fought off a man half his size.

I must have passed out, as he was pressing a washcloth full of ice on my face, and cooing to me like I was a child. I was drenched in sweat and so was he. I had to go pee. He carried me to the bathroom and propped me on the toilet. The light blinded my eyes, and I closed them. He stood in front of me with his hands on my shoulders so I wouldn't fall forward.

I woke again on the bed, face down, a blinding pain in my lower body. I couldn't move, as his full weight pinned me down. When I cried out, he slammed his forearm to the back of my head, grabbed a fist full of hair and pushed my face into a pillow.

He was an enormous man in all aspects, and I was grateful for the drugs and alcohol to quell the pain and fear of how this night might end.

When you are terrorized, your mind moves so fast it's hard to later organize the thoughts into a clear memory, but I know I thought I might die that night, and I didn't really care. I just wanted to die quickly and painlessly. I don't recall if I was able to even speak a protest to him or plead for my life. I doubt it would have mattered.

I awakened to a sharp blade of sunlight across my face coming from between the blackout drapes. I was still face down, naked, and very sick to my stomach. And I was alone. I rolled my battered body off the bed and staggered to the bathroom. I didn't notice the pain in my body until after I'd finished emptying my stomach of its poisons.

When I pushed myself up from the linoleum floor, every part of my body resisted me. I saw bright red drops of blood on the floor, and a small steady stream running down my inner thigh to my ankle. I reached back and brought my hand away sticky with blood and body fluids. I felt sick with panic to see so much blood and realize it was coming from me!

The back of the bathroom door had a full length mirror. I stood in front of it and looked at myself. Blood was smeared from the waist down and I had a perfect bloody hand print on my shoulder. I had fingernail cuts and bite marks, bruises and abrasions all over my body. Only my face had not a single mark on it. He had spared my face. My side hurt like hell and I looked to see a fist-sized bruise as purple as a plum on my ribs, and vaguely recalled the frenzied blow that caused it.

I wrapped a towel around my waist and drew it up between my legs like a diaper to stop the dripping blood. I turned on the shower and went out of the bathroom.

The bed was in tangles, and the white sheets spotted with small droplets of drying blood. My backpack lay near the door, as if thrown hastily, and on the nightstand was the whiskey bottle, a quarter full. Beside it were three twenty dollar bills. I was actually grateful he had left me the money. I imagined that he had felt bad for the state he'd left me in, and that he'd checked to see if I was still breathing before he left the twenties on the night stand for me to find. The money told me he wasn't coming back.

My shirt and underwear lay on the floor in tatters, but my pants were not ruined.

I took a long, hot shower and washed my hair, and the thick fog in my head gradually subsided to a dull throb. The bleeding slowed, and all I was left with was the aches. It would all heal. I had been beaten before. It always heals.

I wasn't mad at him. I was bought and paid for. I was really just dismayed, because I thought he was so nice and charming and I liked him. I was a little mad at myself. He tricked me with the pill and I fell for it. He didn't hate me. I knew that. He just wanted what he wanted and this was how he got it. At the time I did not consider it a rape. Only girls could be raped, I thought, and I put myself in his hands willingly and only had myself to blame.

I've thought of Robert many times in my life, and sometimes imagined it all differently. I imagined that he wrapped me in his big arms and pulled me close and was tender and sweet. That he cleaned the blood away, and covered me with a clean sheet, stroked my unmarked face, and was contrite over what he had done. I imagined he was ashamed of his lustful violence, and vowed to never harm another unsuspecting boy. And I imagined he would not keep that promise to himself and that I was just one of many. He must have at least known I was still alive or he would not have left the money.

I ate the cold leftover food from the night before, and lay on the bed smoking and trying to remember anything I could of what had happened. Thankfully, I remembered very little. The details I do remember are still as clear as if it happened yesterday. There are some things one never forgets.

Before checkout time, I stuffed tissue paper between my legs to staunch the bleeding, straightened the bed and room a bit, put the whiskey in my backpack and headed back out to the street. I didn't want anyone to know what had happened. I despised the idea of myself as a victim. It offended my pride. Until now, I've never told anyone about that night. I played the scene from that night over in my head for a long time to come, and changed the way I dealt with the men that came after Robert. I left New York the next day, and started hitchhiking south to a warmer climate. There was no one to say goodbye to, no one who would notice I was gone, and all I owned was in a backpack.

For the next three months, I wandered the country. My body healed from Robert's assault, but he stayed with me as a lesson learned for a long time after. The lesson that few are who they appear to be and fewer are to be trusted.

Other than a little pot and a drink now and then, I stopped doing drugs, and stayed cautious and alert among strangers. When you're homeless, everyone is a stranger.

I met many interesting characters in my travels, some nice and some not so nice. The truckers always got me to key cities, and often only wanted someone to talk to on their lonely rides. I did what I had to do to keep food in my belly and a pack of cigarettes in my pocket, but nothing more. I did not and would not steal from anyone. I have always carried with me the shame of being caught stealing when I was nine, and again when I participated in the burglary of an innocent family's home. And I could not beg or panhandle. I was too proud to ask for anything from anyone if I had nothing to offer in return. My body was mine to do with as I wished, and those men always got more than I did out of the deal.

All of these years later, I still have very clear recollections of many of the people I met in my travels across America. Aside from the various single men, and sometimes couples, who were looking for sex, I met some memorable characters who made me laugh or touched my heart in some way.

There was a young couple who picked me up along the coast of Georgia. Couples always made me uncomfortable. I understood single men looking for sex, but I have always been pretty traditional when it comes to marriage and monogamy. I'm possessive and jealous in love, and never wanted to share my partner in any way, and can be pretty judgmental of those who do. In my heart, I always wanted love to be so pure and all-consuming that no one else could be a part of it, and no one could penetrate that sanctioned bond.

I don't remember this couple's names. They were young and plain of face, in their thirties, I guessed. They had the kindest smiles, but so did Robert, and I did not trust a smile anymore. They were not looking for sex. They saw a young boy on the side of the road and couldn't pass him by. They were going on a trip to Disney World, and they were happy. They asked me all the usual questions, but they were different. They listened carefully to my answers, and were concerned that my mother was worried, that I should be in school, and that I would be hurt out there alone.

They were professed Christians, and they talked to me about their God, and how He must be watching over me to keep me safe, and I wondered where their God was when Robert was drugging, beating and raping me. Religious fanaticism has always made me very uncomfortable, but they were not fanatics. They were just good, Christian people spreading the word of their God and reaching out to a stranger and sharing their happiness.

They had put off Disney World for years so they could take their first child, but found out recently that they could not have one.

We drove until dusk, and they offered me dinner and my own room in a motel, and I accepted. They took me to a restaurant where we actually went inside and sat at a table. I had done very little of that in my life, and was nervous and embarrassed about my worn clothing and unkempt appearance, but they didn't seem to notice or care.

I had never sat at a table that had two forks for one person, and they explained the difference between a salad and a dinner fork. I picked the least expensive meal on the menu and they encouraged me to eat more, including dessert. It was uncomfortable for me. I have always felt awkward with generosity and charity. They got me my own room at a motel, and she told me to wrap a towel around me because she was going to wash all of my clothes. I showered and slept peacefully, and all of my clothes were clean the next morning when they called my room to invite me to breakfast. I thought they would be gone when I woke up, and I'd be on my own again.

They invited me to Orlando with them, and I went along because I had no place I had to be, and had never been to Florida. They told me they talked about me the night before and agreed that I needed a stable home and a good education. They wanted me to stay with them, go back to school, and "see how it worked out." They wanted a child so bad, and felt God wanted them to take care of me. They were so sincere and kind, and I felt bad for them when I told them I didn't want to go to school or live in someone else's house. I never told them I was gay and they never asked, but I knew being gay didn't mix well with the whole religion thing, and I didn't want any of that kind of restriction put on me. I had already run away from that. I thought it was kind of weird, in a nice way, that they would consider taking a total stranger into their home, but I considered myself quite grown up and not a child up for adoption. They actually seemed slightly wounded when I declined their offer. Perhaps they thought I was interfering with their God's plan. I said my goodbyes to them in Orlando. They made me take money and their phone number. I meant to call and just say hello, but too much time passed and then it didn't seem right. They gave me a Bible, and I read it every day. Sitting on the highway or under a tree in a park, I would open it to a random page and read. It never made much sense to me, but it passed the time.

I thought of them after we parted and imagined what my life would have been had I taken their offer. But I didn't want a new family. I really didn't even want the one I already had. I hope they adopted children. I just knew they would be good parents and raise good kids.

Florida is a great place in which to be homeless. You never have to worry about being cold. I wandered the coast for a few weeks before heading west. I had a destination, but was in no hurry to get there.

I met other hikers along the way, and sometimes paired up for a while, but people are less inclined to pick up more than one hiker at a time, and you were rarely headed in the same direction, so it never lasted. But, now and then, it took away a little loneliness to have a comrade in the war of the open road. I wouldn't hitchhike across the street today, but things were different then. People weren't so afraid of each other.

I did not ever get in a car with more than one man in

it. I could fight off one guy, but knew better than to take risks against two or more. If I didn't like the look or feel of someone, I would decline a ride and wait for the next. Of course, sometimes I was wrong, or just tired of the road, and found myself trapped in a car with someone weird or creepy. Such was the case on a dark, deserted highway in Mississippi.

I didn't usually hitchhike too late into the night. Once it got late, I would find a place to curl up and sleep until sunrise. I was scared one of those big trailer trucks would not see me and run me down in the dark. If I could get to a rest area, I would sleep in a bathroom stall or on a picnic table. If not, a bed of pine straw would do.

I met more than a few men who were in hotels or motels during business trips, and would sometimes stay with them for a few days or a week. Some took me home for a while until one of us got bored with the other, or his fantasies were spent.

All their faces are blurred together in my memory now. But they were almost always between forty and fifty years old. There's something about that age in a man that makes him search for something new. I've seen it too often for it not to be true. I guess it's what's called the mid-life crisis. It's a restlessness, a hunger, a dissatisfaction with what he has, no matter how good it looks to others. It's a void he struggles to fill, often with sex.

I liked older men, and seldom was attracted to guys my own age. Perhaps I was looking for that elusive father figure, and I felt a false sense of security with older men. This particular night in Mississippi I was hitching in the dark. I honestly can't say how I got out in the middle of nowhere like I was. Usually a ride would end at a rest area, truck stop or an intersection of highways, but this was just a long empty stretch of road with woods on both sides. Sometimes a ride would just abruptly stop and say, "This is as far as I go." And you had to get out. There wasn't much point in walking. You would just blister your feet and get nowhere fast.

There were few cars on the road that night, and most would slow down and peer at me curiously and continue on their way.

Eventually a rusty old Volkswagen Beetle, painted orange, pulled to the shoulder and idled while I approached. When I opened the passenger door to greet the driver, I saw the entire front of the car was filled with his bulk. Rolls of fat pressed against the steering wheel and spilled over to the passenger seat, leaving only a small space available for me.

Many times I have seen obese people squeeze themselves in and out of very small cars, and wondered why they chose a vehicle that appeared so uncomfortable and inappropriate to their size. Do they convince themselves that, if they can fit into a Volkswagen Beetle, they aren't too fat?

And he was black.

Until I left home at fifteen, I'd only seen a handful of black people, except on television. Maine was, and is still, the whitest state in the country, having only a two percent black population. I confess to being intimidated by his skin color.

I considered declining the ride but was eager to get off the deserted highway and get to civilization, so I squeezed into what little space was left and put my backpack on the floor between my feet.

We drove for miles making small talk, though I struggled to understand him through the thick southern accent, and could not relax with the closeness of him.

If men were looking for sex, they would usually get their point across early in the ride, so it came as a bit of a surprise when his hand casually settled on my knee and gave it an affectionate squeeze. This was always an awkward moment, regardless of how many times it happened, particularly when it was followed by rejection. I was not only disinterested this time, I was repulsed, and immediately pushed his hand away and said, "Sorry man, I'm just looking for a ride and nothing else."

I had done this enough times and I know that no one wants to be rejected, but you can't blame a guy for trying.

Rejection is always followed by an uncomfortable silence, and then one of several scenarios. Either they laughed it off and pretended I had misunderstood their intentions, or attempted to persuade me into a change of heart with a sad story of their loneliness, or accusations that I had misled them. The end result was always my being put out of the car as quickly as possible.

And occasionally, you had a really pushy one. This was a pushy one. No sooner did I push his hand off my knee than he came right back and dove into my crotch with a squeeze. The car was so cramped I had nowhere to go, and couldn't slide out of his grip, so I roughly grabbed his wrist and said, "You can let me out right here!"

He acted as if he didn't hear me and continued to drive without slowing. He had a smirk on his face and said, "You don't have to do anything to me, just let me do the work. Just slide your pants down."

I was more annoyed than scared, and said, "It's not going to happen, so let me out of the fucking car!"

Maybe it was my cussing that pissed him off, or the knowledge that I was not going to capitulate, but his arm shot out and struck me across the chest the way one does instinctively when you slam on the brakes, but with a lot of force, about three hundred and fifty pounds of force. Pinning me with his forearm right below my throat, he said, "Just do what I said and I'll let you out."

Though I had never had to use it, I still had the switchblade Melody gave me in the front pocket of my back pack on the floor.

I was white hot with rage, and my mind was racing with how I could get to that knife. Robert's attack was still fresh in my mind and body, and I was not going to let it happen again.

I agreed to take my pants down, and he put his free hand back on the wheel. I pretended to fumble with my belt and reached down quickly to find the knife. In one move I had the knife, pushed the blade button, and brought it to his fat neck.

My voice was shaking with rage, and I said, "You stop this car now you fat mother-fucking pig, or I'll drive this right into your neck!"

He stared straight ahead and took his foot off the accelerator.

I think I could have done it. I think I could have stuck him with that knife. I was tired of being treated like a piece of meat, and tired of people putting their hands on me and forcing me to do things I didn't want to do.

As soon as that car came to a stop, I grabbed my pack, got out and started walking without saying a word. He just sat there behind me with the engine idling. I walked about an eighth of a mile and not a single car came by, but his headlights still lit up the road ahead of me.

I wondered what the hell he was doing back there when I heard the engine racing and he started forward.

There was about three feet of gravel shoulder, a steel guardrail, and on the other side of that, a steep embankment. I had a funny feeling about this guy and didn't want my back to him. As he got closer and picked up speed I just knew he was going to come at me, and that's exactly what he did. He started veering onto the shoulder and picking up speed. I had no place to go but over the embankment to the darkness below or get run over by an orange VW bug in rural Mississippi driven by a crazed, obese black man. So over I went, sliding and tumbling, to land in a few feet of black swamp water.

I imagined alligators and snakes speeding through the dark, and scrambled back up that embankment like a bolt of lightning until I hit a dry spot and lay down to catch my breath, think about what happened, and wait until morning to get back on the road.

I have told people here and there of my adventures, and was often told, "it is amazing you're still alive." I suppose it is, but with freeways and airplanes and cancer and serial killers, I think it's amazing any of us are. I just pushed the envelope a little more than most.

All I wanted to do was get the hell out of Mississippi at that point. The next morning a trucker picked me up, and I did just that.

I thought Louisiana and Alabama were pretty states, and it was warm for sleeping outside, but there were an awful lot of black faces peering out at me from the passing cars, and the orange Volkswagen had made me very distrusting of black people. In all my days out on the interstate highways, he was the only black to ever offer me a ride anyway.

My next memorable benefactor will always be known only as "the man with thick glasses." If he told me his name, which I'm sure he did, I have forgotten it. He was a soft-spoken man, and it was difficult to see what he looked like behind his impossibly thick black-rimmed glasses. He appeared slender and of average looks, and though I had learned to trust no one, I quickly relaxed in his company and felt no threat. We conversed with ease.

I learned that people want someone to listen to them, and will tell strangers things they have told no one else. All your secrets are unburdened, then left on the side of a highway. I heard dreams and hopes, triumphs and tragedies, marriages and kids, divorces and affairs, fantasies, and, I'm sure, plenty of lies. God must have been preparing me to be a hairdresser, as I was a pretty good listener. I discussed religion and politics, love and sex, and just about anything else concerning the human condition. I collected dozens of phone numbers from my confessors who felt obligated to consider me a friend after they had told me things they had told no one else. I never called any of them, but kept the numbers until I forgot who they belonged to.

I liked the man with the thick glasses. He was on a week-long business trip in the southeast of Texas, and invited me along as his companion. There was no ring on his finger, and he never mentioned a wife. I'm quite sure he was comfortable being gay, but not in a position to live openly. I imagine his business trips were his opportunities to indulge in his private desires.

He was a gentleman at all times, and did not treat me as the street urchin I was. Most men rented a room with only one bed, so there was no question of what was expected of me. When we entered the room with two queen-sized beds, he politely asked which I preferred. I chose the one closest to the door, and he asked if I would like to shower first before dinner. I did, and expected him to be naked in bed when I emerged. He was not. He was tending to business on the phone and organizing papers in his open briefcase.

He showered, and kept a towel wrapped around his waist while he shaved. Out of his business attire and without his glasses he was quite good looking. His damp dark hair fell over startling blue eyes, and his body was lean and lightly muscled. I lay on the bed watching him shave, and my eyes were drawn to the firm outline of his ass beneath the towel. I felt desire stir in the pit of my stomach. It was rare for me to feel desire for one of the men who picked me up.

He dressed in private, and I was perplexed by his modesty and lack of aggression. We had a dinner with pleasant conversation, and he bought wine to bring back to our room. I had never drunk wine that didn't have a screw top and cost $1.99. I felt a bit embarrassed by his sophistication. He was eloquent, well dressed, and well-mannered, and I wondered what he was doing with someone like me. I know now that he was just lonely, because I have felt it so many times myself.

I wanted to be with him. He didn't have to force, trick, or purchase me. It had been a long time since I had wanted to be with someone. After a few glasses of wine, I stood up and began to undress. He watched me in silence, and when I was completely nude, I lay on the bed beside him. He ran his hand lightly over my stomach and said shyly, "You don't have to do this, if you don't want to."

I looked into his crystal blue eyes and said, "I want to."

What made the man with thick glasses so special, so different, was he was the first person to make love to me. I was seventeen and had lost count of the men I had had sex with, and had done things that would make any whore blush. But I had never made love, and didn't know how.

Every day for a week, I waited impatiently for him to return from his business dealings to teach me more about making love. He was the first to kiss me deeply and passionately on the mouth, the first to bury his face in the hollow of my throat, the first to gently explore my entire body, and the first to show me that my life as a gay man did not have to be shame, pain, or degradation. It could be beautiful. It could be ecstasy.

He did not roll over once spent, but held me through the night, and I woke tangled in his limbs. He told me I was beautiful, and I felt it. I didn't know two men could make love. I thought they only had sex, and had no idea that I was supposed to enjoy myself also. It was exquisite, and it changed me. He made me feel almost normal, and gave me hope for real love with another man. Hope that a gay man's life was not just dark bars, parked cars and sleazy motels.

Before him, the world that everyone else took for granted did not belong to me. The door was closed on white picket fences, wedding bells and babies, holding hands in the street, and telling the whole world you're in love.

And though I could have none of those things with him, he planted a seed in my heart that I might be lovable and I might be of value to someone someday.

And then it was over. He didn't ask me to come home with him. I knew I didn't fit into his life. He was tender in his goodbye and sincere when he wished me a happy life.

He would be around seventy now. I wonder if he ever thought of me, or was I just another boy from one of his many business trips. Did he ever find a lover to stay with, or did he live his life in secret, making love to strangers and leaving them behind?

Recently, a woman I didn't know sent me a 'friend' request on an internet social network. The request was accompanied with a short letter explaining that she met me once when we were twelve years old. She was a cousin to an in-law, and our paths had crossed for only a few hours. She explained that she was a shy and troubled child, and she had seen a kindred spirit in me. That I had listened to her and been kind, and it had meant something to her. She thought of me over the years and had not forgotten my kindness, or me. Thirty-eight years later the phenomenon of the internet assisted her in finding me. I was so moved by her gesture, and honestly embarrassed that I did not recall the day of our meeting. But she proved that we can brush against each other as we move through our lives and have no idea of its affect or meaning on those we meet, however briefly.

So perhaps the man with the thick glasses does not remember me. But I remember him. He has visited me in my dreams more than once over the years. I remember the blue of his eyes, the softness of his lips, a small patch of fine hair on the small of his back, my first taste of a good wine, and the way he made me feel like I was somebody you could make love to.

Texas was not nice to me. They didn't like "hitchhiking hippies," or so I was told by the first highway patrolman who stopped to let me know my kind was not welcome in the great state of Texas. Well, I wasn't about to walk across the biggest damn state in the country, so I did it anyway. If it wasn't for an old man named AJ, I might have had a hard time getting across that state, as I wasn't having an easy time getting rides. Before AJ came along, I was harassed by two different cops telling me I couldn't hitchhike in Texas or they would take me to jail. I guess I remembered AJ so well because he was so nice, and because he was like someone out of a movie about Texas.

He drove up in a car the size of a yacht, had cowboy boots and hat, a Texas drawl and a grizzled old face. I got in the car, and right between us on the seat was a case of beer. He said, "Where ya goin'?" and I said, "West."

He said he was going all the way to New Mexico to visit his daughter, but he had to make some stops along the way, so if I was in no big hurry I could come along. He also said "And don't you worry none, cuz I ain't one of those guys that messes with boys, just lookin' for some company."

That was fine by me, so I popped a warm beer and settled in for the ride.

AJ said he just got out of jail that very morning for slapping his girlfriend across the head because she wouldn't stop "flappin' her gums." He said that girl could nag your face right off. Everything he said was funny in how he said it, and I laughed a lot listening to him talk.

He said he was "gittin' the hell outta Texas 'til that bitch cooled off a little."

He was not happy about being put in jail and was sure he would be going back, if he had to see her face anytime soon.

We went to his house so he could get ready to leave for a while. He had a nice house, but it was plain inside like most bachelor houses. He'd had a couple of wives, but he said marriage fit him "like a hair suit."

We took our time and ate at truck stops, slept in motels, drank beer and talked. He pointed out the sites to me and gave me a native's view of Texas.

I didn't think Texas was a pretty place at all. There wasn't much to look at, but AJ was interesting company. He knew a lot about a lot of things and kept me entertained with conversation. It's funny how I can remember every detail of a conversation from thirty-five years ago and have whole chunks of my childhood missing.

After a few days, we were out of Texas and in New Mexico. He called his daughter to let her know he was coming and bringing a friend. She was hospitable and welcoming when we arrived. I had a feeling her daddy had brought home strays before, and she trusted his judgment of character. Her little girl called him Granddaddy, and giggled and beamed when he pretended to be grumpy and told her he "couldn't have no circus midgets sittin' on his lap 'cuz people would talk," right before he scooped her up in his arms and buried his face in her blond curls.

He was larger than life, and like a character in an old Western movie. He seemed like he was a good dad, and I enjoyed myself with him and his family.

I stayed about five days, then AJ drove me to the interstate, we wished each other luck, and I was on my way again.

I'd been wandering a few months now, and can't say exactly how long. No clocks and calendars were needed, but I was growing weary of it and looking forward to getting to California and starting a new life. I had a place to live this time, and everything else was secondary.

After AJ and I parted, I had a few short rides with forgettable people and crossed into California to a small desert town called Needles.

In Needles, a young guy who looked like Charles Manson pulled over in a rusted and beat-up old car and offered me a ride. He wasn't the usual middle-aged, clean-cut guy with a suggestive gleam in his eye or the scruffy trucker type. He was more the thirty-something pot-smoking hippie type who hadn't grown up yet. He offered a joint as soon as I got in and said, "Welcome to California."

His name was Cliff. I don't know why I remember his name. I forgot the names of most of the people I met traveling. Maybe because he was the first person I met in the state of California this time, and maybe because it was a bizarre experience.

When someone stopped to pick me up, I always gave the back seat a quick glance before I got in, to make sure there wasn't anyone else in the car. This time was no different and, assured he was alone, I got in the passenger side and we headed west. It wasn't until we were a few miles down the road that I glanced into the back seat and my blood ran cold at what I saw. The seat itself was removed and in its place were dozens of plastic boxes stacked neatly on top of each other. Each of the boxes held a rattlesnake or a tarantula. I despise snakes and spiders and actually felt myself go faint at the sight of so many so close.

My first reaction was how do I get out of this car and I'm sure I expressed my horror with some exclamation. I do not remember now. I do remember the slightly amused half-smile on Cliff's face at my reaction.

Cliff explained that he came to the desert regularly and caught the spiders to sell to pet shops and the rattlesnakes went to laboratories to be milked of their venom.

He also had a call service particularly popular in the desert communities, where he removed these unwanted invaders from people's homes. It never occurred to me before the odd things some people do to make a living.

He went on to assure me we were perfectly safe unless we had a car accident. If the accident did not kill us, the spiders and snakes, once escaped, most assuredly would. I think he enjoyed freaking me out.

His beat-up old car wouldn't go very fast, but for most of the trip I rarely took my eyes off that speedometer, and every time a big truck rolled by and rattled that little car, I was seized with anxiety that it would roll us over and all those creatures would rain down right on top of me. I had made it all the way across the country several times and been on and off the streets nearly three years, living a life of daring and danger, and I had never felt more in peril than I did in that car.

Did I mention that those creatures appeared none too happy to be trapped in their prisons? They rattled, slithered and tapped the entire way and, had I not been out in the blistering desert, I would have preferred to walk the rest of the way rather than listen to that sound. We drove about five hours together, smoking pot and talking, with my eye on his speedometer and my hand on the door handle.

Coincidentally his destination was not far from where I would be staying, and he offered to drive me to the door. I called my friends about my impending arrival and they seemed genuinely welcoming. In less than an hour we were in Garden Grove, California. This part of my journey had come to an end, and I was now officially a resident of California. It was February 14, 1978, two-and-a-half months before my eighteenth birthday.

The Spider and the Butterfly

As I lured him to my bed
I whispered, "Welcome to my web."
With a half-heart effort to struggle free,
Butterfly declared his love for me.
With all my limbs I drew him near-
He trembled in erotic fear.
I smiled malicious love and hunger,
pitied his romantic blunder.
I crushed his wings, devoured his heart,
Then wept at his demise.
For even the hungry spider mourns
the death of beautiful butterflies.

E.M.

Chapter Five
As Thousands Died

I knew the couple I was staying with from Maine, but I did not know them well. They were in their late thirties, attractive and modern in their values and style. We had some distant connection through relatives, so I didn't feel like I was at the mercy of complete strangers.

I had my own room and a shared bath in their duplex, and at that time Garden Grove was still a nice place to live. They informed me there were at least six gay bars in the city, and two within walking distance of my new home.

They did not lay down any rules or responsibilities on me upon my arrival, or before, but I was to quickly learn the price of their hospitality. I suppose I was still naïve in many ways, and it did not occur to me when I accepted their invitation that I would be anything other than a temporary guest and would be self-supporting as quickly as possible. The second night after my arrival the price of their hospitality became perfectly clear when, after dinner and drinks, they began to engage in sex in the living room in front of me.

Perhaps they had heard gossip about my prior activity with couples and assumed I was up for it. We never discussed it, and I felt as if I was not being given a choice. I was at their mercy and it was "put out or get out," and I didn't want to be on the street again.

So once again I was to be someone's boy toy and I was not happy about it. It was one thing to be able to turn a trick and walk away, and entirely another to live as an indentured whore day in and day out. It was an awkward and uncomfortable way to live. They were constantly suggestive and lecherous, and though they were an attractive couple, I did not find them attractive at all. I found it annoying that they pretended an image of normalcy that defied the truth of who they were and how they conducted their marriage, and I had no trust or affection for them. I was being used and we all knew it.

My goal was to get out of there as soon as possible and into my own place, but they seemed to discourage my efforts at independence. I imagine their personal agreement was to explore sexual diversity as a couple but inevitably both sought my company individually and requested I not tell the other. They were manipulative and insatiable, though I found him to be less devious in his intentions than she.

Looking back with all of my years of experience, I suspect they were both sex addicts and, not able to be content within the constraints of monogamy, had found each other and bonded because of, not in spite of, their common desires. They stayed married many years and I recently heard of his death from heart failure.

I tried to stay out of their way and out of their clutches as much as possible, but knew I had a debt to pay as long as I lived in their home.

I used the bus system to get around, and found a job as a telephone solicitor. I walked to the local bars at night and, though I wasn't eighteen, I managed to get in. I started to meet people and make some friends and told no one of my living situation. I met a new friend named

James, and he had one of the prettiest faces I had ever seen on a man. He had just obtained his hairdressing license and a job in a salon. I never considered James as a partner and instead loved him dearly as a friend. (It was years later, under the influence of alcohol, that he confessed to wanting more than just a friendship with me, but knew I didn't feel the same. I was embarrassed by his confession. It felt incestuous.)

My social life was limited by my age, so I coerced my brother Bucky to let me use his birth certificate to obtain an ID. I had turned eighteen and he was almost exactly three years older. I was instantly twenty-one, living in Southern California, had a friend with a car, a job and a place to live, and felt pretty damn good.

I did call my mother occasionally but not often. I could tell she didn't approve of my choices, but I never doubted she loved me and wanted me to have a good life.

James helped to groom me with a modern haircut and perfect eyebrows, and we were two young pretty boys roaming the clubs, flirting with men and hustling drinks. He may have been the one to suggest I look into a state-funded educational program called Rehabilitative Occupational Program. I reached the R.O.P. and set up an appointment with a career counselor for an interview.

I wanted to do something with my life now: I had wandered and gone hungry long enough. I saw the possibilities all around me for money, success, beauty and happiness, and I wanted it. The opportunities far exceeded those of small town Maine and its factories. Here, I could make a life on my terms.

I wish I could remember the name of the man who interviewed me. I wish I could find him and thank him for his help and his interest in me. All else aside, I have had thirty years of a lucrative and satisfying career as a hairdresser, and I've always known that that particular man made a significant difference in my life.

I recall feeling awkward in his office, like I didn't belong there. He asked me questions and grew more interested as I shared my background and the last few years that led to my sitting in his office. Though I had always shared my experiences as a matter of fact, I doubt I ever fully understood the impact they might have on others. I believe this man was moved by my history and was determined to help me make a better life. I took an aptitude test, and we went over it together. We discussed several possible career options, and ultimately he and I agreed that cosmetology was something I might be good at and enjoy. Having James as my best friend made it that much more attractive to me, and not for a moment did I make the connection of the stereotyped gay hairdresser during the process.

He explained the process of admission, the various locations of beauty schools, and my heart sank when he explained the costs of uniforms and required tools. I had no money and I told him that. I had no car but one school was close enough to get to by bus, and I would have to find a night job. School was eight to five, Monday through Friday.

He saw me deflate and told me to hold on and picked up the phone. He spoke in a familiar way with a woman named Connie. He told her he had a young man with him that she should meet, and explained that I did not have any money for tools or uniforms. They chatted for a moment and he put the phone down and told me that Miss Connie ran the school and was a fine woman. He told me to report at eight a.m. on Monday, and she would see that I had what I needed. He handed me my admission papers and said, "Ernest, this is an opportunity to do something with your life. These are fine ladies running this school, and you treat them with respect and do as they say and let them teach you. Now go make us all proud of you and what we do."

I will tell you that I walked all the way home that day two feet off that California sidewalk. My feet never touched the ground, I was so excited and scared and hopeful! I was going to be somebody and do something with my life. There were no more factories in my future and no more sleeping in alleys and having sex to survive. I picked up a newspaper along the way and started looking for a night job.

The couple I was staying with did not seem happy for me. They seemed resentful, and I suppose knew I was not happy with the arrangement and was looking for a way out.

I was disappointed when I called to tell Ma and could tell by her voice that she didn't have much faith in me by then to do anything with my life. She didn't know the things I had to do to survive. She didn't know what the world outside of small town Maine could do to a boy. She didn't know how hard I was trying to be more than she thought I was. I think she imagined I was just living like a bum to avoid responsibility or even to punish her.

But my friend James told me I was going to be a great hairdresser and suggested we room together once I got a job. That was the second best thing I'd heard that day.

There is a main street down the center of Garden Grove named Garden Grove Boulevard. I applied for a job as a night clerk at a sleazy motel on one end of the boulevard and was hired for $2.10 per hour. My new school was at the other end and I lived right around the middle, so one bus would get me from home to school and to work every day. James and I found a two-bedroom apartment, and with my first paycheck we moved in.

I had been with the couple for several months and had become repulsed by them and their unusual lifestyle. I left with no remorse, and though I do appreciate that they gave me a start in a new life, I never felt they did it out of the kindness of their hearts but for the lust in their loins, and I never felt I owed them more than a half-hearted thanks.

James and I put together a stained old couch, a beat-up old table and some mattresses on the floor, but we had our own place, and I felt my first great sense of accomplishment. I had my own home, a job, and was enrolled in school, and I did it all myself and I didn't ever have to have sex with anyone again for a place to sleep or something to eat.

And I never have since.

I went to school from eight a.m. to five p.m. and caught the five-fifteen bus to work. I worked until midnight, but the bus stopped running at ten p.m., so I was back to hitchhiking home from work.

School itself was easy and fun, but the long hours and days were tough and I barely made enough money to live on, and relied on my flirtation skills to provide a few drinks now and then in the local bars.

People in California had a great time with my Maine accent, and I made a conscious effort to correct myself when it surfaced. I didn't want to be the poor kid from Maine anymore. I was ready to reinvent myself. The gay world in Southern California in the late 1970s was a different world. There were leather bars and discos, lesbians had their own clubs, and there were little neighborhood pubs to just have a beer after work.

It was the sexual revolution! The Stonewall rebellion had happened, and gays were fighting back and fighting for their human rights. Gays were everywhere, and I was free to be one of them. I found a place where I belonged. I was one of thousands, the tens of thousands.

I was only one of two guys in my beauty school with about seventy-five girls, and we two boys were spoiled by our instructors: Miss Connie – stern, slender and elegant; Miss Pearl – plump, twinkly-eyed and good-natured; and Miss B – our skin and nails instructor, plain and grumpy.

Miss B's full name was Betty Bleyfus, and she suspended me for three days once for jokingly referring to her as Betty Blowfish and for being disrespectful in general. In all fairness, Miss B did slightly resemble a blowfish.

Miss Pearl was my favorite, and I was truly heartbroken to hear of her death about ten years ago. She looked like a big, fat, Barbie doll. She had huge bleached blonde hair piled high in swoops and curls, tons of pink make-up, and thick false eyelashes. She wore bright and bold caftans, and beads and baubles on every finger and wrist. And she smiled all the time. Her husband Jim came to the school every day and brought her lunch, and they sat on a bench in a small park near the school and held hands while they ate. They looked like the happiest couple I ever saw.

Miss Pearl favored me, and the girls were jealous. She would save me part of her lunch and sometimes would slip a bill in my pocket and give me a wink. She would say, "Now don't you forget me, Ernest, when you're rich and famous." I never got rich or famous, but I have never forgotten her either. If Miss Pearl happens to be looking down on me this very day, she can see that I am still making a damn good living on the very skills she taught me. Miss Pearl taught me to do hair with flair. Miss Connie taught me how to be professional, and Miss B taught me you can't say everything you think. Miss B didn't like me much because she taught skin and nails, and I only wanted to do hair. I hated her class, and I took shortcuts and cheated every chance I could just to get through it, and she took my disinterest personally.

They all knew how much I struggled. I wasn't one of the rich kids whose parents were pushing them through beauty school because their grades were too low for college. I was often late, or fell asleep in class from exhaustion, and they overlooked everything except disrespect.

Oh, the drama that was beauty school! The girls and

their love lives and their petty squabbles with each other, the old ladies who had seen thousands of students come and go and had survived thousands of disastrous student hairdos. There were unwanted pregnancies and fainting spells and even a girl who lost an eye to a hot curling iron. We all left beauty school nearly bald from trying out new things on each other, and a few old ladies went out on a stretcher, having had their last visit to a beauty parlor, and saving the mortician some time on styling their hair for the funeral.

It took me eighteen months to graduate, four months longer than it could have had I shown up every day I was supposed to. Some days I just couldn't do it. I was tired most of the time, hungry a lot of the time, and broke all of the time.

I had opportunities to make extra cash at the motel when men would invite me to their rooms, but I had put that life behind me and couldn't risk losing my job if I got caught. A night clerk is a good job for a student. You can study during the slow times.

A cranky old couple named Pat and Edna managed the place, and lived in an apartment on the premises. Edna had a big hump on her back and Pat was an alcoholic, and they fought every night. They were not nice to me, and took advantage of the knowledge that I was trying to get through school and needed that job.

The bus stopped running at ten p.m., and I had to hitchhike home after midnight. During that period it was all over the news that a serial killer was on the loose, and he was killing and dismembering young men and boys in the general vicinity I was hiking. He was killing young, slender, blond boys and leaving their bodies on the freeways. They called him "The Freeway Killer" and he killed twenty-seven or more boys. It was suspected that he drove a white van. I did not accept rides from any vans. People often stopped and admonished me for hitchhiking in such dangerous times, but I had no choice. I had to get home. I had school the next morning.

The Freeway Killers (there turned out to be two of them, Bonin and Butts) were apprehended after I finished school and stopped hitchhiking. I searched their faces in the newspaper, and my memory, trying to recall if our paths had ever crossed on Garden Grove Boulevard when I was trying to get home, and I am thankful that their images did not ring remotely familiar. I had to wonder how come all those poor boys lay dead on the side of a freeway, while I continued to slip through the fingers of fate.

Though we struggled, James and I had a good time. He was building his business as a young hairdresser, and I was trying to finish school. We laughed a lot and partied and danced and dated. I remember this as a wonderful time in my life. It was my time to create and discover my own potential. I grew more comfortable with myself as a gay man and began to develop my own personality and sense of style that was uniquely me, unrestricted by my social conditions or familial obligations.

I had very little contact with my family, just a call now and then, and Tina was the only sibling I remained close to. She had married and had her first child, a stunningly perfect and beautiful little girl named Jenny. That baby had the face of an angel, and the hugest and most beautiful blue eyes that captivated everyone who saw her.

I missed my sister and knew she did not have a happy marriage. We had lives three thousand miles apart, and I was helpless to change the abuse she endured and tolerated from her husband. I beseeched my brothers to intervene, and they did until she continued to return to her husband for more abuse, and they threw up their hands in disgust.

I finished school and got a job in a salon while I waited

to go to the state board and get my license. I also met
and become enamored with a guy named Rick. Rick was
a bartender and was planning a move to San Francisco.
San Francisco was the gay mecca, and I had never been
there. Rick wanted me to go to San Francisco with him,
and I was ready for a new adventure. I had stayed in one
place longer by then than I had since leaving home at fifteen. I passed my state board with a near perfect score,
losing points only on my manicuring skills (which I did not
confess to Betty Blowfish), and was officially a licensed
cosmetologist in the great state of California.

Maybe it was a mistake to leave. The next year was
full of turmoil and trouble, and I felt like I had taken steps
back instead of forward. When I got to San Francisco,
I found that Rick had an entirely different idea of what
kind of relationship he wanted than I did, and I had dis-
mantled my little bit of security to follow a man who found
monogamy old-fashioned and repressive.

We lived in the heart of the Castro district in 1980. It was
the gayest place on the planet, and Rick was a kid in a
candy store.

The gay population was angry and confrontational
at that time. Harvey Milk and George Moscone had recently been murdered, and the gays were calling for the
blood of their murderer, Dan White, and anyone who
defended him. The Castro vibrated with rage and lust,
and manifested itself in overt sexuality and social anar-
chy. The country's first openly gay politician and the pied
piper of a cultural movement had been murdered by a
straight man and his absurd yet successful defense of diminished capacity due to too much junk food, earning
him only five years in prison. His was the infamous "Twinkie
defense." The gay community rioted, and at the time of
my arrival the city had only begun to mend itself.

I found a job as an assistant in an upscale salon, and
shared a flat in an old Victorian with a group of men who

seemed to spend most of their time as activists for the gay community. Most did not appear to have actual jobs.

Though it was enlightening, as a young gay man from rural America, to witness the emergence of power in the gay community, it was not the peaceful and happy environment I had envisioned, and the extremism all around me was overwhelming. I had begun to move through the world as an openly gay man, but had not learned how to live in this all gay world. Everything was about being gay, and that didn't seem any more right than everything being straight. A lot of the militant gays positively hated straight people, and I didn't like that. I had a lot of love and support from straight people in my life ,and I did not want them put in the same categories as the homophobes and gay bashers, any more than I wanted to be put with the child molesters and men performing sex acts in public parks and restrooms. I never wanted to live in a world where everyone was divided up and separated, labeled and put away in his own little space, like the canned goods in a pantry. My idea of a beautiful world was – and is – a riot of color and culture and unique individuality all sewn together in a pattern of harmony like a patchwork quilt. If I wanted to be somewhere where everyone was alike, I might as well have stayed in Maine.

I resented my job as an assistant. I was more of a servant, and I didn't get to do much hair. I know now that it was a very good experience to start out in an upscale salon and watch professionals work and make a lot of money, but at the time I wanted to be the star, not the assistant to the star.

I had decided to go back to Maine, though I knew it was temporary. I managed to save enough money to take a Greyhound bus across the country. That was indeed one of the most agonizingly long and boring trips I have ever taken. It took a full seven days and seemed to stop at least seven thousand times between San Francisco and Lewiston, Maine. Hitchhiking may have been more dangerous but it was certainly more interesting.

I stayed with my sister Rose only long enough to find a small apartment and a job. I took a position in a chain salon at the local mall and found an apartment within walking distance. I was twenty years old and still did not have a car or a driver's license. I could not see the point in getting a license when I couldn't afford a car.

I wondered if home would be different because I felt different. I had some achievement to carry with me, and more confidence and experience. There is an old saying that you can't go home again, and it was true for me. I missed my family, and was a little world weary at the ripe old age of twenty. I thought I had divested myself of the bitter disappointments of my childhood.

I was wrong.

I felt like a failure having returned home, and it didn't matter that I had actually done something with my life. When I was out in the world I could be who I wanted to be. When I was home I was only what I had been before, the poor, country, white trash town queer. It all settled on me like a boa constrictor and squeezed the new me right out. It seemed as if everything I had gone through was for nothing if I was back where I started. I just wasn't the type to settle. I wanted more. Joking, I've often said most children's first word is "mama." Mine was "more."

Chronic dissatisfaction is a double-edged sword. It can drive you to success and it can drive you to despair. In my case it has done both. I was only in Maine about six months when an incident of bizarre fate catapulted me back to the west coast once and for all. I know it was in the fall of 1980. It was getting cold, and I was already wondering how I was going to get back to sunny Southern California before the snow fell.

The incident of bizarre fate that drove me west for good took place in a twenty-four-hour diner. Tina and I had a rare night out together. She had a sitter for Jenny, and we went out for drinks. I will rely on my sister's memory for most of the details, as the only thing I am absolutely sure of is that I was absolutely inebriated. But I do remember what I was feeling, as I had carried those feelings for almost fifteen years, and who would have thought that after fifteen years, and all of my travels, Tina and I together again for a single night would come face-to-face with the man who had stolen our childhoods?

The bars closed at one a.m., and we stopped to eat and sober up a little. I spotted him sitting at the counter as soon as we walked in. His hair had turned gray, and he had put on a lot of weight, but I recognized him immediately.

I pointed him out to Tina. She became nearly terrified, and she begged me not to say anything to him. But I remember the rage boiling to the surface and spilling over. Fifteen years of feeling damaged, tainted and ruined. Being whispered about, analyzed or pitied because this selfish bastard couldn't control his perverse impulses. Why did he get to go out in public and sit in a restaurant and pretend he was just like everyone else, and I had to get through life wondering if things might have been different or easier if he had left me alone? Why did he get to smile and laugh when my beloved sister could not have a healthy and trusting relationship with a man because of the damage he had done?

The anger was all there waiting, the courage fueled by alcohol. I had learned to fight back over the last few years. I guess I grew tired of the humiliation of being beaten, and at some point I just wanted to hit back. Unfortunately, when I drank alcohol, I imagined aggression in others and picked fights that weren't necessary. I'm not sure the bullied had become the bully, but I do remember the satisfaction of driving a fist into an enemy, and it took me many years to learn to resolve my emotions without violence. Perhaps it is my father's blood in my veins, or simply that I grew up in an environment where people hit each other when they were angry.

I approached Roger aggressively. In a voice loud enough to quiet the entire restaurant, I snidely asked if he was still molesting children.

I doubt that he immediately recognized my sister and me when he casually responded with, "Maybe, what's it to you?"

I coldly responded with, "Don't you remember me? Don't you remember my sister, or my mother? You really should remember the people you harm in this world, because you never know when you might have to face them again."

It dawned on him who I was, and I saw no remorse or contrition on the face that had brutalized my family and murdered our pets. I saw only the belligerence and self-preservation instinct of a heartless predator who had not changed at all, nor taken responsibility for the damage he had done, as he rose and attempted to make his exit.

I blocked his attempt, and continued to verbally assault him publicly for his perversions, and apparently the management had called the police already. He was a stocky and strong man, and my small drunken frame was no match for his desire to escape when he seized me by the throat.

I should be embarrassed to admit that one more time my beloved sister rushed to my defense, but I'm not. I am proud of the lioness in my sister. It is my mother in her and has served her and those she loves well through a difficult life. As I fought him, Tina flew into action, heavy stoneware coffee mug in hand, and proceeded to beat him mercilessly over the head, screaming, "You take your hands off my brother!" She cut an artery in his head and blood was everywhere. He fell to the floor, and I remember thinking, "Oh dear God, we've killed him."

The police arrived, and an ambulance took him to a hospital to stitch his wounds. We were not charged at the time, but the police attempted to file charges against Tina. Roger refused to press charges. Perhaps he knew he had it coming and felt he deserved it, but I think it more likely that he did not want the publicity, and wanted his past to stay hidden. I heard he had a very young new wife and twin daughters, and I wonder what he told his wife about that night and his wounds.

The district attorney refused to pursue it once the history of our relationship was explained. Now it was up to us to finally move on. I had a private conversation with my mother where she wept and cursed him for coming back to haunt our family, but she also thought it fitting that he would now bear some scars of his own to remind him of what he had done.

I believe Tina and I to be somewhat luckier than most molested children. Few are given the opportunity to confront and punish the demons of their childhood, and must go through life only dreaming of justice in this world. Perhaps God, or fate, or karma led me home one final time to put closure on an open wound, but now it was time for me to leave for the last time.

I explained to Ma that I couldn't stay there. My ghosts and demons walked those streets, and I suffocated under the weight of the past. She knew I couldn't be happy there, and though she always wanted all her children close, she wanted this prodigal son to be happy and find his place in the world. I wasn't a child anymore, and she knew I had lived too much in a short time and survived alone. Though she may never have understood me, she accepted and respected me, and that was good enough to carry me back out into the world alone one more time. I would not come home again, even for a visit, for five years.

I called my friend and former roommate James and

asked for a temporary place to stay. He offered me a couch without hesitation, though he had another roommate. I had been working and had saved enough to take a plane across the country. It was my first plane ride, and it sure beat hitchhiking.

I got a job right away with the same chain of salons I worked for in Maine, and started building a business. Unfortunately, the manager was a corporate ass-kissing vampire and a huge bitch, so I did not love my job. Chain salons are not interested in creativity or fashion. They are fast food hair salons, and the bottom line is money. Get as much money as you can as quickly as you can. That was not the kind of hairdresser I aspired to be.

I had been back only a few months when I was out with a friend, and we stopped to eat at another twenty-four-hour restaurant – the same chain as the one where I had confronted Roger. The nature of those places attracts drunks and miscreants at night, and after a second incident in less than six months, you would think I'd avoid them.

It is a myth that California is entirely made up of glamorous liberals. It has more than its share of bikers, rednecks and white trash. The difference is that most of them came from someplace else and brought their shitty attitudes with them.

Unfortunately, in places that have a large gay population, you also attract the gay bashers.

I thought my dance attire quite avant-garde that evening and the height of fashion, in canary yellow pants, a bumblebee striped t-shirt and pointy black boots. For some reason the group of bikers a few tables away did not share my enthusiasm for colorful fashion statements, and appeared inexplicably annoyed by our presence, or perhaps our existence. This was made known by the unnecessarily loud and abundant use of the word "faggot."

The other patrons of this fine establishment pretended

not to notice, but my companion was terrified and wanted to leave. I stubbornly refused to budge or cower to these bullies, and gave them my most menacing glare, but it is admittedly difficult to look dangerous in canary yellow.

The ringleader, a particularly hirsute and Neanderthal brute, caught my glare and approached our table. He let loose with a string of invectives worthy only of someone who rarely bathes, and finished his diatribe with an impressive gob of spit directed onto my half-eaten meal.

Before I could reason with myself, I picked up my sturdy ironstone plate and whacked him across the forehead with all my strength. It gave a very satisfying thud but did not break, and I'm afraid the innocent patron at the next table was struck in the back of his head by the remains of my cheeseburger.

I suspected my life was about to end and my pride did not allow flight, so I managed to tear off his sweat-stained t-shirt and land a few more smacks about the head and shoulders before he and his two friends managed to restrain and beat the living daylights out of me. I thought I heard a girl screaming, but later realized it was my less than macho companion who obviously could not be counted on to have your back in a gang fight.

We wrestled our way into the nearby lobby where there was a charmingly decorative fireplace (which was never actually used in Southern California) and the fight came to an abrupt end when one of them struck the side of my face with a length of firewood. I went down dazed but not unconscious.

The police arrived a minute too late to save my face from disfigurement. But at least they stopped my silly friend's incessant screeching which was almost as painful as the blow to my face and the boots in my ribs. The police poured salt in my wounds by stating that I was asking for trouble by the way I was dressed, and that witnesses stated I served the first blow. Spitting in my food did not count as an assault, and if they arrested anyone, they would arrest everyone. The injustice of it pissed me off, but I did in fact deliver the first blow and everyone saw it.

My cheekbone and eye socket were both cracked, both eyes blackened, some teeth loosened, (which later discolored), and severely bruised ribs. Add this to some already broken teeth from previous violence and my quest to achieve a desirable level of physical beauty suffered yet another significant setback.

All healed, but my right cheekbone never again quite matched my left after that, and two visible teeth took on a shade of pale gray within weeks. And I never saw that screaming queen guy I was with again. I guess he thought I was too dangerous to be friends with. Someone told me that that night scared his country ass right back to Arkansas, where he came from.

No sooner had my face healed, about two months after my return to the sunshine state, than I met the man who would change my life in ways I never imagined.

I was out with a friend, having coffee in a diner and chatting, when a group of three – two men and a woman – came in and sat at an adjacent table. He was a good-looking man, but not extraordinary, until he smiled at me. He had, and still has, a thousand-watt smile that takes him from just attractive to handsome. He followed up that smile with a flirtatious compliment, and it was only then that I realized he was gay. He was not at all obvious in his mannerisms and appearance. His male friend, on the other hand, was only one tube of mascara away from being a drag queen.

I returned to my table and finished my coffee, glancing over at him from time to time. Each time, he was watching me. When we passed his table to leave, he stopped me, handed me his phone number and told me to give him a call. I couldn't get that beautiful smile out of my head, but I waited a few days to call, not wanting to appear too eager.

His name was Rod, short for Rodney. He got his olive skin and beautiful smile from his Mexican father, and his green eyes and facial features from his Irish mother.

When I called and identified myself by name, he said, "Who?"

Humiliated and embarrassed I said "Never mind" and began to hang up.

He said, "Wait. Is this the guy from the restaurant?" And I assured him it was. He said, "I didn't expect you to call."

We chatted, and he told me he was leaving for San Francisco for a long weekend with friends and would call when he returned and take me on a date.

Less than twenty-four hours had passed when he called and said he had cut his weekend short and was on his way back. He said he couldn't stop thinking about me and didn't want to wait. Needless to say, I was immensely flattered and agreed to a date that evening.

I was nervous and excited. He was different from anyone I had met before. I could feel it right away. We went to the movies and got to know each other a bit. He took me back to the couch I slept on, and asked me out for the next night.

We went out to dinner the next night: I spent the night with him, and the next six years.

He is a few months shy of ten years older than I. He was thirty, and I almost twenty-one. I asked him recently if he could remember what he thought the first time he saw me. He said simply, "Beautiful."

For me it was not love at first sight, but it was something special, and grew to a love and a friendship that has endured over thirty years.

He has not changed much over the years. From the beginning he's been charming and generous, witty and intellectually brilliant. He exudes confidence without arrogance, and is one of the best listeners I've ever known. He has been a teacher all his life, and he is a phenomenal one. He challenges people without making them feel stupid. I don't remember his ever criticizing me, and he has always been a supportive and loyal friend. He did, as we all do, have some character flaws that challenged our relationship. He lacked simple common sense. He was careless with finances. He was terribly materialistic, but once he owned something he didn't take care of it. It was the obtainment he enjoyed more than the ownership.

And he was not faithful to me. I never caught him, but I always suspected it. I don't know how far into our relationship he remained faithful and he steadfastly refuses, even today, to confess to infidelity. But in every other aspect he gave me a beautiful life. The life I thought I would have to work decades for was mine overnight.

I lived in a beautiful home, owned thousands of dollars in jewelry and clothes, dined in the best restaurants, went on trips and to plays and concerts. And for the first time in my life, I had a life I was proud of and felt I belonged in.

I moved to a privately owned salon, and, with Rod's support and encouragement, my business took off, and I experienced my first taste of success. I had it all, and I was still too young to know what to do with it.

I made friends with a couple of girls in my new salon, who quickly became my closest friends and remain sisters to me to this day. Crystal and Sharon were young and beautiful blondes who knew all the young people in the area and introduced me to a social life outside the gay bars and outside my domestic life with Rod. This was one of the best times of my life so far. Our salon was a solid success, and we were making a lot of money. We were young and pretty and popular. This is what I came to California for. This was the life I dreamed of, and I felt I had truly made it.

Rod and I bought a condo, and my name was actually on a deed. I was a homeowner. I cooked and cleaned, worked and shopped. Rod gave me a car, and made me get my driver's license. I was terrified of the California freeways and would not drive on them. I took the side roads for years before I got the courage to join the murderous chaos of the California freeways. Once I got used to them, I rarely drove at a speed less than eighty miles per hour.

Anything I wanted was there for the asking, and, unfortunately, I had too much too soon and became a bit spoiled. Rod loved to give, and he showered me with gifts. We took trips to Hawaii and Puerto Vallarta, and spent our money as fast as we made it. Rod traveled a lot without me. He was not out of the closet with his job, and I was left out of any job-related activities, and there were many. I resented it.

We could not have grown up more differently. He was one of three kids raised in Huntington Beach, California, to parents who stayed married until his father's death. He was an exceptional student, and went to college on full scholarships to get his teaching degree. His family had suffered a terrible blow with the early death of his older brother, and was simultaneously blessed with the unexpected birth of a baby sister when he was seventeen, but, other than that, they seemed the most normal of families I had ever been around.

Rod's small family graciously accepted me into the fold and I was never made to feel like an outsider, even after we were no longer a couple. His gentle father Louis died of a heart attack twenty years ago at the age of sixty-four, and I remain friends with his mother Geneva and sister Janel to this day. Geneva still refers to me as "My handsome boy" whenever we speak.

It was 1981 when Rod called me at home to tell me about a newspaper article he had read concerning a new deadly "cancer" that seemed to be attacking only gay men. That was the first I heard of AIDS, and it quickly changed the country, and particularly the gay community. It seemed that overnight we became pariahs. The panic and ignorance spread like wildfire. Fear can make people vicious and cruel, and never had it been more apparent than when AIDS hit this country. Some of it was understandable, before we knew how it was spread, but even when it was established that it was not spread through casual contact, gay men were thrown from their homes, fired from their jobs, denied medical care, and abandoned by their own families just for being gay. The self-righteous religious groups used a disease to validate their homophobia and justify their suspicion that God was bringing his wrath to the immoral. Never mind that gay women did not contract AIDS, or that innocent babies were dying also, it was all they needed to set back the social progress and civil rights gays had obtained by 50 years. And they did this in the name of their God, seemingly without shame or hesitation.

My business dropped rapidly, as it did for all male hairdressers, gay or not, and it became that much more crucial for Rod to remain closeted. Teachers were targeted for expulsion, and children with HIV were denied access to school by fearful parents.

It was a nightmare of epic proportions for gay men, and a scarlet letter of shame in the history of this country. Our government did nothing, and President Reagan did not utter the word AIDS publicly until after thirty-four thousand Americans had already died. I scoff when I see Reagan worshipped as a great leader. What kind of a great leader ignores thirty-four thousand dead citizens?

Life had become more serious for the gay community, but for Rod and me things did not change much. We practiced monogamy, or at least I did, and I believe that he did not jeopardize our lives and health, and we both remain HIV-free today, which was no small miracle for gay men in our age group at that time.

My "boy for rent" days were long behind me and other than some brief periods of promiscuity in the future, as a result of drug abuse, I was a serial monogamist. I went from one long relationship to another. If I was not completely familiar with a man and his sexual habits, I played safely or not at all.

We bought a beautiful home in an upscale neighborhood. I had a swimming pool in my backyard and a new convertible in the driveway. I rode the roller coaster of trends and fashion and was known for my flamboyant style of dress, a sharp quick wit, and my indifference to the opinions of others.

I remember secretly feeling that I lived a life of image with no substance, and that Rod, my Pygmalion, had groomed me to a level of sophistication that I did not feel inside. I hid my insecurities about my lack of formal education, though Rod often assured me I was one of the most intelligent people he knew, and I masked the restless shame I carried from a childhood of poverty, violence and ostracism with glamor and false bravado.

I hadn't been home in several years, but I showered my mother with expensive gifts and regaled my siblings with my extravagant lifestyle in an effort to impress them with my success.

Tina, newly divorced with two kids, came to possibly stay and build a new life also. She returned to Maine after only a short stay, and I am ashamed to say that I was impatient with and arrogant toward her country ways and her dependency on me, and did not treat her with the same unconditional love she had always shown me. She was terrified of the city and being away from all she had ever known, and I was caught up in my lifestyle and too self-centered to be there for my sister when she needed me. It was easier to write a check than take the time. This is on my list of regrets, made worse by her never having held it against me.

I felt Rod watching me during this time, and though he never said so, he was disappointed in how I treated my sister. I was disappointed in myself. I realized she was a painful reminder of where I came from, and I was ashamed of where I came from and who I used to be.

As we obtained more, and worked more to pay for it all, we fell into a common trap and started to drift apart. I was partying too much and had discovered cocaine. Though I had played with drugs since I was young, I could never afford to abuse them. Rod liked his alcohol, but was dead set against narcotics, and I kept it a secret from him. It seemed he left me alone more often, and I spent more time with a young party crowd. Nobody considered cocaine dangerous then. It was even believed it was not addictive. Many of those young people have made it to middle age with me, and most watched my descent into hell and never thought I would make it out.

I really do not recall the first time I did cocaine or who gave it to me. I do know that I loved it immediately. The high was so quick, so smooth, so unintimidating. It made me feel confident, energetic, sexy and cool. I could drink all night and never feel drunk. A little toot in the morning and all signs of a hangover or fatigue instantly disappeared. And it was easy to hide from those that disapproved of my drug use. Until I became so addicted I couldn't even fool myself anymore. Cocaine was the beginning of my love affair with amphetamines.

We did not have a mundane life. We had a great life, and he is a good man. He guided me from street kid to sophisticated man who held his own in any social circle. He respected and challenged my intellect and encouraged my creative expression. He dressed and appeared conservative, yet delighted in my peacock persona and enjoyed the sidelines while I took the spotlight.

After a five-year absence, I went home to Maine and he came with me, the first of only three men to be taken home to meet my family, and they all liked him very much. He had an uncanny ability to make others feel comfortable.

I, on the other hand, reveled in my flamboyant image and enjoyed watching my former tormentors squirm in discomfort as I challenged their sedate traditional lifestyles and scoffed at their primitive ideals. What a pretentious little bitch I could be with my crisp Californian vernacular and my razor sharp wit, but never did I lose my desire for their love and acceptance.

Once in a heated discussion my mother told me I was unfair to our family. She said I wanted them to all change to make me comfortable, but I wouldn't meet anyone halfway. She also told me not to "get too big for my own goddamn britches and forget we all came from the same place," and that I was no better or worse than anybody else!

She could put you in your place when you had it coming, and she never forgot to tell you she loved you afterwards. At the same time, she confessed that she was uncomfortable with the lavish gifts I gave her, and told me, "Honey, I can't wear a fur coat and diamond necklace to the shoe factory, and I don't go any place fancy. You spend your money on yourself. All I want is for you to come home more."

But I didn't. In the first twenty years after I left home, I went back only four times. Occasionally a family member came to visit me, but not often, and Ma came only once. She had never flown before and was terrified to fly, but she and Everett's sister, Angie, took the trip together and visited me. It was a great adventure for her, and it was hysterical to hear her tell of their plane hitting turbulence, and she and Angie holding hands and crying while the stewardess assured them they were not going to crash.

Rod and I had ended our relationship as lovers by then, and I lived alone in the big house with the pool. He had another partner right away and I suspected the two of us overlapped, but he insisted they were not together until after we split. We loved each other very much, and it was not an ugly break up. We had several pieces of property that we eventually split up, but for quite some time we continued to own things jointly until I gradually learned to do all the things he had always done for me and insisted on total independence. I stubbornly refused to give up the big house though I could never really afford it alone and should have been more sensible. We still owned the condo, which would have been a better choice for my income and lifestyle.

I developed a daily cocaine habit, and my friends were starting to mention it. Crystal and Sharon, my two best friends and coworkers, tried to intervene, but I was steadfast in my denial that there was a problem. My finances were slipping, my work ethic suffering, and I rented rooms in my house to supplement the income going to drugs.

I had a few meaningless affairs with men whose names I can't remember, but AIDS was marching viciously through the gay world, and I was cautious and fearful. I spent most of my time among my straight friends in the drug world.

Years before, when Rod and I were first together, he asked me what gift I would choose if I could choose anything. I was twenty-two at the time. I was self-conscious about my damaged and discolored teeth. A front one was broken from an incident where a gun was slammed into my mouth, and I had the gray ones caused by the biker's beating. I habitually raised my hand to my mouth to hide my teeth when I smiled. Rod took me to a dentist who fixed all my teeth. It remains one of the best gifts I was ever given. It confirmed once more the true power of beauty, and our ability to transform our physical selves to improve our self-image.

I never thought I was handsome and criticized my features mercilessly. My nose was too big, my chin too weak, and I had hereditary pouches under my eyes. Along with the damage done to my face with the stick of firewood, various other acts of violence, and the self-loathing common among drug addicts, I could hardly bear to look at myself.

I met a young surgeon who wanted to work on my face. People always told me I was good looking, but I only saw my flaws. My already weak self-esteem was further deteriorating with drug addiction and the gradual loss of control of my life. I was like so many others, believing if only I was richer, thinner, better looking, if I had a nicer home, a new car, I would be happier. There is no end to the pointless changes we can make that change nothing until we work from the inside out.

The surgeon augmented my cheeks and chin with implants and removed the pouches from under my eyes. I did look better. There was no doubt about that. But what a disappointment it was to look in the mirror and still see ME! I didn't want to just look better. I wanted to be a different person, and there is no surgery for that. I've chased an image of ideal beauty all my adult life and never caught it. With my second set of surgeries (a brow lift, hair transplant, and second cheek augmentation) now behind me, I have a better understanding of myself and why I did it.

I continued my drug use and I had to be out every night. I couldn't stay home alone a single night. A friend came to me and dared to confront me about my drug use and suggested I was an addict, like he was, and I should go with him to a twelve-step group for cocaine addicts. I agreed to go.

My first meeting on Balboa Island in Newport Beach,

California, was full of spoiled rich kids whining about the trouble they got into and telling stories about getting high. They made me wish I was anywhere but there. I thought them all weak and self-indulgent and quickly dismissed any notion that I belonged there. But in my heart I knew I was one of them. I just wasn't ready to stop. Trouble was closing in on me and my drug habit was common knowledge. I was behind in all my bills, and did drugs to work longer hours to make more money to do more drugs.

I had worked for the same salon for about seven years, and the owner was a squeaky clean but kind and patient woman. Most people would have told me to take my problems elsewhere, but she and her husband cared about me and finally took me aside and offered to help in any way they could, but pointedly explained they could no longer tolerate my behavior in their business. I didn't know what to do. I had insurance that would pay for rehab, but who would pay my bills and cover my responsibilities while I cleaned up?

So was it God intervening, as my believing friends suggested, or just a random stroke of luck when I bought two lottery tickets and instantly won ten thousand dollars?

I had a choice. I could buy a lot of drugs with that money or I could check into rehab. I chose rehab. Wouldn't it be nice if I could say that was all it took for me? That I went to rehab, solved all my problems and had a happy ever after? But I was only twenty-eight. Would the next twenty-two years of this book be worth reading, if I had followed all the rules and been a good boy?

I did go to rehab, and I did get clean, and I joined every twelve-step group I could find, and I picked up the pieces of my life and put them together again. The majority of addicts do not get clean or stay clean, but one thing we all know is, once you have admitted you are an addict, you can never deny it again, and it will totally ruin your future highs with guilt and shame. No one who knows about addiction will believe you, if you say you used to be an addict but now you're not.

I learned about myself and what it means to be an addict in the rehab. One would think the mere memory of withdrawals would be enough to keep you clean, but the lure of pleasure outweighs the prospect of pain. The detox that first time was pretty easy compared to some future ones. The sleeplessness, sweats, shakes and vomiting all passed in a few days under the expertise and care of trained nurses, and after that, each day was filled with therapy, education, and restoration of health.

I wanted to understand myself. I wanted to know why someone who came from nothing and got it all would throw it all away over a bag of white powder. I know I was angry and arrogant and didn't really want to be there, but felt I had no choices left. Looking back, I know I did it for everyone but myself. I did it to keep my job, to placate family and friends, and to get my life straightened out enough to go back to doing what I wanted.

I'm a big supporter of rehab, but thirty days is only enough to get your attention and cannot implement any real change. I didn't know it at the time, but I had a long way to go on the road to recovery. I joined Narcotics and Alcoholics Anonymous and quickly met a group of new friends who enriched my life and helped me stay clean. I have been fortunate in my life to make friends easily and to keep them. I met a group of young, edgy guys who made being clean and sober look fun. I bonded quickly with them.

Robert, Jeff and Nick were three of them, three of the best friends I've ever had. I had so damn much fun with those guys. We never stopped moving. On the go all the time, we lived and breathed being gay and being clean and sober.

Jeff – outrageous and funny, no-holds-barred social glutton, completely uninhibited, in your face, militant homosexual! In twenty-two years, I have yet to meet a single person who did not love him. He approached me with the hand of compassion and friendship as I sat in the very back row of an AA meeting, shaking uncontrollably and trying to staunch a bleeding nose ruined by snorting cocaine daily.

Robert – free spirited, a struggling punk rock star. He was a little boy who never grew up. He delighted in visually shocking people with his Mohawk and leather gear, but further shocked them with an unexpected sweet and affectionate nature.

Nick was tall and boy-next-door handsome, with a booming deep voice and a pensive, reticent, conservative appearance that belied his thrill-seeking side.

I don't know how they would describe me. My fashion changed with the wind. Yuppie, hippie, punk or grunge, fashion was a game for me. Every day was Halloween.

Tattoos were just starting to find their way out of the biker and convict culture and into mainstream fashion. I had that old tattoo on my arm that was obviously home-done, and I wanted it gone. I heard of a woman known for covering old tattoos, and thus began my love affair with body art.

Robert loved tattoos too, and we set out on this adventure together. Nick and Jeff wouldn't get any, and for some reason it annoyed me a little that they wouldn't join our tattooed club.

I still had my close friends who supported my being clean and sober and were not addicts themselves, but I left behind those others who were dangerous to be around. So many of my friends from that period went on to their own battles with substance abuse. Some are still doing it, and some are dead.

The gay twelve-step programs were full of the dying. Drugs and alcohol were often behind the dangerous and careless behavior that infected so many with HIV, and doctors cautioned the infected to help fight the disease by stopping the use of drugs and alcohol that weakened their immune system. For a lot of the guys those rooms were their only source of support and love.

Jeff and Robert had both tested positive shortly before we met. Nick and I decided to get tested together. We did our tests together and ten days later went for the results. There are things you wish you didn't remember and that day was one.

When you went to pick up your results you were called in to see a counselor. If you were negative, it was done quickly. The counselor gave you packets of information, condoms and instructions to test again in six months in case the virus was dormant. If you tested positive for the virus, it took a while for the counselor to walk you through all you were supposed to do once you left his office. I was back in the waiting room in five minutes, negative results in hand, feeling very relieved. I grew worried as the time passed and Nick didn't come out. My heart sank when he exited the office briskly and said, "Let's go." His face was pale and his expression rigid.

Once in the car, he stared straight ahead and said, "Well, that's it. I'm going to die."

I told him I would give anything for this not to be happening to him. Inside, I felt guilty for testing negative.

Nick is alive today. Having survived twenty-two years with HIV, an aortic aneurysm that nearly killed him, and a subsequent stroke that has left an arm useless, I tell him he's like the cat with nine lives and he's got at least six left. He's still quiet and even more conservative in his demeanor, and he's still one of the best friends I've ever had.

Jeff is still alive, having also lived twenty-two years with HIV, still clean and sober, living in Los Angeles, and putting smiles on the faces and warmth in the hearts of everyone he meets. And he is still one of the best friends I've ever had.

Our Robert did not make it. He died of a dozen different diseases that attacked his body when HIV destroyed his immune system. He did not die quickly or peacefully, but valiantly fought death until the end. He was twenty-nine years old. And he is still one of the best friends I've ever had.

With my new friendships in the program, and all the extra time that I'd formerly spent on obtaining and using drugs, I had an extraordinary social life. We went to meetings and program events, nightclubs and parties, gay festivals, and civil rights protests.

The gay community was organized like never before, and growing more angry over our government's failures on behalf of people with AIDS. People were dying by the thousands. My three closest friends had HIV, and if there was a protest or an opportunity to be heard, we were there.

I was renting rooms in my house to make ends meet, and over several years I had a string of single girls living with me. My favorite has got to be Kelli. She was sixteen when we met years before, when I was twenty-one. Jeff had also moved in, and they were two of the funniest people I ever knew. We had a lot of fun together, and Jeff and I really enjoyed tormenting her. We did awful things to that poor girl, and plotted constantly to find ways to punish her for being so delightfully nosy and opinionated. We caught her coming out of the shower once and pulled off her towel, shoved her naked out the front door and locked her out in broad daylight, laughing our asses off while she beat on the door.

She recently dared me to tell the story of my outrage when I went to trim my beard and found some suspicious hairs in my clippers. I stormed out of my bathroom, clippers in hand to confront my roommates for a confession from whoever had violated my personal grooming tool. Kelli looked like a trapped animal, but still attempted to convince me I was over-reacting. I am a natural blond all over, and nearly convulsed when I realized those brunette hairs were decidedly pubic in origin. I had not then or since ever had a woman's pubic hair that close to my face ,and I had no choice but to give the clippers to her and buy new ones. Jeff was definitely on my team with this one, and Kelli's punishment was swift and harsh.

Jeff loved to see Kelli get in trouble, because it meant I was not bitching at him about his messy room. I have always kept a neat and clean house, and his room always looked like a tornado ripped through it. There was a narrow path cleared from the door to the bed, and another from the bed to the bathroom. Otherwise, we did not see the carpet the entire time he lived there. Eventually I just made him keep the door closed so I couldn't see it. I can sit here right now and laugh just thinking of the fun we had all living together. I was single for several years. I had brief affairs and infatuations but nothing that lasted. I was having a great time being clean and sober and running with my sober friends. It was a great time in my life, and I was about to meet a man who would change it all, and not for the better. I did want someone to love and be with, but when I met Donald, I was sure he was just a one-night stand.

I was thirty. I had my nose, navel, and nipple pierced, and tattoos were spreading over my body. I was working out and taking care of myself, and my vanity was reaching a peak of self-indulgence. I loved this new image of hyper-masculinity that was making its way into gay culture and fashions, and I adopted it for my own. Nick had somewhat come out of his polo shirt conservatism as a weekend leather queen, and together we played dress-up and hit a lot of the more hardcore underground clubs.

Robert was part-timing as a DJ and doing background music for gay porn while his rock band struggled for recognition. He always knew where all the weirdest things were happening, and we often followed his lead for thrill-seeking.

The weekend I met Donald, Nick and I went to San Diego for the Gay Pride Festival. We spent nearly every weekend thrill-seeking, usually in LA, but San Diego had a great gay community too, though it was a bit tamer.

I was wearing black leather hot pants, combat boots and nothing else when Donald approached me in a bar. He asked if I wanted to get high, and I said, "no thank you." It was not my style to do one-night stands, but when he invited me home with him I said, "yes." Don was a good-looking guy, had a fun-loving personality, and I was soon to find out that he was exceptionally skilled in the bedroom. Unfortunately, it was not until I was in too deep that I realized that was pretty much the extent of his skills. He was also an excellent cook. Food and sex were all that he excelled at. He was a forty-year-old waiter in a diner and seemed to be going nowhere fast and didn't seem to care.

He did tell me in the beginning that he had never had a monogamous relationship and didn't think he could be happy in one. I also knew that he drank too much, smoked pot, and played with other drugs. He had no ambition, was selfish with his money, and was loud and uncouth when he drank. I went for it anyway. He should have been a one-night stand. I should have run fast and far in the opposite direction. He was not relationship material, but I was tired of being single and he was available, handsome, and boiling over with unbridled sexuality.

Donald was not a really bad person. He was just really bad for me.

I don't blame Donald. But my relationship with him marked the next downward spiral that led to the annihilation of my life as I knew it. He didn't support my being clean and sober, and pushed and cajoled me into joining him in getting high.

There's an old saying that, if you lie down with dogs, you're bound to get up with fleas. Well, this man was a flea circus! Don drank and smoked pot daily around me, and it was getting tough to resist. I stopped going to meetings and hanging with my sober friends. Donald kept telling me about a new drug called Ecstasy, and he wanted us to do it together.

We had an active social life, but once I crossed the line into drug use, it seemed most of our spare time centered around obtaining and using drugs. We used Ecstasy often. Though it gave me terrible hangovers, the sex was incredible. We spent entire weekends without leaving the bedroom. It was so easy to let myself slide back into the drug world with a partner that encouraged me.

We had some good times together. We took a trip to Costa Rica with some old friends of his that both had AIDS and were spending all their savings before they died. They both died within a year after our trip.

We took a trip to Vermont and Maine to see our families. I think both our families realized we were a bad match before we did. He remains the only one of my partners that my family clearly did not like.

We took a trip to Key West, Florida, in August of 1992. Halfway through our weeklong visit, hurricane Andrew assaulted the Florida Keys and devastated Miami. I had never experienced a hurricane before. It was both terrifying and exciting. We were trapped on the island with no communication to the mainland and no clue where the storm would make landfall. Fortunately for us, the eye of the storm veered away from the island and hit Miami, leaving us unharmed. Nevertheless, being on a small island during a big hurricane is an experience one never forgets. That mixture of terror and excitement was about to become a way of life for me as I allowed Donald to lead me on to yet another path of drug use.

We had many days, weeks and months that were lost

in forgettable domesticity. It was not all terrible, but in my memory, it remains the period of my descent, bruised with disgrace and regret.

As is common among addicts in relapse, I was cautious at first, and appeared to maintain control. I told myself I could use recreationally and bargained with myself. I would only smoke pot or only use on the weekends. Predictably, I would not honor my end of my bargain with myself.

After four years together, I could see Donald growing restless, and suspected he was struggling with the boundaries of monogamy. He casually hinted at redesigning the rules of our relationship, and I knew it would be ending soon. I did not love him, and believe now that I never did, because it was so easy for me to end it.

A friend called to tell me he saw Donald exiting a gay bar during the day when I believed him to be working. When I asked him how his day was, he pretended he had worked all day. When confronted with his lies, he looked and behaved guilty, and it was all the leverage I needed to end it. I was generous in helping him to set himself up as a single man and paid for his apartment and the move, along with a cash settlement to assuage my guilt at throwing him out.

I was thirty-four. I was using drugs and drinking regularly, but not destructively. I had moved my business to a swankier salon in an upscale neighborhood of Orange County. The people I worked with were nice enough but not people I would choose to associate with outside the salon. My business was doing well after my trip to rehab, but I had distanced myself from my clean and sober friends and started hitting the club circuit.

I felt like I was reaching a feverish pitch of my sexuality. Donald and the Ecstasy seemed to open a new awareness of myself as a man, and I threw myself into a sexual abandon I never before dared. I was single. I was on the prowl for attention and lovers. I felt like I was letting go of so many of the rules that had held me back from enjoying all the options of pleasure I had denied myself by being clean and sober or in a committed relationship. For just that brief period in time, before it all went to hell, I was hot. I had matured into manhood, I looked better than I ever had before, I was slim and muscular, tanned and blonde, and I had money. It seemed the planets had finally aligned in my favor and I had every intention of riding that horse until it dropped in exhaustion.

It was then that I was introduced to the Demon Lover, the most powerfully addictive and destructive drug I'd ever met. It was like electricity in my veins and an anesthetic to an aching heart. It broke down every boundary of conscience, obligation, and morality. I cared about nothing because I felt nothing but a selfish primal lust to indulge and explore every taboo I had denied myself. It burned my nose, already damaged from cocaine, and someone showed me how to smoke it. That was the end of me. It was a little plastic packet of insanity, and it was called crystal meth.

As Thousands Died

They stood and watched, or looked away,
as thousands of us died.
"We're young and scared, we want to live!"
the dying young men cried.
They scowled and smugly judged our ways,
shouting "You are too full of sin!"
Imagine if they loved their fellow man
how different it all might have been.
So we fought and we cried
as thousands more died,
until one day things seemed to change.
They were all none too pleased
when the dreaded disease
started killing those not quite as strange.
How sad was their hurry, their worry and fury,
when they could no longer look smugly away.
And now everyone knows
as tens of thousands still go,
this killer doesn't care if you're gay.

E.M.

Chapter Six
Addiction

In all fairness to the reader, I must admit that much of the next six years was spent in an alcoholic, drug-induced haze. Specific dates and chronology are sometimes lost to me. There are events that feel more like a dream than reality. I have done my best to piece it altogether in the closest versions of the truth I and some witnesses can provide.

As I put more distance between myself and my quality friendships, the sycophants and parasites took their places. I had money and good drugs, a nice home, and plenty of goods to steal and pawn.

There's an old joke that says, "A meth addict (also known as a 'tweaker') is the only person who will steal something from you and then help you look for it." I had plenty of these types hanging around me.

I had done various types of speed before, and cocaine had the pick-me-up-high I was always looking for, but cocaine was expensive, and the high didn't last long. Meth was cheap in comparison, and a small amount kept you high for a long time. With meth you couldn't eat or sleep or sit still long enough to think straight. It made me feel like Superman. It was the perfect drug. Inexpensive and long lasting. It didn't make you lazy like marijuana, or act like an idiot like alcohol, or unable to function like ecstasy, acid, or all the other drugs available to someone who wanted to check out of real life. Best of all, it made me not care about anything or anyone. Whatever it did to the brain, it shut down the heart and emotionally detached me from the world around me. It is a drug of intense isolation and powerful sexual obsession. I had friends who were brought to their knees by this drug, but like millions of other addicts, I didn't think it would happen to me.

There was never a point when I decided to be an addict and destroy my life. It happened gradually, and the drug told me it was all under control until it was too late, and it was controlling me.

My dear and darling friend Robert was very sick. He had remained clean and sober since we met eight years earlier, but it did not save him from the HIV virus, which had progressed to full blown AIDS.

My clean and sober friends, including Robert, knew I was using again. I spent less and less time with them, ashamed and uncomfortable in their presence. They also knew there is nothing you can do to help a fellow addict unless he wants it. I didn't want it, and they didn't push it.

Robert couldn't work anymore, but still maintained an apartment in Los Angeles. A mutual friend and I went for a visit and discovered he was even sicker than we thought. He could not get out of bed and was painfully thin. My heart sank when I saw him. I could see he was not going to survive this illness.

He mentioned casually that he was bored because someone had taken his TV. I asked who had taken it and why. He looked at me helplessly and said the guys next door took it, and he didn't know why.

I realized two things at that moment. That we lived in a world where people can be so rotten they would steal a television from a helpless dying man, and that Robert could no longer take care of himself.

I went next door and beat on their door until they answered. I threatened to kill them both if they did not return the TV immediately. They threatened to call the police, and I offered to do it for them. They brought out the TV.

I was outraged and horrified at their lack of compassion and humanity to my friend. I was angry at that horrible disease and what it had done to our world. And I was angry at myself for not knowing my friend was so sick. I called Robert's mother and told her what I'd seen that day. She told me Robert did not want to give up his apartment and independence and had kept the severity of his illness secret from his family. They did not know their son was dying.

His parents went to get him and brought him home to die among those who loved him. I was proud of his parents. They loved their son. They were not ashamed of him, and though they were Catholic and Robert's lifestyle violated many of their beliefs, they were unwavering in their love and support throughout his short life.

During the many visits I made to their home, his mother and I spent countless hours swapping stories of the young man each of us knew. Her other children were grown when Robert arrived to surprise and delight her middle age. The grief on her face subsided when she recalled the child that became the life of every party and the heartbeat of their family.

She told me how he became morose and withdrawn in his early teens, and how she and his father worried that he had few friends. When he began to bring home distinctly unusual kids, they realized he was gay. She was so grateful to see him have friends and happy again, that she welcomed them to her home regardless of their odd appearance or their suspected lifestyles.

Robert loved punk rock. He was in a punk rock band.

They called themselves "Latex Love," and even made an album that briefly went to number thirty-two on the alternative music chart. He supplemented his income doing the background music for gay porn and as a disc jockey for the many underground clubs in L.A. He danced to his own beat and spread his infectious enthusiasm to all who knew him. He had an immature and somewhat grotesque sense of humor and delighted in shocking the less progressive. But he was not offensive or unkind. He was a Peter Pan. A perpetually mischievous and comically antagonistic boy who thought most of the world took itself far too seriously.

As his illness rapidly progressed, his mother nervously requested that I procure marijuana in a desperate attempt to improve his appetite and relieve his pain. I did as I was asked, but his diseased lungs were too far gone to smoke it.

His mother wondered out loud why so few of his many friends visited him while he lay dying. I knew why. It was because so many were sick themselves, and because to look into his face was to look into the window of their own terrifying and potentially hopeless futures. I tried to explain to her how frightening it must be for all those beautiful young men to see themselves in the sunken eyes of their peers and still try to get through the day as if there was a reason to go on.

It wasn't like that for me. I was safe from that disease, but another was festering inside of me and it was becoming increasingly difficult to hide.

I had made the transition from recreational user to addict gradually. The next inevitable step in the life of many addicts is to dealing drugs, and I was no exception. The drug takes over. Your old life falls away. It becomes more difficult to maintain a job and a normal life. You must supply your habit but can't function well enough to pay for it. A demon was growing inside me. I felt it clawing at my soul almost constantly. I was keeping it together on the surface but was deteriorating beneath. I lied to myself and others constantly. I told myself I could keep it together. I told others I could quit anytime I wanted. I never planned to let it go so far. I never imagined I would be a criminal. I never dreamed I could be a convicted felon and an inmate.

But it was all there waiting for me, and I drove straight into it.

I met all the right people to set myself up as a drug dealer and, at any given time, was in possession of thousands of dollars' worth of drugs and cash. There is a sickening power allotted to those in possession of something others are desperate to have. That power, in the hands of a weakened and diseased soul, will almost assuredly be wielded destructively. No one can be trusted in the drug world. Your only loyalty is to your habit, and your only commitment is to the obtaining and using of more. I thought my life was all about the power of possessing the drugs and money, and it was too late when I learned how powerless I really was in the grip of addiction.

I did a form of penance at Robert's bedside. I know that now. Several times a week I sat with him, watching him die slowly and struggling to hold on to a life he cherished while I willingly destroyed one I had no respect for.

He knew what I was doing. We didn't talk about it but he knew, and he resented it. It was hard for me to look him in the eye. It was hard for me to take those hours out of my addiction and pretend everything was normal. Only once did he mention it to me. He had his moments of anger and bitterness and had no place to put them but on the few loved ones near.

I remember his father leaning on the door frame of Robert's dying room, staring at his son, silent and forlorn. Robert raised his head from the pillow and shouted, "What the hell are you looking at? Are you checking to see if I'm dead yet? Don't you worry; I'll be out of your way soon."

His father's eyes filled with tears, his shoulders slumped, and he silently retreated. He couldn't even fight back. My heart broke for him.

Fathers are often the chosen whipping boys of gay men. Perhaps it's because they are usually inept at hiding their disappointments and lack the innate sense of forgiveness a mother has for her child. Fathers can be so judgmental of their sons – and far worse with gay sons – but in this case Robert was wrong. There was no judgment in his father's eyes, only heartbreak.

Only once did he turn that anger on me. We were playing cards and he winced in pain at every move. His lungs rattled with liquid when he breathed. His hair was mere tufts of straw, his body cadaverous.

We often spoke of his illness and treatment, but never his impending death. It hung suspended over us, but remained the beast that dared not speak its name. To acknowledge death is to give it life. Neither of us was willing to do it up until now. I felt we must confront the specter. I was wrong.

Watching him I said, "You must be so tired of all this. It must be so awful for you."

He froze, and then put down his cards. He looked at me with fierce indignation, his impossibly large blue eyes flashing with anger and said, "Are you asking me if I'm ready to die? Are you?! No, I am not ready to die! I am only twenty-nine years old. There was so much more to do. So many things I didn't get to do, Ernie! Sometimes I might have an hour a day I am not in pain, and I am reminded of what it's like to be alive and I am grateful just for that hour. And you insult me in your own life by destroying yourself with drugs when I would give anything to have another chance at mine. The answer is no. I am not ready to die and I never will be."

His big eyes filled with tears and I went silent in my shame. What could I say? My impulse was to leave, to run from the ugly truth of his angry words.

Instead I moved the wires and tubes connected to his wasting body to one side and lay beside him. Gently, I cradled him in my arms and tucked his face against my neck. His body nearly burned my skin from the diseases raging through him. His bones were sharp sticks poking through the thin fabric of his hospital gown. They were the bones and the fire of an impending and unreasonable death and the hopelessness and absurdity of my own decline lay obstructively between us in that embrace. I could almost feel us both disappearing, but to different places, him to a place of peace, and me to one of chaos.

Robert was always a very physically affectionate person, but no one had held his body against their's in a very long time. I wasn't afraid. I knew I wasn't going to catch anything by touching him. Meth makes you emotionally dead, but I was very much alive while holding my dying friend, and very much aware of it. He clung to me in naked desperation. We wept together until our tears were spent – two lost and frightened young men, both painfully aware of the futility of our circumstances.

I told him how sorry I was for what was happening to him. He made me promise to find my way back to sobriety. Before I left his bed he said, with a mischievous smile, "Thank you for being my friend. I love you, Ernestine." I said, "I love you, too, silly faggot. And remember, dicks ain't just for chicks, Roberta."

The end was near. I could feel it. And not for the first time did I ask myself, could it be true? Were those awful and hateful Christians right? Did God really hate us because we were gay? Were we being punished for being born this way? How could a loving God visit such cruelty and suffering on someone who brought no harm to others? If this was true, I didn't want to know their damn Gods anyway, and I would rather go to their hell than spend eternity with people like that.

I grew more isolated in my addiction. I wrote poetry, painted, and sculpted to distract me from my neglected responsibilities, and to release the conflict and turmoil of my soul. I still worked and managed to convince my clients and coworkers that my dramatic weight loss and isolation were a choice rather than a relapse into addiction.

I gave away all my pets. I wasn't taking care of them properly, and I couldn't stand the accusations in their trusting eyes when they came to me for the care and affection they took for granted and were inexplicably denied. My writing and creative projects became an obsession. I spent days and nights shut away, vomiting my emotional poison on paper in bizarre artistic expressions I called art.

The glass pipe found its way to my lips over and over, getting me higher and higher, while the life I worked so hard to build sank lower and lower. There were other addicts wandering through my house, stealing my valuables, begging for drugs, and doing my bidding, and the intermittent but steady stream of buyers came to finance my self-destruction.

A few of my old friends who still did drugs came to buy, and even they were concerned at the changes in me and my lifestyle.

My mother had been battling cancer, but I did not go home to see her. I couldn't let my family see me that way. I avoided their calls and lied easily about why I couldn't come home. My mother knew something was wrong. She always knew. When in a healthy state of mind I was an attentive and communicative son. When I was not, I was not.

Some nights I went to clubs and danced alone for hours, blocking out everyone in the club and in the world.

I closed my eyes, and it was just me and the music and my high. Meth gives you inhuman energy and alcohol is ineffective except to take some edge off the meth. Those times I was so high I feared a heart attack, half a bottle of gin would bring me back to Earth, or somewhere in the vicinity. Often those nights closed in the tangled, sweating, and desperate arms of another meth addict who also didn't know when to quit.

It was the morning of June 5th of 1995, about 6:00 a.m., when I was startled out of a deep sleep. Those deep sleeps are hard to come by for a meth addict. My heart was racing, and I couldn't figure out what had awakened me. The house was silent, I was alone, but I was sure I'd heard a loud bang on the door. I investigated and found nothing, and concluded it must have been a dream. I lay back down until I was again awakened by the ringing phone. It was 8:00 a.m. It was Robert's mother. He died at 6:00 a.m. that morning. She asked if I would like to see him before he was taken away. I asked if she minded if I didn't. I didn't want to see him dead. I told her I would be over after his body was gone. It occurred to me he died at 6:00 a.m., when I had been awakened by the loud bang. Was it him leaving this world? Was it my dear friend giving us all one last big punk-rock bang, heralding his exit?

Robert did not die peacefully or willingly. I wish I could say he did. He struggled and fought for eight months and hoped for the miracle that never came.

I made the forty-five minute drive to their home in silence and contemplated this particular example of death. I was high. I was always high, and I wonder now if I felt it the way it was supposed to be felt. Did I give the entire experience the respect, the emotional commitment and consciousness it deserved? Did I do my best by my friend? I was there for him, but not all there. And he knew I loved him. What more was there?

When I arrived, the expected pall of silence shrouded their home as the family comforted one another. His mother's weary face wore a weak smile of resignation and despair.

I went to his room and lay on his bed, now stripped bare. I tried to feel him in the room, to see if his soul or spirit was still there. There was nothing but finality in that room. I glimpsed just a hint of something colorful peeking out from under his dresser. I got up and pulled it out. It was a photo of him and me, our arms over each other's shoulders, our smiles brilliant and youthful. It was taken at Disneyland years before. I put that photo in my pocket, and that is the picture of Robert I have kept in my mind and heart these past fifteen years, not how he died, but how he lived, dancing to his own beat, spreading laughter and love, and throwing a curve ball to the conservatives and the ignorant.

He had a leather jacket I coveted. It was decorated with chains and spikes and softened with age and use. His mother said he wanted me to have it, and gave it to me. I left his house for the last time with a leather jacket, a photograph, and a profound sense of loss, and returned home to call his many friends to tell them he was gone.

That very afternoon, at 2:00 p.m., my youngest brother John called and told me our niece Jenny, Tina's eldest daughter, had been in a car accident and was in a coma.

There were times I can almost believe my drug addiction was a blessing. In times of such enormous grief I might have gone insane if I had had to fully feel it all without the anesthetic of narcotics. Tina was my favored sibling and her first daughter, Jenny, the favored of her generation. We had a special relationship. She was a beautiful child, and was becoming a beautiful young woman. She kept good grades in school, was a popular cheerleader, was in love with a handsome boy and, other than some typical teenage attitude issues, was a cooperative daughter.

Jen's father, for the most part, was absent and uninvolved in her life, and I informally adopted her as my own. Only a few summers earlier she'd spent an entire summer with me in California. It was around that time that I had taken charge of my four-year-old godson, Jaime. My old friend Sharon – his mother – and his father were both having their own drug problems, and were incarcerated. Those two children were the closest I ever came to being a parent. I have photos of twelve-year-old Jenny holding four-year-old Jaime, both so beautiful and innocent. Both doomed to tragedy before they were grown.

I was still reeling from the impact of Robert's death when the call came about the car accident that put Jenny in a coma. They did not know if she was going to survive, but it seemed unlikely. I could not imagine what Tina was going through, and I couldn't let her go through it without me. How could this be happening, Robert and Jenny on the same day?

I was to be a pallbearer at Robert's funeral in two days. I arranged to fly home to Maine immediately after. My sister assured me there was no need for me to come sooner. There was nothing I could do that couldn't wait two days.

Robert didn't want to be buried. He wanted to be cremated. His Catholic parents did not believe in cremation, and defied his wishes. I did take time to wonder if he was watching and if he were pissed that they put him in the ground. It was not my place to interfere in their family decisions, and they buried him in a beautiful spot in the shade of an olive tree. I was glad it was in the shade. He didn't like the sun. He was very pale-skinned and burned easily. It was a peaceful place, and I visited now and then for a while, but I couldn't feel him there so I stopped.

When my plane landed in Maine I went directly to

the hospital. Jenny's room was dimly lit. The bed moved gently, like waves or a gyroscope, always in motion. Tina sat across the room, her head bowed in her hands. She didn't see me come in. I looked to the floating bed expecting to see damage, disfigurement, or a specter of near-death.

But there was not a single mark on Jenny's beautiful face. Her tiny frame nestled in a cloud of white bedding, her thick, dark hair fanned out around her head. Her long dark lashes lay motionless in sleep. She was flawless in her ethereal beauty. If not for the breathing tube parting the bowed lips she'd inherited from my mother, it would have been impossible to believe she had suffered trauma severe enough to hold her at the brink of death. All the fairy tale images of the sleeping beauty were captured in her countenance. She was sixteen years old.

Her chest rose and fell artificially, air and life forced into her lungs with a machine. The monitors beeped and chimed, the floating bed whirred, the respirator breathed rhythmically to culminate in a chorus of electronic cacophony.

I felt faint with the enormity of what I was witnessing.

Tina raised her head. The weary grief on my sister's face pulled all the strings of my heart and my throat closed, stifling a sob. I embraced her, and she did not cry. I did. The last few days of death and a funeral, the flight to Maine, wondering what scene awaited, my spirit shredded with loss, my body and mind weakened by addiction, all came together in an explosion of unwanted reality in the arms of my big sister. And in a preposterous reversal of propriety, she comforted me.

The impact had torn Jenny's brain stem and injured her brain.

The doctors could not tell us much of the injury or a prognosis. She could die any minute or lie there indefinitely. And there was always the possibility of a miracle that would bring her back to us the way she was before.

But I could feel her there. She couldn't move or make a sound, but I could feel her there, just beneath the surface of this sleeping beauty. She was not completely gone, and I knew it. Her heart monitor sped up when I touched or spoke to her. The doctors insisted it was insignificant. Perhaps I just wanted it so badly that I dismissed their incomprehensible jargon and continued to search for signs that she was still with us.

I was painfully thin, pale and unhealthy from drug abuse and stress. My family was in upheaval. Jenny's condition was a tragedy of humongous proportions, and I only added salt to their wounds with my appearance and withdrawn behavior.

I knew what they thought. It was what everyone thought in those days when a gay man suddenly lost a lot of weight and looked sickly. They thought I had AIDS, and I let them think it, though I never said anything one way or another because I was too much of a coward to admit I had once again succumbed to addiction. I let my poor mother believe her son was dying of AIDS rather than confess to my self-inflicted illness. Chalk one more up for my list of regrets. When the truth was finally revealed, she was so relieved that I wasn't dying, she immediately forgave my deceit.

I sat beside Jenny and talked to her. The doctors told us it was not good to leave her in silence. I bought a CD player and CD's. I sang songs to her and held her hand. I held vigil while Tina took short breaks and tried to tend to her other daughters and a life put on hold. Tina rarely left her side for the four months she slumbered. She was afraid Jenny would wake up and not see a familiar face. Even after the doctors told us there was no hope for recovery and recommended removing her from life support, Tina did not give up on her child.

During my stay I continued my drug abuse, sometimes feeding my demon in the bathroom of Jenny's hospital room. I spent scant time with my family, avoiding them whenever possible. I walked the city streets and my old haunts at night, and one more time was reminded that home always brought me pain.

I went to the old Blue Swan and saw some of the same men who were there twenty years before when I was a boy just coming out. I had traveled the country, seen other countries, lost my Maine accent, and built a whole new life, and they were still sitting on the same barstool as when I left. It seemed a haunting tableau from the twilight zone of my boyhood.

Every head turned when I entered, and I'm sure not a one remembered the boy of twenty years before in the man that stood before them. Rail-thin, tattooed and pierced, spiked bleached hair, I embodied the look called "heroin chic" back then. I ordered a drink, stripped off all but my shoes and pants, and found my spot on the dance floor. I danced for hours under the strobe light, bathed in sweat, and spoke to no one. Men wandered close to me but I closed my eyes and felt only the beat of the music and my pounding heart. Dancing was part of the reason I was so thin. I used it as an escape, a way to be out in the world but alone and not touched by it. I danced in fury.

At last call I chose a man. His name was David. I went home with him and lost myself some more. David was another of my bad choices, and he was to come back to haunt me later.

I left Maine after a week to return to my crumbling life in the West. I left a failure. For all of Jenny's life I was her hero. I fixed things. I made a call or wrote a check and fixed things for a little girl with no Dad who cared. I was the great and powerful Uncle Ernie. But this I could not fix. I imagined I would rescue her. I would be the Prince

Charming to kiss her cheek, whisper her name, and her eyes would open and all would be well. I could leave without guilt. My family would be intact, and I would continue to at least have the security of knowing everything was the same at home and I was not needed.

But all I did was make it worse. Now they added me to their list of worries, and I was relieved to board my plane and leave the questions in their eyes behind.

The next five years of Tina's life were a series of tragedies, and I was not there for her. I wasn't even there for me.

Jenny awakened from her coma on her seventeenth birthday, after four months of sleep. Tina was by her side every day of the four months. She had been moved from the hospital to a long-term care facility two hours from home, when the doctors determined there was nothing more to be done and the insurance money ran out. I believe it was not a coincidence that these two events were simultaneous.

At Tina's request the family gathered to celebrate Jenny's birthday. As they stood around her bed and sang the birthday song, a tear slipped down Jenny's cheek. Her fingers on one hand were moving furiously and her eyes followed her sister as she crossed the room. It was a joyous occasion and the entire family, except me, was there to witness it.

I called regularly during the four months she slept and Tina held the phone to Jen's ear so she could hear my voice. I called on her birthday to join the celebration and received the news that she was coming back to us.

When Jen was ten years old, she befriended a deaf girl. She learned sign language to communicate with her friend. She taught Tina some of it. Tina recognized the furious working of her fingers as signing. Jenny couldn't speak, but desperate to communicate, somehow pulled forth from the depths of her damaged brain this memory of signing. Tina translated the movements of her daughter's hand. She said, "Mommy, what is happening?"

It was not like you see in the movies. The waking was very slow. And she was not the girl she used to be, and she never would be.

Extensive damage to the brain left her paralyzed in all but one hand and one foot. She was like an infant in many ways and had to learn to hold her head up and speak, and eventually to feed herself with the one hand that still worked. She cannot care for herself at all, and cannot be left alone. When it became obvious that the care facility was not taking proper care of her daughter, Tina fought opposing forces to bring Jenny home, and has cared for her every day for fifteen years now. Whatever life, freedoms, and even relationships Tina might have had, were, and continue to be, sacrificed for her child to be with her family. Jen's ability to stay at home hangs by a precarious thread through a state program that pays Tina a little more than minimum wage as a personal care attendant to care for Jen in the home. Without this program it would be impossible, and she would be left to the mercy of state facilities.

Jenny remains one of the great loves of my life. It was ten years before I could see her, or even tell her story, without breaking down.

Even now I recall the beautiful little girl who loved her Uncle Ernie so much more than I deserved. And I see the young woman in the wheelchair watching the world go by and living with the memories of how she used to be, and the fear that something will happen to her mother, leaving her remanded to the custody of strangers. And still she loves her Uncle Ernie more than I deserve. Because I could never do what my sister has done, perhaps because I never had a child of my own and cannot comprehend such sacrifice as that of a mother for her child.

Jen looks at me with an idolatry that shames me with

unworthiness. She still looks to me for answers I don't have, and hope for a cure that will give her back a life cut short. Just looking into those enormous and trusting blue eyes reduces me to tears and heartbreak, and anger at how unfair this damn life can be.

Three days after Jenny emerged from her coma, Tina's house and everything she owned, burned flat to the ground.

Over the next several years her long-time companion committed suicide, and another daughter got pregnant at fifteen years old with Tina's first grandchild. The child, Gabrielle, born with a heart defect, died at three months old. During this period, Tina fought and failed a lengthy battle with a neighbor who had molested her two younger girls. I don't know how she faced each day.

While my sister fought her battles on one side of the country, I fought my own on the other.

Robert's death and Jen's accident marked a point where I lost what little faith I had in a God, and in myself, and set out on a full-scale war of self-destruction.

Addiction

Isolation bathes me in silent security.
Inwardly deeper I move.
Breathing through the phallic glass
I nod, melting, all my cells sparking in ecstasy.
A slow-motion excitement builds,
My drug-lover caresses away the pain.

I pretend to live, wearing a frozen smile of half-truths.
I awaken naked, starving, ashamed,
to a moment of startling clarity.
Degraded, disgusted, desperate, determined,
moving cautiously toward my ruined world.
I step back, frightened,
And again, the wheel begins to turn.

I am lost.

E.M.

Chapter Seven
Punishment School

My choice of companions was plummeting to the social depths of bottom feeders. I did not see them as my equals, but accepted them as a necessary evil of drug dealing. They all behave as if they are your most trusted friend to stay close to their drug source, but they are not friends and not to be trusted.

There are a few key players in my downfall, but I'm cautious not to place blame on anyone but myself.

Shortly after I returned from Maine, David, the guy I met at The Blue Swan, showed up at my door. I had in fact invited him to "come see me," but I didn't mean it when I said it. I thought I was safe, over three thousand miles away, when I made the casual invitation. You have to say something after you sleep with a stranger. I should have said "call me."

David was a troubled man, and he brought his troubles with him. As if I didn't have enough of my own! He took to meth addiction like a fish to water, and now I had two habits to support. He drove me crazy, or crazier, I should say. He tended to lurk and spy on me. He gave me the creeps, and he wasn't going to be easy to get rid of. I asked him how long he was visiting for, but he avoided giving me a precise date.

He was one of the tweakers we called "a picker." Pickers pick at their skin, imagining bugs or foreign matter underneath. It's a bizarre affliction for some meth heads that results in hours locked in a room disfiguring their bodies with a sharp object. I have seen people bore holes in their faces and arms with a needle or pin, pull their own hair out in clumps, and starve themselves to skeletons. Obsession is a common affliction in meth addicts. A mundane object or pointless activity can distract and fascinate for absurdly interminable lengths of time. The sexual side effects go far beyond the boundaries of normalcy, even for one as experienced and adventurous as me. In the drug world meth is often called "queer juice," as it easily entices an otherwise heterosexual man into homosexual behavior by removing all sexual inhibitions and opening a gateway to the deepest of fantasies unrealized. It is a difficult high to let go of in many ways, and I have time and again heard ex-meth heads wistfully recall the outrageous and copious sex while on meth.

David became agitated whenever I suggested he had overstayed his welcome, and confessed he had jumped parole in Maine and would go to prison if he returned. I never learned what his crimes were, but they were severe enough to put him on the state of Maine's 10 Most Wanted List. Maine may have wanted him, but I sure didn't. His bizarre behavior, coupled with fugitive status, made me a nervous wreck, and I wanted him out of my house and life.

Richard solved that problem for me. Richard was tall, dark, handsome, charming and dangerous. He took over my life as my protector, and within a short time, my life manager. He removed David from my house and other than a brief visit to a motel to retrieve things he had stolen from me, I never saw David again.

Richard removed a lot of people from my house. Not because they were using me and stealing from me, as he said, but because he didn't want to share the wealth. Richard sought complete control over me, my house, my money, and my dope. He brought in his own gang of guys, and they were some serious criminals. Most, if not all, of these guys had been to prison and obviously had not been rehabilitated. From the moment I let them in, I could not get them out. They made sure I stayed high enough to remain defenseless. They wanted to use my house to build a meth lab. They said we could make a lot of money and never run out of dope. I needed both. My house was going into foreclosure, and my income was severely compromised by my drug habit.

I was assigned body guards. I wasn't sure who I needed protection from, but I knew I was playing with the big boys now, and a lot was at stake. These men carried guns. They knew no one would ever suspect a meth lab in my quiet upscale neighborhood and were careful to keep a tranquil appearance.

Most of the drug dealing was done off the premises to keep attention off the house. Meth was exploding in Southern California, and lawmakers were frantic to control it. Labs were busted in the desert communities, and penalties were increasingly harsh in an effort to stem the growing popularity of the drug. Meth was hard to control because anyone could make it in their kitchen with easy to obtain and legal materials. The chemicals used are toxic and cancer-causing, and the process explosive and extremely dangerous. We did it anyway.

A Mexican chef was brought in from a local gang to do the cooking. He was short and fat, spoke poor English, was very nervous and quiet, and his hands and face were already peppered with cysts and tumors from exposure to the chemicals. A meth cook's life is a short one, one way or another. He set up shop in my garage and went to work. I had no real idea what to expect, but I imagined windfalls of money solving all my problems.

I stayed busy trying to maintain my suffering hairdressing business and actually found a market for the art and crafts I was turning out in my sleepless nights. My addled brain created countless oddities that others found appealing and wanted to buy. I crafted bizarre furniture, sculpted items of décor, and created images of dark emotion from wire, glass, wood, metal, plaster, and paint. I built my art from materials other people threw away. My hands were cracked, bloodied and scabbed from hundreds of hours of working with harsh materials.

I often walked through my house where strangers lay about smoking meth and crack and never bothered to ask who they were or why they were in my home. It wasn't my home anymore. It was just a very high-end crack house.

They all smiled in my face and made a show of having my best interests at heart, then walked out with pieces of jewelry for the pawn shop, and pieces of my life to feed their own demons. I was host to a parade of parasites.

The money did not come rolling in. The larger portion of the drugs was leaving the house in the pockets of the parasites, and I was fed enough to keep me paralyzed into submission and to satisfy my personal clientele of buyers.

The days and weeks all melted together. Some marked only by the petty dramas of drug addicts, and a few marked by not so petty ones that, in retrospect, signified the beginnings of the end.

Richard was actually almost brilliant. Had he applied his ability to manipulate people in a traditional business he might have been a CEO on Wall Street. But drug addicts are unpredictable and not so easy to control. The only successful drug dealers I've ever seen don't do drugs. They keep sharp, clear minds for business, do not snort or smoke their profits, and easily control and exploit the addicted.

Of the not-so-petty dramas, I suppose the cook setting himself on fire must qualify as a big one. Meth labs are highly flammable, and fire extinguishers are part of the necessary equipment. Fortunately, he was put out before he could set fire to my house. He may have suffered minor burns – I don't remember – and his clothes were tacky anyway. I know it sounds callous, but I really didn't care about him or any of them. I hated what was happening in my house, and I felt powerless to stop it. I was caught up in a game I didn't know how to play, where everyone made up their own rules. The trust was low, the tension high, and everyone was out for himself.

The explosion in my kitchen qualifies as a not-so-petty drama too. Red phosphorous is a chemical commonly used in cleaning horse stalls and is sold at farm supply stores. It is also used in making crystal meth. It's toxic and flammable. I came home to find my all-white kitchen looking like a murder scene, stained red from floor to ceiling, and several men frantically cleaning. I looked at Richard and said, "I am leaving for the night. When I come back, I want this kitchen painted and everyone gone. I've had enough." He knew I was serious. Several days prior, extremely agitated, I had pointed a gun at his face and given him an order in the same tone of voice. He didn't argue with me this time.

I had been given a small pistol by a well-meaning friend after he visited and assessed the type of people around me. He gave it to me to protect myself. I was growing past the point of fearing these men or caring what happened to me. I just wanted to be left alone.

I had a favorite gangster I was sleeping with at the time. He was supposed to be my bodyguard and became my lover. His name was Tony. He was big and handsome and dumb as a rock.

I took Tony with me and went to a motel for the night. I had also removed what was left of my pawnable valuables and put them in the custody of a trusted friend. I had already lost thousands of dollars in jewelry and cash to these thieves, and some sense of self-preservation had clawed its way to the surface, and I began to take control of my home. It was too little, too late.

I was stashing dope away, and had a large cache hidden in my house. I had not come even close to the profits I was promised or imagined, but was ready to cut my losses, get these idiots out, and try to clean up the mess. When Tony and I returned, the kitchen had been painted and most everyone was gone.

Richard explained that the cook was in the middle of producing a large batch of meth. It would take a few days to finish. When it was finished they would dismantle the lab and leave. I agreed to a few more days if only a few key players were allowed to participate. I had a deal in the works where I would unload a large quantity of meth in a single sale and the proceeds would pull my house out of foreclosure and I could get back on track.

As we were getting ready to wrap things up, Richard came to me to say they suspected the cook was stealing meth from us. He was not producing what he should have from the measure of ingredients supplied. My response was to hide a video camera in the garage rafters. The video confirmed our suspicions. He had a false bottom in the overnight bag he carried and stuffed thousands of dollars' worth of drugs there. He was also clearly observed stuffing more in his underwear.

Richard made a call, and within minutes two very dangerous looking gangsters arrived at the door. They asked me what I wanted done with him. I told them to take the dope, take him out of there, and make sure he was scared enough to never come back.

I was seething with rage, but remained calm. The cook was fairly rewarded for his role, as was everyone involved, and for the first time I had undeniable proof that our agreements were being violated.

I may have been a criminal, but I was an honest one. I produced and sold the purest dope to be found, and sold it at a fair price. From the inception of this business venture, I suspected I was being used and taken advantage of by everyone involved, and I was disgusted by all of them and by my own naiveté. I was not a good criminal. I trusted too easily and expected others to respect my values. I believed in honor among thieves and a counter-culture unity that really only existed in the movies where the bad guys really weren't so bad in the end.

As the cook was packing up to leave, he was asked to join us in the living room. He knew something was up and was very nervous. He had always worked alone and was never part of the network. He came, he cooked, and he left. His bag was taken from him, and he was placed on the couch and the video tape was set in motion. When he saw himself stealing on camera, he looked like a terrified, trapped animal. He shocked and annoyed me when he started to cry.

He was ordered to strip, and he refused. They stripped him and handed me the bag of dope hidden in his underwear and two more, one in each sock. This alone was several thousand dollars in street value, and there was no telling how long it had been going on.

He had been allowed to pull his shorts and pants up but remained shirtless and shoeless. He broke free and attempted to run from the house. He was caught and tackled at the front door before he could open it. I stood back and watched the ensuing struggle in the foyer dispassionately.

One of the gangsters pulled out a gun. I barely took a step forward to stop him when the gun went off. The explosion was deafening. Blood spattered the white tiled foyer. Everyone froze and fell silent. The Mexican cook lay on the floor. It was so surreal. It seemed all in slow motion. Sound was muffled. Life snapped back to real time and panic erupted. Only seconds had passed.

The cook was not dead. Only grazed at the temple and stunned. The shooter swore it was an accident. He only meant to scare him. They all wanted to run, envisioning the cops arriving momentarily. A calm came over me and my head was clear, my mind razor sharp. I raised my voice above the others and ordered them to shut up and listen.

I knew my neighborhood. I'd lived there a long time. It was mid-afternoon. No one would expect or suspect a gunshot in this neighborhood; it would have been noticed and dismissed as a car backfiring or a sonic boom from the nearby El Toro Air Force Base. It's what I would have thought as a resident. In nearby gang-infested Santa Ana, it would have been recognized for what it was but not here. If everyone had raced to their cars, it might have raised suspicions. Too much activity in a quiet neighborhood is sure to be noticed. I warned everyone not to leave. It actually amuses me now to recall the fear on the faces of these men who had instilled so much of it in others. Ultimately, they were cowards.

Richard was a familiar face in the neighborhood by now. I told him to wait ten minutes and back the car into the garage, put the cook in the car, take him back to his neighborhood and dump him. That is exactly what they did. The others were instructed to help me clean up and then gradually disperse. As I predicted, the cops didn't come. My house was quiet and empty. It occurred to me to search for the bullet. I found it lodged in the center of an antique Chinese inlaid table. It also occurred to me I was far more upset over the destruction of a beautiful piece of furniture than I was over the shooting of the cook. I was not a well man.

Months later someone told me the cook was found dead in an alley in the barrio. Apparently he had not learned his lesson, either.

The meth lab was out of operation, but I continued using and selling drugs. I'd gotten rid of Richard and his parasites and found a small pack of my own.

Donald, my ex, was coming around. He claimed he wasn't enjoying single life as much as he thought he would, and wanted me to consider taking him back. We did drugs together and he reminded me how good in bed he was with copious, drug-induced sex, but I never considered a permanent reunion. He was just someone to share my drugs and my bed for the moment. None of it mattered anymore anyway. It was all falling apart, and I was too far gone to fix it.

Around 2:00 a.m. on February 19th, 1996, a half block from my house, a cop pulled me over for failure to use my turn signal. I was stoned as usual. He searched me and my car, found an ounce of meth and assorted paraphernalia, and arrested me. They obtained a warrant to search my house and tore it apart. They found a lot of drugs and the remains of the meth lab.

My life was now officially ruined. Cops did not sit in my neighborhood at 2:00 a.m. and pull people over for failure to use a turn signal. He was waiting for me. Someone had given them my name. They were too confident; too sure of themselves when they searched me without probable cause, and the warrant to search my home came quick and easy. As if it was already issued. I had heard Richard was busted a few days earlier, and I have no doubt he gave me up in exchange for a deal. Richard was that kind of guy. There's an old rule in drug busts the cops use vigorously. They call it "Name three, go free." A small time druggie gets busted, agrees to name three dealers, and he'll be cut loose for snitching. When I was busted they told me, "Give us three dealers who are bigger than you, and we will get you a lighter sentence." I told them, "I don't know anyone bigger than me."

I was charged with possession, sales, and conspiracy to manufacture methamphetamine, possession of cocaine, marijuana, PCP, mushrooms, paraphernalia, and various lesser charges that were eventually dropped in the bargaining process.

It was called, by the newspaper, one of the biggest busts in Orange County history, but I am absolutely sure that was an exaggeration, and it is not possible I was in possession of the quantities stated. It doesn't matter. Everybody lies. The addicts lie, the police and newspapers lie, the lawyers lie, and somewhere in there is a grain of truth, so everyone can convince themselves there is justice and justify their paychecks.

There was a suitcase in my closet with a lot of drugs in it. I really didn't know how much was there, but it was far too much to claim personal use only. All the drugs other than the meth were, in fact, for personal use.

The Orange County Jail was my home for the next three months. In county jail, inmates are separated and identified with colored wristbands, red being the most dangerous or highest security risk. White the least. I was blue banded. Blue bands are for P.C., protective custody, which meant separated for a myriad of reasons, none of which are held in high esteem among the other inmates. Snitches, homosexuals, death penalty cases, sex criminals, and anyone else who must be kept safe from the more elite class of criminals in the general population are blue banded.

The inmates living quarters are called "mods" (as in module). The mod is constructed in an octagon with eight pods, or sections, to a mod. It is entirely glass, and a control tower stands in the center of each mod, which holds twenty cells. There are speakers in the cells to communicate with the tower. The cell fronts are glass. The bunks and toilet are visible to anyone outside the cell. There is almost no need for an officer to have any physical contact with an inmate. Everything is controlled from the tower electronically. The officers are generally quite bold and abusive given the lack of opportunity for retaliation by the inmates. Most are arrogant pricks.

Twenty-three hours a day locked in an 8x6 cell with another inmate. One hour per twenty-four in the day room to shower, make a phone call or mingle with your neighbors. A lot of them knew each other from the streets or their many prior visits to County Jail. I knew no one.

For the first few days, I was so dope-sick I didn't even get off my bunk except to throw up now and then. Kicking drugs is not easy. Kicking drugs in a jail cell is hell.

I must have been suicidal, because they put me in the crazy ward of the jail for those first few days. They give you a paper dress and a mattress on the floor. You don't even get sheets, in case you try to use them to hang yourself. You're in a glass cube and monitored at all times. You sweat and shake and puke and shit until you can't possibly have any fluid left in you. The inside of my body felt like I was being stuck with a thousand knife points. All those deadened nerves coming to life at once and screeching for drugs that were out of my reach.

Coming off meth, there are two things your body can't get enough of: food and sleep. In jail you are fed just enough to keep you alive and nothing more. The food is garbage I wouldn't feed my dogs. You eat it because that's all there is. But you can sleep all you want if you're lucky enough to have a quiet cellmate. I wasn't so lucky.

My first cellmate after the crazy ward was a Vietnamese cross-dressing prostitute and petty thief. He spoke little to no English and talked incessantly. My nerves were raw and my body worn out. After three days of his clicking, clacking, and undecipherable screech, I gave him one good punch in the stomach and he stayed quiet until he left for the streets a week later. He tried to tell a deputy I punched him in the stomach, but they had no more patience trying to understand him than I did, and just ignored him. This was my first exposure to prison "girls."

There's a street corner in the ghetto of Santa Ana, California that is known for and patronized by its unique breed of whores. These girls are all boys. These boys are not prissy little drag queens dressing up for attention, either. These are hardcore, knife wielding, needle-packed bitches who can hold their own with any man. Most of them had girls' names, lived as girls, and had been making a living and surviving on the streets since they were very young. These girls were regulars in the revolving-door life of the Orange County Jail.

A pretty Mexican "girl" called Yolanda told me her mama started injecting her with female hormones at nine years old and put her out for sale on the streets of Tijuana to help feed the family. She was so pretty even the deputies were taken by her and couldn't believe she was really a boy. She was so uncomfortable with her penis that I held up a sheet for her, to block prying eyes, so she could use the toilet in private and not spoil her illusion. I adored her, and she tugged at my heart strings with her stories of a childhood far worse than my own.

Our Mod was certainly the most fascinating and colorful section of the jail. There are two tiers, double cells on the bottom and single cells on the top. The single cells on the top were reserved for the most notorious of prisoners, who had no physical contact with other inmates. Most were death penalty cases.

During my three months awaiting trial, I came face to face with several of California's more high-profile murderers of the time, and one of the most celebrated serial killers in California history. He looked like a cartoon version of a fat little Chinese professor, with big thick horn-rimmed glasses and a bowl haircut. Charles Ng tortured, dismembered, and even cannibalized dozens of people. But he was always really polite to me. Of course I was awfully thin and not much more than a snack for Charles, and he couldn't get through the bulletproof glass to eat me anyway, so why not be nice?

I briefly had a Cuban drag queen for a cellmate named "Vickie." Vickie was terrified of Charles Ng, and I amused myself by telling her Charles was looking at her and licking his lips. Charles had the first day room call in the mornings, and therefore had first access to the newspaper all the inmates had to share. For some reason unknown to me, Charles decided he would give me the paper when he finished with it. He slid it piece by piece through the thin crack under the cell door. When Vickie bent down to retrieve the paper I grabbed her ankle from behind and yelled, "BOO!" That queen let a scream out of her that brought the deputies running to our cell. Charles Ng actually smiled a little at her terror and my hysterical laughter. The deputies were not amused by either of us. Jail and prison are full of gallows humor. It helps alleviate some boredom.

County jail is a very tense place. Most of the guys are awaiting trials or have been convicted and are on their way to state prison and waiting for the chain. There's nothing to do and that makes men mean. I suppose its best they are locked in a cell most of the time or there would be no end to the violence.

I read a lot of books, played a lot of cards and slept in between trips to the court house for the endless motions and legal meanderings of my lawyer and the prosecutor.

Court days are hell: awakened at 5:00 a.m., hand-cuffed and chained for a short bus ride to the courthouse dungeons, freezing cold cells with concrete benches and one toilet for a dozen guys. A fifteen minute court appearance is twelve hours of extreme discomfort. I was tempted to just accept the first offer to not have to do court days. My lawyer suggested otherwise.

I usually had the unique privilege of being placed in a single-man cage, roughly the size of an old phone booth, for my own protection, of course. Though other prisoners couldn't touch me, they could talk to me. The first question was always, "Why are you a blue band?"

I would simply answer, "Because I'm gay, and apparently the rest of you have a problem with that."

They rarely did. I believe gays are separated in county because they don't want the guys having sex. Of course, there are plenty of men who don't admit to being gay who are in general population and undoubtedly having plenty.

A lot of the men on their way to prison try to "hook up" with homosexuals who are going back to the street, hoping to find someone to do their bidding while they're in. Many are just playing games to amuse themselves and their buddies and alleviate some boredom.

Such was the case with Shane.

In California facilities the races do not mix. Adjacent to my cage at the courthouse dungeon, roughly twenty blacks occupied a holding cell. They made a few comments to or about me, and I ignored them. I was used to jail banter by now, and they were harmless.

One in particular sauntered over while his friends watched in amusement. He was only inches away, separated by steel mesh. I was struck by his unusual beauty and his obvious awareness of it. He appeared confident and sly. Other than his braided hair, he did not look black at all. His striking eyes were neither blue nor green, but both. They reminded me of opals. High cheekbones and a broad Cheshire grin, black hair and lashes, all combined in a captivatingly menacing exoticism. His arms, hands, and throat were heavily tattooed. I was intrigued.

He asked me if I was gay. I answered, "Most of the time." He could tell I was defensive, and his demeanor softened. I asked if he was black. He said, "Most of the time." We both laughed. He had my attention. He told me he lived in the same Mod as me and had seen me before. He said he would send me a "kite." A kite is a letter carried from one inmate to another secretly. Kites are illegal communication between inmates intentionally separated.

Shane and I became jailhouse boyfriends. Only once, in the visiting room, were we actually in each other's physical presence, without glass or steel between us. Shane was just a fantasy, born of boredom, loneliness, and fear. My future was waiting to be written, and his was non-existent. He was facing twenty-five to life for a petty cocaine charge, under California's absurd and overzealous three strikes law, and is now fourteen years into that sentence. Shane knew he was going to prison. He was playing a game with me, looking for someone to use in the outside world, but we grew beyond that and formed a bond of friendship.

My lawyer had procured a deal. Though I had serious charges against me, I was a first-time offender and, prior to my arrest, considered an upstanding and productive member of society. I got a break.

I was considered for and accepted into an alternative sentencing program, and would do my time in a recovery center. We were waiting for a bed to become available for me. I didn't care if they sent me to Alaska, as long as I was leaving that damn jail. The only positives were that I was clean when I hit the street, I didn't smoke for three months, and I had caught up on my letter-writing. I could write volumes about the crazy people I met in those three months. I had many fascinating conversations with men awaiting trial for murder. Though each had his own peculiar background, I was consistently struck by how normal the perpetrators seemed. Just your average, common man who happened to chop someone's head off, or was curious what human flesh tasted like. But they still showered and shaved and wrote letters to their mothers like everyone else.

I despised those shapeless orange jumpsuits, all those lonely men and me with only one outfit, and orange has never been one of my colors. The female inmates wore a deep blue. I asked for a blue jumpsuit, but they stubbornly denied me. One gets so pasty without sunlight for three months, and orange really only works well on someone tanned. I made the best of it with some alterations. Cuffing the hems, cinching the waist with shoe strings, and standing the collar gave it a bit of personal style. I was admired for my aesthetics by the few other inmates who appreciated such things.

There is no grand farewell when someone leaves county jail. The most common salutation is, "See you next time." Jails and prisons in this country might as well have revolving doors on them for all the success we have not achieved in rehabilitation.

After finding myself on the wrong side of our judicial system, I studied the inner workings and discovered the system feeds itself with failure. Imagine all the lost jobs and revenue provided by the two million inmates in America if we actually rehabilitated? There's no incentive to change things if it will cost someone his job. The very people who make and enforce the laws have the most to lose if other people stop breaking them. Their goal appears to be to cripple and incapacitate by cutting off all opportunities and avenues to the already socially handicapped, forcing them to rely on the survival skills of crime, subsequently using them as an example of substandard humanity and undeserving of our compassion or assistance. I came to realize the correctional system has no desire to correct anything. They like things just as they are.

A disturbing and memorable quote from a lawmaker I met: "We do not have a justice system. We have a legal system. They are not the same thing."

Of course, I speak in generalities. There are some who find a way out. There are people out there who care enough to seek change and offer assistance, and there are plenty of people who have no desire to better themselves or their circumstances, and are not deserving of opportunities. I have certainly rubbed elbows with those who belong behind bars and wouldn't change if you handed them a better life on a silver platter, but I do believe they are the minority.

I was fortunate to meet a woman who embodied the force of positive change, particularly with addicts. Nancy Clark never met an addict she didn't think she could help. She had a career in the public defender's office and saw a gaping hole in the system. In that hole fell the men and women who were not criminals, but addicts. They had broken the law, but were not candidates for prison. She created the medium of the Alternative Sentencing Program, a place to carry out a sentence and be exposed to Twelve-Step recovery simultaneously.

We were allowed to keep our jobs and maintain limited and controlled exposure to the outside world while living at the Recovery Center and filling our free time with rigorous education and recovery programming. We reported regularly to probation or parole. One dirty test or failed responsibility could result in revocation of this opportunity and result in finishing one's sentence the traditional way, behind bars.

My house was in foreclosure, the contents seized by the police, and the rest picked over by the tweakers as soon as the police vacated. I had little to no material wealth left. But I had a reasonable facsimile of freedom, a place to start over, and a handful of people who still cared about and believed in me.

I lived at the Recovery Center for a year. I had a great time there, and met some truly wonderful people. I forged friendships that I still enjoy today and, unfortunately, witnessed more than a few who didn't make it. One way or the other, they made an exit.

Nancy was not a harsh taskmaster, but I thought she was at the time. I resented a controlled environment, and pushed her to fury more than once. She had seen hundreds, maybe thousands before me, and she knew more about me than I did myself. One more time I pulled the sexy, funny routine to get everyone to like me. People are easier to manipulate when they like you. I kicked manipulation into high gear, but I was among people that were far too experienced with people like me to fall for my charms, and they held me accountable at every turn.

I do think I'm a genuinely nice person, but control issues are a character defect I'm still working on and probably always will. I was still pretty spoiled and used to getting my own way. I hadn't sunk low enough to appreciate what was being offered to me. I could have saved myself a lot of ensuing pain had I realized this at the time.

While I was in the program, I did manage to get my business back on track and begin to clean up some of the mess I'd made. I built a foundation in recovery and, though I was still not ready to stay clean for good, I had learned what it really meant to be an addict, and became part of a fellowship of people who understood me, maybe for the first time in my life. And one more time, I had to fuck everything up over a stupid man. I was still carrying on with Shane through the mail, but he was not my future. He was someone I could have just to feel like I had someone. Relationships with someone incarcerated are perfect sometimes. You always know where they are. Your relationship is never challenged by the daily petty and mundane things couples fight over, and your partner has nothing better to do than write you love letters and tell you all the things you want to hear about how wonderful you are.

Toward the end of my sentence, I met Scott. He was my new roommate at the Recovery Center. The first time I saw him, I walked into my room and he was sitting on the other bed, playing a guitar. A curtain of black hair fell over his face. He was shirtless, and had a smooth, toned body, and when he looked up, the irises of his eyes were solid black. He looked every part of his Native American heritage. He wasn't handsome, but he had that dangerous feel about him that gets my attention every time. My tattoos grabbed his attention and were the open door to conversation. Scott had a fascination with tattoos and had a few of his own, which he proudly showed off to me. When I removed my shirt to show him the ink that was not immediately visible, I was disconcerted when he ran his hands lightly over my tattooed skin with an overly familiar and vaguely erotic touch. We hit it off right away, but I had no plans or inclination for it to go beyond a friendship.

He was divorced, with a daughter from his first marriage and had a second daughter with his current girlfriend. I believed him to be completely straight. I liked his girlfriend. She was a sweet girl, and had been through hell with his alcohol problem. We became fast friends, went to our meetings together, and lived harmoniously as roommates, until Scott started secretly drinking. He came home obviously drunk one night and begged me not to tell anyone. The Recovery Center would make him leave, and he had no place to go. I put him to bed to sleep it off, but in the night, he left his bed and crawled into mine.

There I was, with everything in me telling me to run in the other direction, and I didn't. I turned to him and set in motion yet another relationship with the completely wrong man. Emotionally unavailable, sexually confused, and spiritually bankrupt, Scott was familiar to me. He was all the other men (with the exception of Rod) I had been with, and would bring me nothing more than the same heartaches.

I was readying myself to finish my sentence and set back out into the world on my own. Nearly a year clean, and back on track, I let my guard down. I began to think I had it all under control and could do what I wanted again.

Scott asked me to get a place together when I left, and I foolishly agreed. Meanwhile he continued to drink, and I continued to cover for him. I exited the Recovery Center with fanfare and a confidence I did not feel. Nancy Clark tried to convince me to stay as a non-sentenced resident. I'm sure she knew I wasn't ready to take over my life, but I was determined. I rented a small house and moved in. I managed to salvage some things from my former home to furnish the house, and my hairdressing business was slowly recovering yet again.

Scott brought nothing with him except his guitar and drugs. Within a week after leaving the center, I was getting high. I was still on probation and reported and tested regularly. I was barely free a month when probation arrested me for testing dirty. Nancy Clark went to bat for me one more time at the probationary hearing, and after a few weeks in jail I was sent back to the Recovery Center for five more months. I maintained the rental house, moved Scott out and roommates in to pay the rent, and settled in for five more months of programming.

I loved being clean and sober. I loved the fellowship and my sober friends. I never understood what kept driving me back to self-destructive misery, and I still don't. With so many years without drugs behind me now, I have forgotten what that insane drive feels like. Once in a while I get an unexpected wave of desire that never fails to take me by surprise, but it is never powerful enough to act on. I have become a person who obsessively tries to fix things instead of one who destroys.

Thinking back sometimes, I wonder if I was not in a profound depression. I had lost most everything I had worked for and what I thought was my identity. I could not muster what it took to care about my life enough to keep it together. I was angry at the authority that ruled my life and believed it to be my right to destroy myself if I so chose. I was tired of the parole department and the Recovery Center telling me what to do. I wanted to be totally free again. I am glad to be alive today, but I still don't think it's anyone's business if I choose not to be. And I don't think keeping drugs illegal has done a damn thing to solve the problem. A lot of people on both sides of the law make a lot of money off drugs and drug addicts in America. As long as it's profitable that's not likely to change.

I did my next five months at the Recovery Center like a gentleman. I followed the rules, gained my freedom once again, and moved back into my rental house. I went to informal probation and did not have to report or test. No more pissing in a cup with a stranger watching. It wasn't long after that Scott showed up again with a pocketful of dope, and I was high again.

On my most recent trip to jail I met John. John was on his way to prison for a relationship with an underage girl, and I was on my way back to the Recovery Center. John recently reminded me of the first time he saw me. He was a jail trustee. Trustees are the few jail inmates who have jobs and privileges inside the jail. One of John's jobs was to help feed the rest of us. It was easily an hour earlier that I had pressed the intercom button to request a visit to the jail nurse. Sitting on the bottom bunk, I had stood up quickly and nearly knocked myself unconscious, gashing the top of my head on the steel rail of the top bunk. My head was pumping blood and I was nauseous from the pain. The deputies did not respond. I managed to quell the flow of blood on my own and, when the deputy and John arrived an hour later with my food tray, I launched into an unprecedented tirade of rage at their lack of response to my medical request. The deputy was visibly unnerved at my blood-soaked head and face and comically chastised by my verbal assault on his job performance and the inefficiency of his employers. He immediately had me escorted to the medical facilities. John was absolutely delighted by my tirade and told me he had never seen anyone talk to a deputy that way and get away with it, and he insisted that we be friends. I gave him my address, and we kept in touch while he finished his sentence.

John is not the sharpest tool in the shed, but he has a good heart and is a long way from a menace to society. He was soon to be released and had no place to go. He had few friends and no family in California. I agreed to take him in until he could find a place to stay.

I have seen a great deal of unfairness in our legal system throughout my years of miscreant behavior. Not unfairness for myself, I was guilty of everything I was ever accused of or convicted for. I knew the law, I broke it anyway, and I did more than my fair share of punishment for my crimes. But I've always felt John's predicament is unjust.

John embarked on a relationship with a fifteen-year-old girl when he was twenty-nine, resulting in her pregnancy. The girl's father gave his blessing to the relationship, hoping it would calm his wild teenaged daughter down, and the three shared a home. When the young girl's mother re-entered her life, after years of absence, she was outraged by the arrangement and had John arrested. Though both the girl and her father testified on his behalf, John was convicted of lewd and lascivious acts on a minor and branded for life as a sex offender.

John was the first registered sex offender I'd known, and my heart went out to him for how difficult his life was for that single indiscretion. Sex offenders are our modern-day lepers, our Salem witches, and our scourge on social and moral order. Regardless of the severity of their crime, they are branded for life, exploited by the media, and denied access or opportunity to the most basic survival tools in the free world. They are never allowed to put their past behind them or look forward to paying off their debt to society and being an equal member. They are simply too offensive. Even the most liberal and compassionate shy away from publicly defending the sex offender. Even though we all know peeing on the side of the road, drunkenly grabbing the wrong boob, or accepting a sexual invitation from an undercover cop is an unfair reason to brand someone for life, we remain silent lest we appear sympathetic to sexual deviants and taint ourselves with their misdeeds. My friendship with John gave me an inside view of the harsh realities of the life of a sex offender. Though the conditions for gay people are considerably less debilitating, I can certainly relate to being labeled sexually offensive by the more judgmental members of society.

And I believe you can defend a person without defending their mistakes. People do it with their children all the time. It's easy to do with someone you love. The real challenge is to find compassion for someone you don't care about.

Today, John lives in a van in a parking lot. In California, a sex offender can't live near a day care, school, church, or park. They have a hundred other rules that prevent them from having a place to live, a job, or any semblance of a normal life. They are pariahs. And each time one commits a new crime, it gets that much worse for the ones who are behaving. Lawmakers are eager to put them away for the slightest error to relieve themselves of the cost and effort of monitoring and managing them. Paroled murderers have more freedom than an average sex offender. My opinion has always been, if our billion dollar correctional system believes someone is still a menace to society, don't let them out. But if they do let them out, let them have a life. Don't torment them and place impossible demands that ensure failure. The prisons and the streets are full of dangerous people, and they're not always who you think they are. I have met many who do not deserve freedom or opportunity. It is the state's responsibility to know the difference, and they fail miserably. That's what I've seen with John for twelve years. In and out the revolving door, never having committed a crime worse than stealing something to eat, taking a shower at a friend's home too close to a school, or being out past a curfew.

John was staying with me when Scott started coming around again. He didn't like Scott at all, and Scott didn't like him. He was protective of me, and sensed Scott was trouble. But John is a follower, not a leader, and could not sway or persuade my behavior. I intimidated him and I held all the power in our relationship.

Scott was pure lust. He lusted for excitement, money, sex, drugs, danger, and anything else that will destroy you. He never said "no" to anything. He was the straw that broke this camel's back, and helped push me down the path of no return.

I started dealing again, almost right away. I had what I commonly refer to as the "fuck-its."

I'd been down this path too many times before to pretend I didn't know what was coming. There was heat on me from the start. I was a known drug dealer now. I refused any offers to involve myself in manufacturing, but hooked up right away with some local gangs to get my new sources for dealing. I had met a few guys in jail and rehab who were back on the street and rolling big.

This time I was not the prissy hairdresser hooked on drugs and easy to take advantage of.

I was dealing with LA gang members, black and Mexican, who would shoot you for $500, a bag of meth, or for dealing in their territories. I was just scared enough to be mean, and kept a gun nearby at all times. I was told that some local Mexican gangs were not happy about my dealing in areas they claimed, and I was in danger of their retaliation. But I had the "fuck-its" and was not about to quit while I was ahead. It wasn't even close to the quantity I was moving before I went to jail, and I wasn't interested in anything more than paying for my habit, but my habit was expensive.

I was depressed and ashamed to be using again, and once again I submerged into isolation. I picked up my arts and crafts and writing again. My obsession to express myself through creativity was a direct contradiction to my obsession to destroy myself. It was almost as if I was compelled to create beauty to justify the ugliness. Or at least distract from it. But nothing made me feel better. I contemplated suicide often. I can't say how many times I sat with the glass pipe in my mouth and the pistol within reach, wishing I could get high enough to put it in my mouth and pull the trigger. I fantasized and planned my death but couldn't gather the courage to make it happen. I did have a second failed attempt through overdose during this period. I had the gun but I didn't want to make a mess, and I wanted to look good at my funeral. My vanity was the only thing that never deteriorated. I figured the pills would make me just as dead without disfiguring my face. I had written another of many farewell letters in my usual dramatic fashion and put it on the nightstand before swallowing a bottle of pain pills, a few at a time. I drifted off, ready to be done with it all.

I don't know how many hours passed before I woke, violently ill. I was so disoriented from the overdose I didn't even know why I was sick. I leaped out of the bed to the bathroom to vomit and my legs went out from under me. They were either asleep or numb from the drugs. When I went down my chin slammed against an antique trunk at the foot of the bed, and I blacked out again. I woke again to daylight streaming through a window, in a pool of blood and vomit, disgusted to still be alive. I carry a scar on the underside of my chin today from that night, a lifetime reminder of the depths of my despair.

Things were spinning out of control again. I was dealing with a black gangster from South LA who introduced me to a new drug. Actually, PCP was an old drug, but it was being used in a new way. It came in a liquid form, and they called it "whack." You dipped a joint or cigarette in it, smoked it, and it took you to another planet. You couldn't find it much outside the black community, and they couldn't get good crystal meth, so we set up a trade deal.

Thinking back on the nights I spent in the meanest streets of Los Angeles, the only white face for miles in any direction, I am truly amazed I never caught a bullet or a knife for daring to walk their streets. I recall a particular night where I was to meet a gangster for a deal on the very street Rodney King was beaten by the police. Dressed like a hardcore punk, with electric blue hair and rings and chains decorating my emaciated and pale body, I strutted down those streets like I owned them. But I had the "fuck-its," and you can sense that in a person in a neighborhood like that, and they stared and talked shit, but left me alone. And a lot of them knew who I was. People know the regulars on a street, and they knew I was bringing the best meth in town and I was bringing it to a man who would kill them if they interfered with me. As I returned to my car that night I was confronted with a pathetic creature blocking the path to my car door: a scarred, starved, and flea-ridden blue pit bull. I stopped dead in my tracks and eyed her. She dipped her head and whimpered pitifully, her tail between her legs. I spoke softly to her, and coaxed her to me. She smelled like a garbage heap. I scratched her head and petted her for a few minutes. I felt so sorry for her, but I couldn't help her. I couldn't even help myself. I got in my car and began to back away. She slowly trotted beside the car and never took her eyes off my face, pleading with me not to leave her. Through all my insanity and the chaos of my life, my love of dogs and my soft heart for the wounded prevailed. I opened the car door and said, "Goddamnit, get in girl." I took her home, cleaned her up, named her Cali, and eventually found her a good home. I knew she was better off with someone else. I knew where my life was going, and she wouldn't have a permanent home with me.

I learned in prison that the most dangerous men are the ones with nothing left to lose. I had begun to feel that I had nothing left to lose. I knew there were only two ways for this to all end, prison or death. And the clock was ticking on me for one or the other. I couldn't quit, but badly wanted it all to end. I needed someone to take charge and steer me in the right direction, but all the good people in my life had given up on me, and the rest were no stronger than I.

I kept my family in the dark and pretended all was well in the little contact I had with them. They had their own lives and problems. My mother had successfully beaten two bouts with cancer back to back. When she had finally retired from a life in the factories, and with her kids grown, my stepfather finally took the reins of running their finances and lives. I imagined her at last having the life of comfort she deserved. The last thing I wanted was for her to worry about me. Whenever we spoke, I did my best to dredge cheer from the depths of my dark spirit and placate her concerns for my well-being. If she pried, as my mother tended to do, I became short and irritable, and she backed off. It had become easy to cut myself off from people. The less they knew the better. I lived in a world of secrets.

John brought home a Mexican convict named Arturo, an ex-prison boxer just coming off a ten-year term and crazy as all hell. Arturo was my pit bull. I should have been afraid of him, everyone else was. But I wasn't. He was somewhat enamored of me and as loyal as Cali. He was a raw, powerful, and dangerous man. Stupid, primal, and angry, he was two hundred pounds of rock-solid muscle and paranoia. He spoke poor English, and his inability to communicate frustrated him.

Over the years I've seemed to have developed a knack for calming the raging bull in that type of man, through either imperious authority or feminine and non-threatening manipulation. Soothing affection and sincere concern, coupled with a carefully orchestrated appearance of submission to his masculine authority gives the savage man his much-needed respect and gains his devotion. Once you have dared to enter the inner sanctum of his troubled violent heart, without fear or judgment, you rise above all others in his eyes, and make him feel less alone and less angry. And he will kill to protect that.

Arturo was a beautiful man. Dark gold skin, black eyes, sculpted body and impeccably groomed. In a different life he might have been a Latin film star. He came to me frequently and unannounced, and told me nothing of his life away from me. He was my "tax man." Addicts will take advantage if they can, and the best drugs you can find are ones you don't pay for. The tax man is the dealer's debt collector. He comes to where you live, he intimidates and roughs you up, and then he takes anything of value he can find to cover your drug debt. He must be frightening and nearly heartless to do his job well. He is a necessary evil for the dealer. Arturo badly beat a man in my backyard, in front of a group of people, for an imagined slight, and established himself as volatile and dangerous. People walked cautiously in his presence, and it was known that he was my protector. He quickly became my lover.

John and Scott were both on friendly terms with him, but I'm sure even they knew he was unpredictable and extremely dangerous. I did not fear him, because I knew his heart. I knew his secrets and desires. I fed his desires with my drugs and my body. I pried his fantasies out of him and became them. I was not a young boy anymore, and I took him places he had not been before, outside of the most secret parts of his mind. His fantasies of aggression, bordering on sado-masochism, were easy for me as long as I felt in control. We were both men who lived our lives barely controlled. An understanding linked us in ways no one imagined. Our sicknesses bonded us. I teased and provoked him to hurt me, and I manipulated his shame when he was spent. He was the Scottish man Robert, and I was back in the motel room in New York, only this time I understood him. I welcomed his bruises and his bites. I smiled while he sweated and bucked and moaned with sexual ferocity, and I walked the razor-sharp edge of knowledge that at any moment he could go too far, I could lose control, and he could kill me. His pain, and the pain he gave me, was something I could actually feel. It was better than feeling nothing at all, and it reminded me I was still alive.

Though I knew his inner self, Arturo still kept some things secret from me. I didn't know where he lived, if he lived with anyone, or if he had a job or a skill beyond the world of drugs and crime. He came and went like a ghost. He did my bidding and left with his rewards. He often appeared in the wee hours wearing a look of guilt and hungry desperation. I imagined he lived in the barrio when he was not in prison. In the barrio, the macho ex-convict could not allow himself to feed the hunger he acquired in prisons, where women were just a picture on a wall and boys had no choice but to play his games. I imagined he lived with his large Mexican family, and his immigrant parents watched him warily for signs of the familiar behavior that would take him back to his real home in prison. I was wrong in my imaginings. He did live in the barrio, but not with his parents.

We were curled up together on my bed one morning when the phone rang. I answered, half asleep, and the girl on the other end asked if Arturo was there. Thinking he had given someone my number, I said he was. I prodded him awake, handed him the phone, and said, "It's some girl for you."

A look of guilty terror came over his face and he whispered, "I am not here."

I told her he wasn't there. It sounded as if she was crying. She explained that she had found my phone number on their bill and he would be very angry she called, but they had a new baby and no money or food in the house and she had not seen him for several days. She was worried and frightened. She was his wife. She said she thought he was sleeping with me and would I please think of their baby and try to get him to come home. I said of course I would. And I meant it. He watched me furiously through our short conversation and when it ended he wanted me to tell him what she said. He was very upset that she knew about me. I told him to go home, take care of his family, and not come back. I wasn't angry with him. I didn't love him, and never asked him about his life away from me. I didn't care. Our relationship was business and sex. At least that's all it was for me, and he never indicated it was anything more for him. He pleaded with me not to banish him, but I felt so sorry for his wife and child and didn't want to be a part of hurting them. I had enough bad karma already.

I saw Arturo one more time after that, when he came in my bedroom window in the night while I slept, and sexually assaulted me with ferocity unmatched by any I had previously submitted to. In my usual state of drug-induced delirium, I first wondered if I was dreaming. I had allowed his fantasies of sexual dominance to flourish and should have known that I might not always be able to control him. I believe he had to come back one more time to show me he was in control after all. His pride would not be sent away. It had to walk away victorious. Afterward, he sat with his head in his hands and explained the drugs made it difficult to control his urges, and he knew he had to quit before he did something terrible to someone else. I did not see myself as victimized. Again, I had brought this on myself, and I was relatively unhurt in relation to what he was capable of. He went away, and I did not see him again. There is no doubt in my mind that he indeed remains a menace to society, and though I have no idea what happened to him, neither do I doubt that he is behind bars and always will be. Nothing short of a miracle could save that man from the violence of his own nature. He was a bull, and the world his china shop.

He was only one of a string of men: gay, straight, confused, or just-don't-give-a-shit kind of guys who came around for the drugs and stayed for the party. Scott had a favorite game he played with the straight men he befriended in bars and invited home to party. He knew the kind of men I liked, and, once procured, he challenged me to seduce them so he could watch. We placed bets on how long it would take me to get them into my bed, and we joked at how quickly I took them down with the "queer juice" and the unbridled debauchery of our lifestyle. Scott was an unapologetic voyeur and marveled at my skills of seduction. The hard part was getting them to leave that house of unrestricted fantasies once we were done with them. They always came back for more.

I started smoking the PCP along with the meth, and drinking peppermint schnapps by the gallon. I craved sugar, and lived on schnapps, Pepsi, and chocolate cupcakes. I do not remember eating a real meal for months on end.

John returned to prison for another of many minor transgressions. Scott was back and forth between his girlfriend and my house. Most of the people around me were involved in some criminal activity or another. It's part of the territory. One of them was using my computer to produce some pretty sophisticated counterfeit money. It was surprisingly easy to do before the government changed to the new bills we have now. I kept my distance from that business, but admit to being fascinated by its potential. These guys were printing out thousands in small bills and selling them at twenty-five cents to the dollar. They said small bills attract little attention and were easy to pass. They took tens of thousands of dollars to Mexico, where they could easily pass without detection.

Surrounded by junkies, ex-cons, pimps, whores and counterfeiters, was this really my life? How could it have all come to this? From the days of social status, success and dignity, I had come down so far, so quickly.

Scott's girlfriend made a scene in my front yard and drew the police. She had found some poorly hidden photos of Scott and me that confirmed suspicions she had of what might be going on in that house, and she was rightfully upset. I was furious that his drama brought unwanted attention to the house, and told both of them to get out and not return. I had made it a policy to avoid married men and family men. They brought an extra set of troubles with them, and I still had enough of a conscience left to feel bad for their families. At the time, I had few moral boundaries left which had not been violated, and that wasn't one of them. She was a sweet girl, and I was genuinely ashamed I had been a part of hurting and deceiving her. I told myself and others that it was not my fault or problem. But I felt the contrary. And later on, when a trusted friend slept with my partner, I couldn't help but wonder if karma had paid another of her vengeful visits.

It was only a few days later when lady karma paid her epic visit, and I found myself staring down the barrels of a dozen assault rifles and began my journey through the California prison system.

Punishment School

With eyes of shame and sadness,
we walk the edge of madness
within these walls of time and rules
here, robots are awakened
individuality's forsaken,
we are only seven digit numbers
in a punishment school.
The devils spawn? Fear not.
Just souls locked away, forgot
To society, mere specimens of fool

E.M.
inmate # p24400

Chapter Eight
Nightmares

I woke the first morning at Wasco State Prison to the sound of the cell door unlocking. My new cellmate, Al, said brusquely, "Breakfast." I said, "Not hungry," and went back to sleep.

There are several counts a day. At count time, all inmates must stand inside the cell to be counted. After each count I climbed back up and resumed my sleep. I dreamed beautiful dreams. I dreamed of friends, and family, and freedom. I dreamed of everything except my reality. I did not have nightmares, those were for the waking hours.

Each time I was awakened to perform a simple order or task, I did so in half-slumber, eager to return to the safety of my dreams. Other inmates attempted to engage me in conversation or invite me outside the cell, but I politely refused. Even Al seemed to be growing concerned by my withdrawal, and he didn't even know me. My depression was profound, and I felt incapable of responding to the life happening around me. It wasn't a life I wanted to be a part of. Al went to the yard often and I had the cell to myself. I managed to nibble on a sack lunch, use the toilet in private (which was a luxury), and stare at the ceiling for hours on end; thinking, dreaming, wishing, and regretting.

Reception's purpose is to observe and evaluate an inmate to determine an appropriate facility for long-term incarceration. After the third day without showering, going to chow, or leaving the cell, I was ordered to the counselor's office. She explained everything I could expect during my stay at Wasco, asked some standard questions concerning my mental and emotional state, and prescribed anti-depressants.

Before I could scurry back to my dark cave, I was stopped by two Mexican "girls." They introduced themselves as Gina and Polla. Obviously, they were biological males, but they looked, spoke, and behaved like girls. Gina was actually quite pretty. They were very friendly and curious to know more about me. They asked me what my "girl" name was. I told them I didn't have one and I didn't want one. I was invited to join them in the large open area called the "dayroom," where inmates socialized, played cards, traded and bargained their meager possessions, or sat on hard steel benches to watch a communal television.

So began my education into the daily life and drama, rules and regulations, codes of conduct, and methods of survival, as apply to homosexuals in the prison social structure.

Gina and Polla (pronounced Poya) were seasoned convicts. They had a lot of time behind them and much more ahead. Polla was an armed robber and Gina a heroin addict, prostitute, and petty thief. I confess to smiling inwardly at the idea of being robbed by a transgender, but I suppose her victims were not concerned with her gender identity when she had a gun on them. They were gangster girls. Prisons were their home. They spent most of their lives inside and they had learned not only how to survive, but to live more comfortably than your average inmate.

Using their vast experience with the criminal class, coupled with their polished feminine wiles, they exploited machismo egos and lonely hearts, titillated libidos, and alleviated some boredom with their bad-girl antics. They seemed so comfortable in their environment, so in control. I watched them as they went to extraordinary lengths to create and maintain their feminine illusion while commanding respect and endearing themselves to the right men. They instinctively knew which men to discard and which to ingratiate themselves to. They knew how to make the right men feel important, and which ones to put in their place. They procured material goods they might otherwise have had to do without through flirtation and implied subjugation. I remember the girls telling me the importance of hiding our "junk" (our male genitals), so as not to spoil the illusion of feminine authenticity. Gina spotted my obvious bulge and shrieked, "Girl, you got to hide that thing! These men don't want to be with no girl that's got a bigger dick than them! You got to learn how to tuck it away."

I found them wildly amusing. It seemed so long since I had laughed: it felt strange to my face. We became fast friends, and I an eager student. This was my life for now, and I needed to make the best of it. I wanted to know how to do it right and do it well.

They told me to go upstairs and make myself pretty, and they would save me a seat at their table at chow. It was time for me to start living again, even if it was in a prison.

When Al returned from the yard, he was visibly surprised to see me awake, showered, and groomed, writing a letter to my mother, and waiting for chow call.

Al was an intimidating man. I remained cautious and quiet in his presence, letting him initiate and lead our conversation. It's awkward to be to be locked in an 8 x 10 space with a complete stranger, and it sure doesn't take long to figure out if you're going to get along. He also became essential in my education on incarceration, but from a different perspective than the girls. He was my education on prison gang life. Al was a long-time member of the Aryan Brotherhood. I had heard of them and met a few in county jails, but had never been close to any.

Prison is an extraordinarily racist society. The AB is the oldest white supremacist group, and the most feared and powerful of all prison gangs. Once I was educated on their culture I wasn't especially afraid of them, as they did not seem to have a problem with homosexuals as long as they were white.

I didn't understand why the guards seemed to single Al out for special attention. Several times they came to our cell, ordered him to strip and photographed his body. Later he explained he was being examined for gang-affiliated tattoos. The various gangs have identifying tattoos reserved for members only, and woe is the man carrying one who hasn't earned it.

Over the next few days I spent my days with the girls and my nights with Al.

He was amused by my prissy "uptown" ways, and particularly my refusal to use the toilet when he was present. I remember him rolling his eyes at me and saying, "Girl, it's going to get worse before it gets better. You have a lot to learn."

Convicts coined the now widely used moniker "Dawg" as a term of brotherly affection. One of Al's homeboys casually referred to me as Dawg, and provoked an amused Al to say, "Bro, that's no dawg, that's a little princess puppy!"

"Princess" was quickly dropped by everyone except Al (he continued in private to refer to me affectionately as Princess), and I was tagged "Puppy" by all the other inmates.

Just about everyone in prison has a tag: a prison name. Gang members all have them, and in prison everyone is part of some group. Few men stand alone.

I don't know the origin of prison aliases, but I suspect it started with the gangs, and somehow became a way of distinguishing the separation of who we are on the street from who we are in prison, two different names for two different worlds.

Al was a tall man, lean and muscular and in excellent shape for a man in his early fifties. He was a dangerous man with a brutal past, present, and probable future, but he was gentle to me in the privacy of our cell. He barely acknowledged me on the yard, and I came to understand it was nothing personal, it was just his way. He did not allow the other inmates, including his own people, to glimpse one iota of kindness or sensitivity. He believed it didn't pay to care for anyone in prison, and to never let anyone see your heart. Everyone was just passing through and few could be trusted.

He asked me many questions about my life on the street, and he was the first of many, staff and inmates both, to say, "What's a guy like you doing in a place like this?"

He was born into a world of crime and violence and never got out. My stories of material wealth and social privilege were like watching a foreign film with no subtitles to him.

It didn't seem to matter to the people I met in prison where I started out, only where I got to. I felt I had a similar background of poverty, substance abuse, and social and economic underclass to claim legitimate inclusion in their midst, but it only seemed to matter to them that I found my way out, and not with crime, but with success. The facts that I started out like many of them, and at present was in the same predicament, were discounted by the time between, when I achieved and lived the dream that eluded them. They saw me as some miscarriage of social order. The pampered pet mistakenly caged with the lions and hyenas.

In an unexpected and not unpleasant turn, they seemed protective and admiring rather than dismissive and resentful. In me, they inspired compassion and gratitude, and a desire to understand their lives in the revolving doors of prison life. The feeling of making a friend, regardless of where you are, is a cure for loneliness and fear.

I suppose I was not your average inmate. Well-spoken and groomed, with an air of sophistication, self-assurance, dignity and humor that served me well in the free world, I was determined to retain my sense of self and extend the very same to my fellow inmates.

They said I looked and smelled like money.

I had friends and family outside who sent me money for small comforts not easily obtained by most, and I shared it freely with those close to me. I didn't share to gain favor or friendships, but perhaps more out of guilt. It wrenched my heart to see old men scavenging the yard for cigarette butts to break apart and roll a single smoke. It made me feel a little better to roll a few and slip them under a door and be rewarded with a toothless smile or a grateful nod. Seeing decrepit old men slowly hobble through the crowds of tattooed muscle made me especially sad. At least they were left alone and not bullied or abused for their vulnerability. The prison code considers it unmanly to abuse the weak or feeble. The occasional upstart who violates that code is quickly reprimanded by the men in power.

Al appointed himself my guardian. Not my husband, but my protector. He schooled me on the appropriate way for me to behave as a convict and a white person. Though he never threatened or harmed me, there was an understanding that even I must adhere to the rules or suffer strict consequences, probably directly from him.

He said very little about his life outside of prison, except he often mentioned his "red-haired girl," whom I assumed to be a woman he loved.

Within a week of my emerging from my shell of depression, Al triggered my soft spot for hard men, and we became lovers.

I understood he was not gay. There was something essential missing in our coupling that suggested it was a matter of convenience, and subtle desperation, rather than any real emotional attachment. It seems the straight and not completely straight men have often gravitated toward me and taken comfort in my acceptance of a simple attraction that defied traditional boundaries and did not pressure them by making more of it than it was, or laying claim of ownership that insisted on uncomfortable social labels.

I understand simple physical need and gratification. I understand fear of commitment and responsibility. I understand the mistrust of love. I understand a desire to connect and release. And though I have always searched for that special someone who wants to go all the way, I understand that most are just passing through, and it need not be more complicated than a satisfying but temporary embrace of two lonely people, regardless of gender.

He closed his eyes when he made love to me. Perhaps he thought of his red-haired girl. It didn't matter to me. I was just grateful to feel something other than the prison walls around me, something warm and alive, something human, and something that was completely mine for a moment. And just like so many men before him, once I let him inside of me I owned a little piece of him, and he could never take back the power he gave me. His body was all heat and hard muscle: he was handsomely endowed and surprisingly adept. He made love with an urgency that implied guilt. I got the impression he simultaneously could not stop himself but wanted to. I felt powerful after seducing him. I owned a piece of him that lay in the core of his manhood. Sex is the Achilles heel of many a man, and I didn't need to go to prison to know that. I had found and tapped his weak spot and exploited it only to gain some footing in our close quarters, but not outside of it.

He spoke very little about the Aryan Brotherhood. The prison system was determined to eradicate their organization, and had worked for decades to undermine their power. They were sought out and separated from each other as often as possible.

A gang or group in prison is called a "car." To ride in someone's car is to belong to their group. There are requirements and initiations to become a member of a gang like the Aryan Brotherhood, but the secrecy honored among their members prohibited Al from sharing any details with me, and I preferred not to know. Whether one chooses to be or not, one is a member of a group determined by one's skin color, and no initiation is required.

With both Al and the girls schooling me, I learned I belonged to my race. I could not ever allow a man of another race to touch me. I could not eat, drink, smoke, sit, or shower with a man of another race. These rules did not apply to the girls. We were almost considered a race unto ourselves. We were the only group allowed to mix socially, and had our own place on the yard. But when it came to choosing a husband, even we had our own very strict code of conduct determined by race, Any girl who crossed racial lines by getting too close to a man not her color was in grave danger. Ostracism was unquestionable, and beatings or death at the hand of her own people a viable possibility. Racial tension is a constant in prison life, and such behavior can easily spark wars.

The "girls" consist of "he-she's," men who look and live as women but are biologically male; "queens," feminine and flamboyant men; and "gay boys," men who look and behave as men but are openly gay. I fell somewhere in between the queen and the gay boy.

We are all referred to as the "girls" by most of the inmates, and a lot of the officers as well. The butches, studs, and straight men who take us as their mates are not part of our group. Their code insists they are not homosexuals as long as they are the aggressor and dominant partner.

Many men do not engage in overt sexual activity in prison. For others, it is merely a game, and we are trophies to be competed for, won, and paraded as a prized possession. To some, we are slaves to clean their cells and satisfy their needs. We can be bought, sold, traded, or loaned to their friends and debtors; beaten, raped, or held captive in their cells. I witnessed only a few of the more sickening arrangements. The unfortunate souls so enslaved are called "punks." They walk quietly behind their husbands, eyes cast downward, reeking of powerless misery.

But to some, we are treasured and loved as partners, friends, and wives. The men who have done a lot of time, and the lifers who will never be with a woman again, appreciate the feminine illusion of home we bring to their lonely lives, and treat us with a jovial reverence.

There is a constant good-natured banter between the men and the available girls, and only occasionally an ugly battle over one of us. A girl not taken and unprotected, particularly an attractive one, will constantly fight off unwanted advances, and rape is always a possibility. Usually the men do not harm the girls. Again, it is considered unmanly to attack the weak, and we are equal to women in their eyes. Most men do not want to chance a fight with a girl. If a man should lose a fight with a girl he is ruined in the eyes of his peers, and must leave the yard ashamed and disrespected. I have seen some vicious and bloody battles among the girls themselves over a man or some petty slight, but for the most part we supported each other and got along well. There was strength and safety in numbers, and we were a small car.

Gina and Polla insisted I needed to look more feminine to appeal to more men, and set about creating my new look. We removed my facial hair, arched my eyebrows, altered my jumpsuit to fit snugly in all the right places (but not show my junk), and I was instructed to grow my hair and nails and shave my entire body. All the girls grow their nails for fighting. At night I lay on my bunk sharpening them into talons on the rough concrete walls. They proved useful shortly thereafter.

Al seemed amused by my transformation into one of the girls, and relieved that I was emerging from my depression. I suppose it was no fun for him to be in such close quarters with someone so morose. We spent our nights talking about our lives and views, hopes and needs. He cautioned me repeatedly to keep a safe distance from the petty soap-operas of the prison. He was a good teacher.

The anti-depressants I was taking did alleviate the depression, but one of the side effects seemed to be increased aggression. Twice a day, morning and evening, was "pill call." All inmates, prescribed medication for any reason, formed a line at a window in the dayroom, where you recited your inmate number to a nurse. She handed the pills with water, and they had to be swallowed with her watching. Before leaving the window, you had to open your mouth and lift your tongue to prove you had swallowed. Of course, some of the men managed to get around the examination, save the pills, and sell or trade them for tobacco or desirable commissary goods.

My first fight at Wasco happened at pill call.

I can assure you prison is full of some very odd people, and more than a few are just plain crazy. I could fill another book with stories of bizarre and peculiar incidents and people behind prison walls. I'm positive there are just as many or more in the free world, but in prison it's far more difficult to avoid them.

Every morning at pill call, the same man insisted on standing or sitting uncomfortably close to me. He spoke a foreign language I did not recognize, Russian, or something like it, and stared at me relentlessly with crazy eyes. Other people noticed and told me he was a "jaycat" (a prison term describing crazy people), and to just ignore him. After about a week of it, I became irritable towards him when I realized he seemed to enjoy antagonizing me.

One morning I had enough. I looked him in the eye and said, "What the fuck are you staring at, Psycho? Get the hell away from me!"

He muttered some gibberish and threw a cup of water in my face.

It might have been the weeks of pent up anxiety and frustration, possibly exacerbated by the medication I was taking, that surfaced in a flash of white-hot rage.

The TV benches were behind him, and he backed up between two of them. I jumped onto a bench to gain some height advantage, and was looking down when I drove my fist into his face. He went down between the benches. My intention was to jump on his head and knock him senseless before he could get back up, but an officer witnessed me hit him, and immediately set off the alarm and ordered everyone face down on the floor. We were both cuffed and taken to the captain to be disciplined. We were found equally responsible and each lost thirty days of good time credit.

After a fight, inmates cannot be returned to the same building or yard. You will, from that time forward, be designated as known enemies, and it will be in your file.

I was returned to my building, and he was placed elsewhere.

Though my reprimand read "mutual combat," I felt wronged. I felt it was self-defense given the water in the face. I lost my appeal.

What I didn't know was that any reprimands or loss of credit resulted in additional points on a point scale, and I had just jumped to a higher level of security. But it sure felt good to hit someone.

I got a little more respect after punching him. Now, the other inmates knew I was willing to fight. You don't want a reputation as a troublemaker, but you do want other inmates to know you will defend yourself.

The mutual combat with the jaycat was minor by prison standards, and I settled back into the monotonous routine of life in our building.

Reception is constantly changing. People are shipped off to their final destinations and somebody new takes their bed the same day. You don't have a clue when or where you will be assigned, and are usually informed of your move less than twenty-four hours in advance.

The days just roll in to each other. The only thing that changes are the faces. There are no clocks and calendars, no weekends or special events. The only breaks in the monotony are the fights and petty wars that break out among the inmates.

Reception is a waiting game, the purgatory between county jail and full scale prison life.

There are no phones available for reception inmates, and an exchange of letters from the outside world could easily take a month to find its way to you.

I had spoken to my mother only a few times since my arrest. The collect calls from an institution are so costly that my conscience wouldn't allow me to call often. The last time we spoke was after my sentencing. When I told her of my three-year sentence, she cried out in distress. I reassured her that three years was a light sentence compared to what I could have received, and I would only do a little more than half of that with good time credits. Regardless of what I might be feeling, I kept our conversations positive and lighthearted to minimize her worry. I sent letters regularly to assure her I was well and safe. Old age and illness had begun to attack her, and I hated the feeling that I was making things worse. It was foreign to my mother to have one of her children in the position I was in. We all went through our typical teenage delinquencies, but not as adults. It was ironic that the one who had climbed the highest had fallen the lowest.

I didn't hear from my siblings during my incarceration, but neither did I contact them. I had an unreasonable notion that they might be enjoying my fall from my lofty perch. I was ashamed to recall my arrogance at their simple country ways throughout my years of success. Ma always assured me I was asked about and loved, but I didn't believe it. When I indulged myself in infrequent self-pity, I imagined that my siblings didn't think of me at all.

Al was merely a circumstantial lover rather than a chosen mate. When I reached my final destination I planned to choose, not be chosen. Part of Gina and Polla's education was to teach me which men were suitable husbands and which ones to stay away from. Within my race the playing field narrowed. The short-termers might be fun to play with, but they cannot compete with men whose power is established with a lot of time and earned respect. They don't have the kind of connections one needs to have a comfortable existence, and are quickly dismissed as inconsequential. The girls warned me to stay away from the men who sold and used drugs. They are a source of much of the violence and most all the gang activity. A man addicted to drugs in prison can almost never afford his habit. Just as on the streets, he must eventually do things he would rather not to support his habit or pay his debts.

Several uneventful weeks passed without incident. Every day I wondered if this was the last at Wasco and I would be moved to a new prison full of strangers.

I received a letter from a friend informing me my former friend and lover, Scott, and some of his drug buddies, had stolen or sold everything I had left at the house I was renting when I was busted and had left the place in shambles. I shouldn't have been surprised. Scott was an opportunist and an addict. But I did resent him for his betrayal. I was doing time for the things we did together, and he pushed drugs in my face the moment I left rehab. I should have known better but I thought he cared for me. I thought we were at least good friends. I became angry and combative as I realized how easily my world went on without me and I spent hours on end imagining my revenge on those that damaged and deserted me.

Thus far, my personality seemed to serve me as well on the inside as it did in the free world, and I established a circle of friends. All had done a lot of time and recognized the various stages of emotion I was experiencing as I attempted to adapt to institutionalization. Al encouraged me to let go of the world outside while I was in, and often reminded me there was nothing I could do about what's going on outside and I needed to let it go or it would make doing time a lot harder. He knew how to do time and he knew I was making myself crazy over things I had no control over.

A new guy arrived on our block. I took an instant disliking to him. He was a self-described gay boy and fancied himself tough and important. He was automatically included in the circle of girls but obviously had no education on the rules we lived by. He had a maverick attitude that offended and challenged a way of life established long before all of us and wasn't likely to change on his say so. He was headed for trouble and the girls were concerned he would bring that trouble to all of us.

There are no real shot callers in reception. No one stays long enough to create a hierarchy of power. Still, with all groups there are leaders and followers, and I have always been cursed with the personality of a leader. The staff, along with the men, expect the experienced inmates to educate new members of your group.

Even though I disliked the new gay boy, I was friendly when I counseled him. Unfortunately, he was belligerent and resentful of my interference and saw me as an obstacle between himself and his determination to run his own program. As a white gay boy, he assumed a position of superiority he hadn't earned and an attitude of condescension toward the non-white he-she's and queens that created conflict within our group and elicited too much negative attention from the men and staff. He was manly in appearance, arrogant with self-importance and without subtlety in his pursuit of a husband. None of these characteristics served him well among the straight men. He didn't know, or wasn't willing to play the game.

We are expected to appear subservient and show respect to masculine authority. We are allowed flirtation and the subtleties of sexual provocation without violating a man's image among his peers. Our own image of femininity is carefully constructed. The more feminine we appear and behave, the less challenging it is to the masculine ego and the easier it is for the men to convince themselves and each other they are not engaging in real homosexuality.

I found it quite easy to allow my feminine side her freedom. I walked the edge of androgyny many times in my life in fashion and demeanor and was comfortable with role playing. The beauty salon is a stage and I was an accomplished actor with years of experience. I resented this new punk's attitude that somehow he was above our rules and I resented his intrusion into what had become a relatively peaceful existence. My second conversation with him did not go well.

I tried to let him know that he was not making himself look good to the girls or the men, and there would be repercussions if he continued alienating and offending his fellow inmates. I thought myself non-confrontational and diplomatic. I really didn't care what happened to him, but had taken on the responsibility of informing him of his position on the block. He interpreted it as a direct threat from me and decided I was his enemy. He decided to assert his authority by attacking. He told Polla he would come to my cell for the next unlock (the cells are not left open for inmates to come and go at will, but are unlocked each hour on the hour) and attempt to kill me by throwing me off the tier to the steel and concrete below. She, in turn, told me of his plan and I went to my cell to wait for him. I watched him from the window of my cell as he headed in my direction.

He was ten years younger and much larger than I and I had no idea if he was a skilled fighter. I do know growing up with five brothers provided me with some skills at self-defense, and backing down is not an option, if you want any respect from your fellow inmates.

I looked for something to use as a weapon. I had nothing heavy or sharp except a pencil. I wrapped a washcloth around the base of the pencil and left two inches of the sharpened point to stab with. Not a deadly weapon, but capable of doing some damage driven to the right spot. I opened the cell door and stood inside as he approached. Adrenaline coursed through my veins.

He stood at my cell door but did not enter the cell. He knew if he entered my cell he would be held completely at fault as the aggressor. Inmates are not allowed in any cell they are not assigned to.

He saw my crude weapon and invited me to step outside on to the tier. I graciously declined the invitation but told him he was welcome to come inside if he wanted to talk. It's hard to believe it now, but I had every intention of driving that pencil into his throat. In a fight or flight situation, and the option for flight is unavailable, winning is the only thought in my mind, and this punk was not going to cripple or kill me without a fight.

He refused to enter, but stood outside insulting and threatening me. The final straw came when he promised he would get me on the yard when I didn't see it coming. He had his chance to come at me like a man, face to face, and he was threatening to come at my back like a cowardly bitch. I would not live having to watch my back and decided to finish it there and then. He was a punk, a bitch, and a coward for threatening my back, and I willed myself to go to that white noise place with rage. I attacked.

I threw down my weapon and drove my sharpened nails in to his eyes and raked downward. He raised his hands to his eyes defensively and I kicked him in the knee. He staggered back and crumpled against the tier railing.

I was not about to let him get up and fight back. I mounted his chest and pummeled his head with my fists. Blood ran in his eyes and he lashed out at me blindly and ineffectively. The noise in the building came through my rage. The officers had seen us fighting and set off the alarms. The other men yelled and cheered and a voice over the loudspeaker ordered everybody down. I heard the sound of keys jangling and footsteps pounding up the metal stairs, but did not stop raining blows on him. I bit my own tongue and the taste of my own blood spurred my fury.

As the officers bore down on me, they yelled for me to get off of him. I dismounted only when threatened with pepper spray.

Once released, he attempted a halfhearted lunge at me from the floor, so I kicked him in the eye. We were both cuffed within seconds. As I was being cuffed I looked him in his bloodied eyes and said, "The next time I see you, I will rip your fucking throat out, bitch." And I meant it.

I was just trying to do my time and did not look for trouble, but I was not about to let some punk make a name for himself with my blood.

We were led away in cuffs and put in cages several yards apart outside the captains' office. He ran his mouth a bit from the safety of his cage until an officer told him to shut up or he would beat his ass again. I just smiled at him. He lost this one and would lose what little respect he might have had in this prison. But I was now getting a reputation as a fighter.

I lost three more months of credit and gained more points for what went on my record as an assault. I thought this genuinely unfair and appealed the decision. I felt it was at least a mutual combat, if not a self-defense.

When interviewed by the captain, I explained the new guy provoked the fight and threatened me. His response was, "You should have told an officer you were being threatened and let us handle it."

I laughed in his face and said, "Ha! We both know telling an officer and being branded a snitch is not an option in here. You don't make the rules in here and you know it."

That pissed him off. My appeal was denied. Damned if I wasn't adding on more time than I even had behind me yet.

The officers of my building opted once again to have me back, and the new guy was moved to another yard.

When I returned to my block, I was somewhat embarrassed and secretly pleased when the officers good-naturedly played the theme from "Rocky" over the loudspeaker and all the inmates clapped and cheered my win. One of the officers shouted over the speaker, "That ain't no puppy, that boy throws down like a pit bull!"

I had earned my respect at Wasco State Prison, but I paid a heavy price when my points rose to a level that ensured I would be transferred to a place more dangerous than I would have originally done my time.

It was March of 1999. From County jail to Wasco, four months had passed and I had lost four months of good time credit. The outside world was slipping away and I was falling in to the rhythm of prison life.

My fellow inmates often talked of which prisons they hoped, and hoped not, to be sent. Some were in more desirable locations for potential visitors, some were known for better food or treatment of inmates and most important, some were known for less violence and danger. No one told me I was lucky when I received the news I was being shipped to Soledad State Prison. The general consensus was, "It's not too bad."

Soledad is a Spanish word meaning solitude or loneliness, an appropriately ominous name for the third oldest prison in the state that reportedly held Charles Manson for fourteen years. Only San Quentin and Folsom have been operating longer. I was actually going to the same prison Manson once lived? I was apprehensive about adapting to a new environment but also eager to reach the final leg of my journey and get it behind me too.

I said my goodbyes to the friends I made and collected all the names and addresses of the people I would never write or see again. Saying goodbye is a constant part of prison life. Gina and Polla had been good friends to me and our goodbyes were teary and dramatic as befitting three drama queens. All these years later I still think of them and smile at their antics and with gratitude for the valuable survival lessons they taught me that made that time in my life bearable and endurable. I wonder if they are still doing time or if they found a way out.

Only Al was left to bid farewell to, and that was left to the privacy of our cell.

Of the thousands of men that passed through Wasco while I was there, only Gina, Polla, Al, and the men I fought, remain in my memory. The rest are just a kaleidoscope of faces and orange jumpsuits.

Al and I had always been separate outside of our cell. We did not eat, shower, socialize, or walk the yard together.

He was cold to me our last night together. I was a little hurt, but understood he was not comfortable with emotion and I was just another of thousands of goodbyes in his life. I asked him for his contact information so I could write when I was free and he refused to give it to me. He said he didn't want to be one of those guys standing at the window waiting for mail that never came, and it was best we forget each other quickly. He never told me why he was there this time, or for how long, and I never asked. I wonder if he would be surprised that I am remembering and writing about him eleven years later.

The next morning I caught the chain one last time. He didn't get up from his bunk or even look at me as I left.

Nightmares

Do not weep for me in sorrow,
Things are not as they may seem.
Though it appears I live a nightmare,
nightmares are just a dream.

For in the early hours of morning,
when the sky turns black to blue,
I may gaze out the window of a prison
but I am just as free as you.

For freedom is a state of mind.
My mind remains untethered.
This prison is not the worst of storms,
this weary man has weathered.

E.M.

Chapter Nine
A Handout

Soledad, viewed from yet another long and uncomfortable bus ride, did not appear as desolate and barren as Wasco. The entrance was landscaped with trees and flowers, and denim-clad inmates tended to them. Mountains created a purple back drop for the infamous old prison. It lifted my spirits for a moment to see some color and life. The buildings were very old and everything was surrounded with a double row of electrified chain link fencing and topped with the lethal glint of silver razor wire. Some of California's most notorious criminals had lived within those walls.

Soledad is in Monterey County, California. Sometimes you can smell and feel the nearby Pacific Ocean in the air, but you can't see it. It would have been nice if you could see it, even from a distance. But there are no oceans in hell. Seagulls reel and scream over the yard, looking for scraps left behind by the inmates, and hungry stray cats roam the perimeters hoping for – and receiving – kindnesses from soft-hearted inmates. Many of the inmates adopted these strays as their own, though it was discouraged by staff as the cats were considered pests. I was told later that kittens were often secreted away in

cells but would be taken away if discovered. I was horrified when told a particular guard had been known to
flush the kittens down the toilet to punish an inmate for
disobeying the rules.

That was eleven years ago. When I got off that bus at
Soledad I didn't know what to expect. I certainly did not
expect to meet someone who would change the course
of my life yet again, and permanently. I did not expect
everything I believed it took to be happy would change,
or that I would discover some of the best parts of me in
the worst imaginable circumstances. And I did not know
that I would finally become a man of substance and en-
durance, possibly worthy of the merit I looked for in others
but never saw in myself.

In my most raw and primal self, I am a survivor. I am the
odd boy in the country school, the bewildered teen on
the streets, the determined young man far removed from
the roots of my birth competing in a harsh world to succeed. From the embattled drug addict, to the convict,
to a new life in the free world, I became finally aware
of who I really was and what I am made of. I found that
when the entire world falls away and you are left with
only you, it can be frightening, enlightening, and even
strangely exhilarating.

One more time my determination to survive and con-
quer the world around me returned when I stepped off
that bus. I was going to hold my head high, I was going
to make them laugh, I was going to turn them on, I was
going to make them think and feel, and I was going to
make them like me. I decided survival was not enough,
if this was where I was supposed to be then I would do
more than survive, I would live and succeed.

I didn't care if I was judged in prison. Why should I care
anymore? Sure, I felt like I was better than some, because
I was. And I may have been worse than a few others, but
those are the kind of thoughts best kept to oneself when

attempting to win the hearts and favor of several thousand convicts. In prison, you had to at least pretend to care what others thought of you.

The drugs had left my veins and I was back to me. I needed to pull out all the weapons in this place. I needed to be smart and strong and perhaps a little devious and manipulative, if I was going to get out of there in one piece. After all, as Gina and Polla once said to me, "A girl's gotta do what a girl's gotta do to survive."

A new inmate, commonly called a "fish," is not immediately placed in the general population. Upon arrival one must first endure the process of "classification." For two solid weeks I lived in a cell alone. Fed three times a day and allowed to shower for five minutes every three days, my only human contact was provided by the inmates whose job it was to serve my meals, and the nurse that came by once a day to dispense my medication.

There were no books or television and no one to talk to. The days were agonizingly long. The workers engaged me in brief conversation through the door, but were admonished harshly by staff if they lingered. Homosexuals seem to inspire a great deal of curiosity, so there were men at my door as often as they could get away with it. I was unaware that these workers had already spread the news to the general population that a new white "girl" had arrived. Information spreads like wildfire in a prison, and there are few secrets among the inmates.

Though racial division is clearly defined in all California prisons, it does not prohibit the men from amusing themselves at the expense of homosexuals, regardless of race. A minor incident, involving myself and two Mexican workers, inspired some controversy I would later answer for when I joined the general population.

While in classification, an inmate may not have access to any personal possessions, nor may he be allowed to obtain commissary goods. I had no access to tobacco unless assisted by someone on the other side of the cell door. Two young Mexican men asked me if there was anything I needed. I thought they were simply being compassionate. My immediate response was to ask for cigarettes. There were plenty of other things I would have liked to have, but it had to be something they could slip under the quarter-inch space at the bottom of the door.

Tobacco has since become contraband in California prisons, but at that time it was still allowed and commonly used as currency among the inmates. Smoking was one of the few pleasures I had left. When the two Mexican men told me they would give me cigarettes if I showed them my ass, I was a bit surprised but more amused. If they waited until I had shower day, they could see it for free. The showers offer no privacy from passersby. Guys are naked so often, it didn't seem like a big deal, and those cigarettes were like heroin to a junkie. What I didn't know was I would have to answer to the white men for my racial indiscretion when I hit the yard.

Those were two very long weeks. The days melted into each other, and I often wondered how men kept their sanity during long periods of punishment in administrative segregation, also known as "The Hole."

Sensory deprivation is certainly more torture than punishment. The urge to beat on the door and scream like a mental patient washed over me in waves. I paced the tiny cell, counted until I lost track of the numbers, sang every song I could think of, and exercised myself to exhaustion to stave off the boredom, restlessness and loneliness. I would have given anything to have a stack of books or a pad of paper and pen. Reading and writing would have killed all those hours alone with my thoughts and quieted my mind.

I was finally allowed a bible. I read the bible many times while incarcerated, when it was the only reading material allowed, and I read it front to back when I was a teen hitchhiking around the country. For years I carried a bible stolen from one of the many motels I'd spent the night in making money to survive. With all the time I spent reading that book, I never really understood it or derived any of the real solace others claim it offers. Perhaps it was because I only turned to it in desperation rather than desire. Perhaps it was because I lived my life being told, and believing, that God did not love me and I was damned anyway, so what would be the point in believing.

There can be a spiritual experience in extreme solitude. At least there was for me. The deprivation of any and all distractions from the self, and the removal of all distractions and interaction with others, drove me deep into my own psyche. It forced to me think all my own thoughts and feel my own feelings without interference or influence. I had never really believed there is a God, and, if there was, then surely he had abandoned the human race to its own ugly demise. In my solitude I came to believe there is a God, but He is not to be found in a book or a church. He is not Christian, Muslim, or Buddhist. He is only to be found in the deepest reaches of my conscience and self-awareness, my innately human ability to recognize right from wrong, and to practice that knowledge on a daily basis and to acknowledge when I fall short, regardless of the circumstances. If I am, in fact, created in the image of God, then I find it reasonable to believe God exists within the fabric of my own existence and not outside of it. I do not believe there are any pure hearts and minds outside the womb, but I believe we can achieve a pure conscience in day-to-day life, and that may be the closest thing to Godliness I've been able to comprehend. I am not troubled by the question of God's existence, but I am sometimes troubled by the questions of my own. What is my purpose in life? Why has my life been so difficult? Why do we exist only to die? The question of how I exist is irrelevant to me. It is why I exist that haunts me, and I suspect it is a question without a satisfactory answer.

After two weeks, I was assigned to G Block and released into general population. It was finally time to settle in for the rest of the ride. My next move would be to the free world, and that was nearly a year and a half away.

My orange jumpsuit days were over, and I was issued my prison blues. My meager possessions were returned to me and I was assigned to a cell. On my way to the cell I felt all the men watching me. Only a few said hello.

In my cell lived a pale, white-haired old man named "Red." I assumed correctly that his tag was given years before, when his white hair was still red. It turned out Red was only fifty-eight. He had been down twenty-eight years for a double murder conviction. Almost three decades of prison life and an addiction to heroin had aged him beyond his years. He could easily have been mistaken for a man in his seventies.

Once we grew comfortable enough with one another, I asked him why he killed those two men, and I have often repeated his simple response since. He peered at me from under his bushy white eyebrows and said, "Well, Pup, some people just need killin'."

I supposed he was right.

He was long past dreaming of freedom, and had let go of the outside world. He didn't want to be free anymore. Prison was the only life he knew. He had no place to go and no one to go to. He had been at Soledad a long time before I met him, and had a coveted clerical position with the staff. I found out later he used that position to manipulate my assignment to his cell. He was looking for a cell-wife, but I made it clear to him right away that was not going to be me. I was indeed husband shopping, but he was not even in the running. There were over seven thousand men in Soledad and twenty-five hundred on my yard. Some were the best looking men I had ever seen, and I was not about to settle for a broken-down old heroin addict. As one inmate so distastefully put it, "I was a fag on Dick Island and I could pick them like fruit off a tree."

Red was a good old guy, and nice to me, but I found him and his lifestyle stressful and depressing. Heroin was everywhere. I was surprised how easy it was to get drugs. Needles were much harder to get than the drugs, and I was horrified to personally observe dozens of men sharing one.

Red may have been respectful to me, but many of his heroin friends coming in and out of our cell were not. I spent far too much time fending off unwanted advances, and on one occasion woke to the crushing weight of a very big, very stoned, and very determined man on top of me. I kicked, flailed, and cussed him off the top bunk. He was angry at my refusal to submit to his demands, and I made my first enemy at Soledad.

I complained to Red that his friends were disrespecting my personal space and I would be looking for a new cell to move to. He came to understand I was not going to partake of drugs or sex with him, and didn't really care what I thought or felt beyond the basic code of conduct every inmate can expect in his own cell.

On my first day on the yard I was approached by a menacing group of young, white skinheads. They called themselves the NLR (Nazi Low Riders), a relatively new white supremacist gang in prison society; they were intent on asserting themselves on new inmates and establishing an image of power and threat. The Aryan Brotherhood looked down on the NLR and considered them upstart punks, but they were allowed to flourish as they supported the white cause. I, on the other hand, was successfully intimidated by our first encounter.

The leader of their group asked me if I was "down for my race?"

I responded honestly with, "I have no idea what you mean?"

He said, "Are you down for your race, are you with the whites?"

"Well I suppose I am, isn't that the way it works around here? I don't consider myself a racist but I understand the rules"

"We heard you showed some Mexicans your ass in classification, and that can get you killed. We don't care if you're a homo, but you belong to your race. When you choose a man he better be white, or you will answer to us for disrespecting your own people."

I heard his threat and chose my words carefully.

"I didn't think it was a big deal at the time, and no white men came around to ask me if I needed something. Perhaps you guys should make sure your girls are taken care of before you demand their loyalty. I have every intention of choosing a white husband that will take care of my needs as quickly as possible. Is that satisfactory to you?"

They were obviously amused by my direct response and choice of words. Everyone visibly relaxed, including me. They asked me a few more questions about myself and made the usual sexual innuendos before apparently deciding I could live a while longer, and I went on my way.

The yard was like nothing I had ever experienced before. Unlike county jail, and even far more so than Wasco, this prison had a strict division of races and a code of conduct I was only partially prepared for by Gina, Polla, and Al.

My very first day on the yard, I sat on a patch of grass in the sun, and was immediately told I was sitting on grass that belonged to the Northern Mexicans. Apparently it was a major faux pas to step on another race's grass. I thought it thoroughly absurd, but apologized and asked to be directed to my appropriate place on the yard. He asked if I was gay, and when I assured him I was he pointed me to the girls section of the yard. It looked exactly like all the others except, once again, it was the only place the races mixed. Girls and gay boys of every color sat together and talked, snacked, primped and flirted with the men. Some were familiar from my block. There were dozens of girls, and I took my place among them and began to learn the ways of Soledad.

We didn't have to wear orange jumpsuits at Soledad. We were issued our prison blues – denim pants and chambray button-down shirts – or you could wear gray or white sweatpants and t-shirts if you could afford to buy your own or someone gave them to you. The girls were very creative in redesigning their allowed clothing to maximize their feminine allure. There were hot pants and crop tops, knee socks and Capri pants. Some of the girls fashioned lip gloss and eye shadows with baby oil and Kool Aid. They bleached their hair in the sun with grapefruit juice from breakfast, and lined their eyes with lead pencil. They fashioned jewelry out of foil and string and stones that would easily sell in any gift shop on the streets. I was very impressed with their ingenuity. There's nothing like a group of queens to make the best of a bad situation

I was always told I had great legs, so I copied some of the other girls and cut off a pair of sweats as short as possible to show them off. I have a large green serpent tattooed on my right hip and thigh which was revealed in the short shorts. I was promptly tagged "The Snake Lady" by the superstitious blacks, and asked many times if it was a voodoo symbol. I gathered the snake is significant in voodoo, though I'd never known before.

Hundreds of men roamed the yard. They were in groups separated by race. They were every shape, size, color, and age. They played football and baseball, basketball and tennis. They worked out, ran, and walked the circular track that enclosed the perimeter of the yard. They made deals of drugs and contraband and discussed the politics of prison. The atmosphere was heavy with testosterone and the potential for violence.

Even though everyone knew the racial lines, it didn't stop the men of other races from sexually harassing us. Most of the time it didn't go beyond good-natured ribbing, but some of these men were extremely dangerous and not to be toyed with. Men can be so vulgar and immature without women around to encourage them into a semblance of civility.

All my life I wanted to be an object of desire, I think most people do, and at first I enjoyed all the attention, but it didn't take long for it to become tiresome. My grand epiphany was in realizing that to be an object of desire is to be an object. To be objectified is to be dehumanized. I found it ironic the men complained of the system dehumanizing them, and repeated the same behavior toward each other. I realized I was way out of my league with some of these men, and that the simple act of taking a shower could be dangerous without a husband to protect you.

The faces and time blur in my memory now as my old self fell away and I became a person who even today feels so foreign to me, but who I know was always there and, to some degree, always will be. Perhaps the boy from the streets was never really gone and had resurfaced when I needed him again to remind me of the survival techniques that had helped me twenty-five years before. There's no place for a person like me to hide or lay low. I'm just too noticeable and I always was.

Some of the men were tattooing and piercing each other on the yard. There was a horrifying new trend among the younger men for disfiguring their penises. Plastic dominoes or stones from the yard were filed down to small spheres and inserted into cuts made with a razor blade on the shaft of the penis. They were intended as built-in French ticklers and the men promised the girls enhanced pleasures with the increased girth and deformity of their manhood. I watched the procedure only once out of sheer curiosity, and was amazed at the spectacle of a dozen young men standing in a ring watching this bizarre rite of passage and cheering the recipient on. It felt very tribal. I thought it disgustingly unsanitary and juvenile. With disease rampant in the prisons and medical care minimal, these were dangerously foolish games. I never allowed anyone to touch me in prison for a tattoo or piercing. I had plenty already.

I was only there a few weeks when I spotted a handsome muscle-man on the yard wearing a pair of white denim cut offs and asked one of the girls who he was. She said they called him Boone. She thought he was a lifer. He was quiet and played sports all the time and she did not think he had a cell-wife, or know if he was interested in one.

There were a lot of men on that yard, and I was getting a lot of attention, except from Boone. He seemed to not notice me at all. I wanted a pair of those white denim shorts and I wanted Boone's attention, but I didn't have the nerve to approach him yet, so I mentioned to one of the other men I would like to have a pair of those white shorts and wondered aloud how I might get them.

The very night I admired the muscle man in the white denim shorts, he delivered a pair to my cell. They were kitchen workers' pants. He worked in the kitchen. I got only a glimpse of him through the door and was barely able to thank him before he was gone. I planned on keeping an eye out for him on the yard.

Before I left classification, I was counseled by my new captain. I vividly recall our conversation. She told me what I could expect when I hit the yard. She said guys like me can cause a lot of trouble among the men, and that men will kill each other over a homosexual. Possession, jealousy, disrespecting someone else's property, are all catalysts for violence, and a gay guy can fuel some raging fires and go down in flames himself for playing games with convicts. We have value and power within our realm of usefulness, but we are still disposable.

The captain advised me to find a husband quickly, move into his cell and behave myself, or she would put me in the hole for the duration of my sentence, if I was the cause of trouble among the men. I was flattered she thought I had that kind of influence, until I hit the yard and understood what she meant.

I had plenty of men vying for my attention and offering gifts, drugs, and protection. Whites were a minority in that prison, especially among the girls, and only a man of a certain stature could really compete for our attention. He had to be a man the other men respected or feared, not only to walk the yard confidently with a male lover, but to defend and protect him at any cost.

From the moment I spotted him on the yard, I was interested in only one man, the muscle man who gave me the white shorts. The man they called Boone. He seemed different from the other men.

I watched him stride confidently across the yard, dressed in white shorts, shoes, and a ball cap, his perfect physique tanned deep golden brown, tattooed torso rippling with muscles and shiny with sweat, images of the iconic gay porn star assaulted my senses. I was smitten. It would be absurd to deny it was anything more than pure lust at first sight. But it was more than that too. It was in the way he carried himself. He had an air of detachment that fascinated me, and the first time I had the courage to get close enough to initiate conversation, I swear he blushed.

I was captivated.

He was soft-spoken, well-mannered and slightly awkward in response to my overt flirtation. He immediately seemed the most unattainable man on the yard, and I immediately set out to win him. My personality has always gravitated toward the most challenging men, and I have paid heavy dues for my victories. Boone was no exception. I was to pay some very heavy dues for winning his affections.

I got butterflies in my stomach just being near him. My eyes searched the yard for him each time I went out. He was almost always to be found engaged in some type of athletics. He played quarterback for the football team, captain of the baseball team, plus tennis, basketball, and handball, when he wasn't working out.

I rarely saw him inside the building. He worked in the kitchen, played on the yard, and did leather crafts in his cell at night to make some money. He had a small circle of friends who were almost all lifers.

Most of the long-term inmates had jobs in the prison, usually the longer the time, the better the job. The top jobs paid up to twenty cents an hour. Many had hobbies and crafts they sold to staff, other inmates, or in the prison gift shop located in the visiting area. I have seen amazing talent and creativity behind those walls, and thought it a shame it was not shared with the world. Boone created and sold beautifully intricate, hand-tooled leather goods that allowed him to have a few extra comforts without asking anyone from the outside. Only his mother had not abandoned him, and he refused to ask her for money.

Not long after we met, an incident in the showers significantly enhanced my devotion, and my commitment to have him as my cell-husband.

The building is three tiers. Each tier has a shower room. The ground floor shower is for blacks, the second Mexican, and the top floor for the whites. The girls showered together or with their husbands for obvious reasons, but a girl can only shower with people her own race. Mornings, and after the yard closes in the evening, the showers are crowded, and unsafe for an unprotected girl. Mid-afternoons are quiet in the buildings and in the showers.

This particular day, I seized an opportunity to shower alone, a rare luxury. The showers are a large, open, tiled room with six to eight shower heads. It was not unusual for twenty men at a time to crowd in together sharing those shower heads. One would rinse while the other lathered. I found it to be uncomfortably homoerotic and palpably dangerous for someone like myself, and avoided it at all costs.

No sooner was I naked, wet, and soaped up, than three Mexicans walked in. They were Southern Mexicans. They had shaved heads. The Northern Mexicans wore fade haircuts. The Southern Mexicans tended to side with the whites in conflicts, and the Northerners with the blacks, so they were not my enemies. Regardless, they were not supposed to be in the white showers. The white showers were the safest place for illegal activity because most of the guards were too lazy to walk up the two flights to reach the top tier.

They were there to shoot heroin, and my presence did not deter them. I have never been able to stand watching someone shoot up. It turns my stomach. But they stood in front of the single exit to watch for guards, so if I attempted to leave I would have to go through them.

I continued to shower while they shot up and silently prayed for them to finish and leave.

Once the drug hit their veins they turned their attention to me. I was never terribly shy about nudity, and prison will cure you of it quick, but I still felt more vulnerable for my nakedness.

The guys were laughing and whispering to each other before moving closer to the showers and boldly examined me with heavy lidded eyes. Next were the lewd comments suggesting the various ways I might entertain them all. I kept a light banter going to let them think I believed they were only joking, but I knew they were not. I had seen that look in a man's eyes too many times before. I managed to fend off many men in my life and many more during incarcerations, but I didn't have much of a chance if these guys attacked.

One of them gleefully and graphically described what the three of them would do to me and I could see an obvious erection becoming visible in his sweat pants as he verbalized his threat. I was deadly serious when I told them, "You can try, but no one is fucking me without an invitation, and I promise you I will go down fighting."

The glee disappeared from their eyes when they realized I considered them a threat, and I'm afraid they took my aggressive response as a direct challenge. I should have just told them I had herpes or syphilis but I didn't think of it in time.

Suddenly, Boone appeared at the door. I was never so glad to see someone in my life. He told me later he saw me go to the showers alone, saw them follow, then came to investigate.

The three guys greeted him coolly, but with sheepish guilt on their faces. They mumbled something about being in the white showers just to get high. They did not appear to want a confrontation with Boone.

Boone looked at me and asked, "You okay?"

I told him I was fine and he offered to wait while I finished and he would walk me back to my cell. I felt suddenly shy and a little foolish for being afraid, but he made me feel better when he said, "You shouldn't be any place all alone, Puppy."

I hadn't been at Soledad long and had only skimmed the surface of what it was like there. It took a little while to see what was really going on. There is a way of life that is established which has evolved over a century that is only gradually revealed to the inexperienced. I was wrong when I thought earlier there are no secrets in prison. There are a million secrets, and most you don't want to know.

The inmates essentially run the prisons, but do so in unison with the staff. There are the written rules and the implied rules. A single inmate or a single guard can upset the precarious balance and create havoc.

The racial lines run deep in Soledad. Blacks separate themselves in three groups, Crips, Bloods, and Muslims. Mexicans are also three groups. Border brothers are non-citizen Mexicans who will be deported after finishing their sentences. California Mexicans separate by north and south: Bakersfield is their border. They are mortal enemies, and create the lion's share of discord and violence with their senseless war. They don't even know why they hate each other. It's just the way it's always been.

Native Americans are a separate group, whites are all one group with different factions among them, and all other races are categorized as "other" and may be found mixed in with various non-white groups. Christians formed a group of their own, as did the homosexuals. As with Wasco, one did not ever cell with another race. Showers, tables in the chow hall, areas of the yard, and the telephones are separated by race. Races only mixed with job assignments and the sporting teams, and that was because the prison staff was instructed to create a balance of color to avoid accusations of preferential treatment.

When job assignment became aware of my haircutting skills, I was assigned as the white barber. I was not allowed to touch or be touched by another race and I was assigned a guard to watch over me while working. I was paid nineteen cents per hour, and the men were expected to tip me with commissary goods.

It was surreal to live in such close proximity with such severe restrictions based on skin color, but after a while it becomes a normal way of life.

I was annoyed that black and Mexican men amused themselves and threatened the peace between the races by crossing the lines of appropriate behavior with me. Lewd comments were just a part of daily life for a homosexual, but many went further, exposing themselves or brushing against me, and even attempting to coerce me into sexual situations. I rarely complained or even mentioned it, except to the other girls, as I did not want to be the guy the captain warned me about and cause fights among the men.

When I was finally able to use a phone for the first time, the only person I really wanted to talk to was my mother. I hated calling collect, Ma always worried about money, but I had no choice. All calls from prison are collect and expensive. The telephone companies that contract with the state for inmate phones exploit their families by charging three times more than a free person's call. It's shameful to capitalize on people already economically depressed, and many inmates' families simply could not afford it.

I wanted to hear my mother's voice, and I wanted her to hear mine and know that I was okay. The first time I called, she cried at the sound of my voice. I reassured her I was fine and she was not to worry. She said to me, "When you call, I wonder if it will be the last time I hear your voice. When I don't hear from you, I think someone might have killed you or something awful has happened."

I put on all the bravado I could muster, and with confidence and humor, I said, "Oh silly woman. It's just a bunch of overgrown boys here. I've been handling men since I was fourteen years old. If they really wanted to scare me, they should have put me in a women's prison.

I hear those bitches are evil! I'm going to be just fine, and you don't need to worry."

It always made her feel better when I joked about my situation, and it made me feel better too. It is my way to joke about bad things, to find irony and humor in life's difficulties is part of survival.

All of it seemed quite absurd to me anyway. It was like I had been dropped in an alternate universe of bizarre primitive customs among the socially disordered. I marveled that the most anti-social of society imposed and observed strict social order among themselves and each other. It is a paradoxical culture, the most grievous of rule-breakers establishing an impenetrable code of conduct without question or compromise. But I suppose even in Hell there must be rules: no society can function in chaos.

I wrote many letters to those I loved, and devoured their responses, however brief, and read them over and over. Ma was having more health problems. It seemed just when she should have been having an easier, softer life, her body began to betray her. And I was adding to her worries and didn't feel too good about it.

I hadn't spoken to my father in many years. I wondered what he thought of my predicament. Eventually I would write my father for the last time in either of our lives, and unsurprisingly, would receive no response.

I came to a point where my mind settled and cleared. I had too much time to reflect and regret. I read once that the Quakers who created our prison system intended them to be places of penance, a place of reflection and solitude. Thus the word "penitentiary" was born.

I wrote many letters of apology to loved ones. My letter to my father was not one of apology, but one of forgiveness. My hate and fear of him had poisoned too much of my life, and with that letter of forgiveness I let it go. I did not hate him. His was a sad life deserving of pity. I could not love him either. I was indifferent, and it was a relief to make that step. He couldn't even pick up a pen and write his own son in prison a word of encouragement or support. It was time to let it go. It was time to let my whole life as I knew it go.

Boone came to me on the yard one day to say his cell mate was being transferred to another prison. He shyly asked me to move in with him. He said he expected nothing from me, I didn't have to do anything I didn't want to do, and that he just liked my company and the way I conducted myself. Without hesitation I said yes.

I was eager to get out of Red's cell and away from the drug addicts in and out of there. I was eager for the protective comfort of a husband. I was lonely, and I wanted someone to feel close to.

The other girls were jealous, but it was a good-natured jealousy. I had captured one of the most desirable and aloof men on the yard. He was known as a nice guy, and liked by inmates and staff alike. To be liked, and also respected, is no easy feat, as kindness is often mistaken for weakness. He was not a weak man. Boone had been in prison fifteen years when we met and had established his respect in some of the harshest prisons in the state. I had no idea why he was there and I didn't ask. I showered, ate, played cards, and walked the yard with murderers, rapists, thieves and addicts on a daily basis, long enough for it to not matter anymore. One does not ask another inmate what they are in for. It's considered invasive, and a violation of prison etiquette. If a person chooses to divulge that information, chances are you are considered a trusted friend.

Seasoned convicts look down on the ones who brag about their crimes. It appeared to me that no one with stature and respect was proud of his crimes, and most would take it all back in exchange for freedom.

When I agreed to move in with Boone, I knew that a man who had been down fifteen years, with five more to go, was not a petty criminal, and must have done something terrible to get a sentence of that magnitude. I didn't care. I didn't judge the men I lived with every day for what they did, only for the way they treated me. We had all been judged already and were receiving our punishment. And it was only temporary. I would leave that place, and leave all of them behind when I made it back to the free world, and I would never look back.

I made a new friend named Chris.

Chris looked like an all-American boy, the boy-next-door type. Blond-haired and blue-eyed, tall and skinny, no tattoos – he looked even more foreign there than I. He was a sweet, gay boy in his late twenties. He told me right away how he came to be at Soledad.

He and a girlfriend got drunk and robbed a friend who worked at a convenience store with water pistols and masks. He claimed it was a joke gone badly. The friend did not want to press charges, but the police didn't find the joke amusing. Chris got eight years for armed robbery. He was halfway through his sentence.

His lover and cellmate, Randy, was a lifer seventeen years into his sentence. Randy hoped for an appeal to set him free someday, for "accidentally" stabbing a man in a bar fight when he was barely twenty-one years old. I remember expressing sympathy for his plight to another inmate, prompting him to chuckle and say, "Don't feel too bad for him, Pup. He 'accidentally' stabbed the guy fifty-two times."

An inmate's version of his own crimes is not always reliable. They do tend to gossip about each other's crimes, but just don't often speak of their own. I took what I heard with a grain of salt, as the men could be unreasonably judgmental of each other, particularly if they didn't like someone.

If the men, and sometimes the guards, didn't like a particular man, they might "throw a jacket" on him;

meaning they would spread rumors that he committed a particularly distasteful crime that would ostracize or endanger him with the other inmates. The guards were not exempt from playing the same games as the inmates. In fact, my observations concluded you could hardly tell the difference between the inmates and the guards if it were not for the uniforms.

It's a fishbowl life, where everyone is looking at you and curious about your secrets. And everyone has secrets.

Our request to move me to Boone's cell was immediately granted, but it took a few weeks before his cell mate was transferred. In the meantime I took my meals with him, showered with him, and spent my days near him on the yard. It was necessary for him to show the other men that I was no longer available. Often he left me with the girls while he played sports, but kept an eye on me all of the time. If another man approached me, he seemed to appear out of nowhere within minutes to coldly inquire of the man's intentions and intimidate him away from me.

I liked belonging to someone and knowing I was protected. I felt truly safe for the first time in a long time. He was taking some ribbing from some of his sports buddies over me, but I think most of the guys understood a man can only go so long without someone to call his own, and still others were jealous it wasn't them, and he didn't lose any friends over it. We were not publicly demonstrative – that kind of behavior is frowned upon – but there was no question of the nature of our relationship. The entire atmosphere of my life in prison changed once I was considered married. I was treated cautiously and respectfully, lest my husband and his powerful friends be offended.

Finally, the day came when I moved my meager possessions to his cell.

We went to yard together for the day, and when we returned late that afternoon, someone had put a "Just Married" sign on our cell door.

The guards did it as a joke and were quite pleased with themselves and our embarrassed reaction. Boone and I both had good relationships with most of the guards. Practical jokes and humor were enjoyed by men on both sides of the law to help everyone get through the days.

The guards live there, too, every day and all day, and it's easy to forget they are the enemy. Some are over-zealous assholes who think it's their job to make our lives miserable, but most are just trying to get to retirement without a shank in the neck. If you treat them right, they will usually do the same. I had verbal confrontations with a few of the new guards who didn't yet know their place, and one or two homophobes, but when I was given the position of staff barber, and gained the ears of their superiors, most of that stopped. The commanding officers are more likely to learn the truth of activity in the blocks from the inmates rather than their staff.

I did once tell an overly friendly officer that though I liked him, we were not friends, (being overly friendly with staff could get you branded a snitch), as I knew when the shit went down and the shooting started, he would shoot me deader than hell. He laughed and said, "But Pup, I wouldn't shoot you first."

Life got much easier after I moved in with Boone. I laughed a lot more.

Our first night together he was so nervous. In his first attempt to kiss me he bumped his head on the steel frame on the top bunk. It ruined the romantic moment but diffused the tension. Embarrassed, he said to me, "Be patient with me, I'm kinda new at this."

I laughed at his boyish awkwardness and said, "Just relax, handsome, I'm not new at this at all. Just follow me and take over whenever you're ready."

When no one else was looking, and it was just him and me, he was a very different man from the one I knew on the yard.

One of the first things he did to make me happy was devise a curtain I could pull around the toilet for privacy. All the men made fun of me because I refused to use the toilet in front of anyone. It was just one more example of my prissy nature to them. They could laugh all they wanted and I didn't care. I've been bathroom shy all my life, and have always thought men vulgar with their bathroom habits. I was horrified to see men use the open air toilets on the yard. Prison or not, I was embarrassed to see a man drop his drawers and pop a squat in broad daylight while hundreds of other men loitered around him. I would sooner explode in constipation than allow myself that public vulnerability. I don't even leave the bathroom door open when I'm home alone. Boone teased me relentlessly about it, but placated me with maximum privacy. Those times when I could not be alone in the cell I pulled my curtain and made him put on his headphones, lest the tiniest sound of human nature escape my delicate bottom and destroy my illusion of feminine decorum.

I set out to make our cell a cozy and pretty little home. I stayed in our cell when he was working and busied myself with books, writing, and my domestic duties.

I crafted rag rugs out of old sheets and sponge painted the walls. I made a mobile of the sun, moon and stars out of toilet paper, soap, and dental floss. I made a toilet seat out of cardboard, framed pictures from magazines, and made toss pillows out of old shirts.

Boone taught me to craft leather. We played cards, watched our little TV, made love often, and talked away hour upon hour of our lives before we met.

We found we were born only six days apart, and came from similar backgrounds of alcoholism, violence, and family dysfunction.

He told me about his marriage and the pictures on his wall of the three little girls he left behind when he went to prison, all young women now, and I could see his heart break when he spoke of them.

It wasn't long before I realized I had made the most grievous of mistakes. I was falling in love with a convict. I suppose it was inevitable. He made me feel safe when I had forgotten what it felt like. We had hours, days and months of each other. He had not known love in fifteen years, and I felt as if I had never known it at all. The whole world was shut out. Our old lives were gone, our futures a blank. All we had was each other.

He made me feel like the most important person in the world, and appreciated the smallest gestures of kindness and affection. Every possible thing he could obtain, beyond what the prison provided, he did his best to get for me. He brought me good food from the kitchen, handmade gifts from other inmates, leather goods he made especially for me, polished stones and pretty feathers he found on the yard. Every day, it seemed, he gave me a token of love.

But he did not tell me he loved me, and I wondered was it all just what convicts do to keep their cell wives happy?

He was an enigmatic man. He shared only bits and pieces of the puzzle that was his life. He was so kind, gentle, and soft-spoken, it seemed impossible he had committed acts of violence. But that was a common impression as I went about my day-to-day life among men who appeared as average people you would meet on the street, but had perpetrated heinous acts against their fellow man.

He came to California from the Southeast with the military, married young, and had had three children when he came to prison at twenty-three years old.

He came from a small family, and it appeared only a mother and grandmother kept in contact. He was always solemn when he spoke of his loved ones, except the memories of his daughters always brought a winsome smile to his face.

I found myself eagerly awaiting his return from his kitchen job in the early afternoon. I couldn't get enough of him. We were inseparable. He left for his job in the kitchen at four a.m. The cell was so cold in the winter months: he put all his blankets and pillows around me before he left for work, and I woke swaddled and warm. It shocked me when I realized how happy I was, considering I felt this to be the lowest point in my life. I was learning how little you really need materially to be happy, and that so much of happiness is built on a sense of security and well-being. Boone gave me that. I knew I was safe in his company, and he did his best to see that all my immediate needs were met.

Boone told me stories of his early years in prisons far more violent than Soledad, and I was amazed he was still alive to tell the tales. He earned his way through good behavior to a softer environment, and the massive growth of California's prison industry has instigated regulations making them considerably safer than in his early years.

Outside of our cell were the daily dramas of drug dealing, racial hostility, fights, suicides, stabbings, gang warfare, and the occasional murder.

Before prison, I enjoyed reading crime novels, and was particularly fascinated with serial killers. I lost all interest in that type of entertainment when I lived day to day among the very people I used to read about. I cannot read or watch films where people do horrible things to each other anymore. It's all too real now, and I don't find it entertaining.

"Doc," a former doctor who had chopped his ex-wife up in pieces and buried her under their house after catching her with another man; "Jimbo," a sweet, collegiate young man from a good family who had shot two men outside a bar for touching his girlfriend; and

"McFadden," the old man who wheeled around an oxygen tank, and had killed his drug-addict son-in-law for repeatedly stealing from him. He got eighteen years for second-degree murder, but was already seventy years old and suffering with severe emphysema. He would never make it home alive.

The stories went on and on, and so often the crimes made sense, things that could happen to anyone. They were just regular people, living their lives, then something happened and everything changed. They never saw it coming. Lives ruined on both sides of the law. The stories are not so entertaining when you are looking straight in to the eyes of someone who took a life and lives with it every day. Not everyone in prison is a career criminal or came from a bad home or neighborhood. Some are just victims of circumstances. And others are pure evil.

When Boone told me stories of the hard prisons he'd lived in before Soledad, I was grateful to feel as safe as I did there with him. There were places much worse.

He told me a story of a man in a cell near him, when they still had bars instead of doors. It was night when two men crept quietly into the cell in his line of vision. They believed its occupant had swallowed a large quantity of valuable heroin. While one garroted his throat with a length of chain, the other gutted him from neck to na-vel. Boone told me he could hear the guts splatter on the concrete floor and the men whispering while searching the gore for the heroin. He laid motionless, feigning sleep, watching through slitted eyes, lest he be spotted as a wit-ness and next on their hit list. They found no heroin. When questioned, he saw nothing.

He brought me to tears when he told me the story of a young boy running across the yard, bleeding to death of multiple stab wounds, crying out for his mother while he died.

He told me his stories with a detachment that only comes with years of life in a world of violence, but I was relieved to see he was still human enough to be disturbed by the memories.

I didn't want to hear anymore, it all made me sick and sorrowful, but I felt he needed to tell someone all the things he had seen over the years, all the things he pretended not to see or been affected by, all the scars and wounds he carried. And I was that person he told. So I listened, and sometimes wept at the horror of it all, and curled my body against his, to ward off all the evils that men do, and all the sadness that had been both our lives.

There was that singular moment in our early days together that marked the point of no return for my heart.

We lay together on his bunk. The day room closed and quiet, all inmates locked safely away in their cells, the block was quiet, preparing for sleep. He then, solemnly, told me a story of his boyhood.

He told me of his father beating his mother around the house during one of their many fights. He told me of him, as a little boy, following behind them picking up pieces of broken glass and putting furniture back in place. He told me of himself, at five years old, finding his mother naked and bleeding in the bathtub, with wrists slashed from one of her many suicide attempts, and of the shame of finding her passed out from drink on the front lawn for all the kids on the school bus to witness. He told me of his father's brutal dominance over everyone in their home and his constant criticism of his family. As his stories unfolded, I saw beneath the hardened convict. In the deep blue pinwheels of his eyes, I saw the damaged little boy haunted by a childhood gone terribly wrong. And I saw some of myself there. All the disappointments and painful memories that wove the fabric of my own childhood into the long tapestry that led to us both being there, in that place and time, that very moment, to crash into each other's lives, and grasp on to something hopeless but impossible to let go of.

I took the leap. The one I swore I wouldn't take. I looked into those pinwheels of ocean blue and said, "I love you, Boone."

He turned away, but not before I saw a tear slip from his eye. Ever so softly he said, "No one has said those words to me in over fifteen years."

I said, "I'm not asking you to love me back, I just want you to know you are loved."

Still not looking at me, he whispered, "If you knew who I really was you wouldn't love me."

I imagined he was referring to his crimes. I thought for only a moment before I said, " I don't know who you used to be, any more than you know who I was, but I know who you are right now, and that is who I love. And that is how I love. Right now, right here, with all the past in the past and the world shut away, I love you."

I received a letter from my mother telling me that Roger, the man that molested my sister and me, was dead of a heart attack, and she thought I might like to know. I didn't think it mattered to me one way or another, and believed I had dealt with it and put it all behind me many years before. But in my solitude, as I read her words, I was flooded with memories and emotion, and found it not to be true at all. It was all still there waiting for me. All I had to do was reach in and touch it. I didn't want him to be dead. I wanted him to say he was sorry for all he took from me. He never did, and now he never would.

I let myself remember his hands on me. I felt the rough stubble of his beard on my tender skin, the calloused hands parting my tiny buttocks, his genitals enormous in my child hands, and I remembered the smell of stale alcohol mixed with his man's sweat.

And the aftermath, the string of events that disintegrated what few positive memories I had as a child, and the piercing shriek of shame that lived inside my head, surfacing at every thought of him or mention of his name. And at his death, I knew that I may have dealt with it, but I could never put it behind me. It was a part of me and would go with me wherever I go. He altered not only the course of my life, but how I saw myself and the world around me. He altered what I thought about love and trust, family, relationships, and sex. His touch contained promises he didn't keep, he whispered secrets that were found out and destroyed us both, and he sensed my need and he used me. I thought I was special. I thought he loved me. But I was just a child, and I didn't know that men like him don't know anything of love.

I told Boone the story of Roger after I finished reading my mother's letter. He listened in silence. His eyes welled with tears when I told him of the killing of the animals and my innocence.

He said to me, "My sweet Puppy, I am so sorry those things happened to you."

I don't ever remember feeling closer to another human being as that first time we both allowed ourselves to go back to those two little boys, born only six days apart, at opposite ends of the country, and remember, feel, and share the demons of their destruction. I was moved by his compassion. I assumed it stemmed from the many issues he had from his own childhood. I didn't have any way of knowing it was so much more than that. By the time I found out, I was desperately in love and didn't have the heart to turn away.

The life of a man in prison is one of fantasy. The longer he is in, the more unrealistic his view of the outside world becomes. Most all the men we spent our time with were friends Boone had made over many years of mutual incarceration.

I found them to be childlike in their simplistic, and often glamorized, visions of life in the free world. The world had frozen in time for them when they entered those gates, and they were frozen in their maturity. Their reasoning, humor, temperaments, and self-absorption were those of boys, and not the seasoned, experienced men they thought themselves to be. They had little experience in the real world, and little understanding of how difficult it is to obtain even the basic tools of survival, let alone the complications of the success and affluence they appeared to believe were simply waiting for them to partake of.

It bothered me to think how disappointed they would be if they ever got out. But I stayed quiet because I knew most of them never would.

Again, Boone was no exception. He had no idea what awaited him outside those walls. He was twenty-three-years old when he went to prison, and would be forty-four when he got out. I knew how much the world had changed while he was frozen in time. I knew how expensive things were, and how competitive the job market was. And I knew how much harder it was for a man with a criminal record. I tried not to rain on his parade with too much of the truth when he regaled me with his imaginings of the life we would have when he was free, though I did try to inject some reality whenever I could.

In everyone's life there are defining moments. I was about to have one.

Christmas of 1999 was on its way. Boone and I lived happily together. We established a routine that kept us together every possible moment. He showered me with attention and affection. He made me feel better about myself than I had in a long time. Other inmates and even many of the guards admired and envied our devotion to one another.

The violence continued all around us, but it didn't touch us. There were fights, stabbings, petty squabbles, and even the occasional suicide. Suicides were jokingly referred to as "an early parole" by inmates and staff, but I was not jaded enough to find any humor in it.

I recall one in particular. He was a man in his fifties. His name was Terry. He had been in a long time and was sure he would be paroled home on his next visit to the board. He was denied, and hanged himself that very night in his cell.

No one is allowed to touch the body until outside investigators can determine the cause of death and exonerate the staff and other inmates of responsibility. The investigators took their time getting to the prison, and in the interim he hung there while everyone went about their business.

I was morbidly fascinated by the violence, and more so by how casually it was accepted by the men around me.

Boone called me Snoopy Puppy, and admonished me to mind my own business when I leaped from my bunk and rushed to the door to peer out the window at the slightest sound of upheaval. He became more annoyed when other inmates started to come to me for information on the latest drama. I usually knew everything that was going on in our building, and Boone knew it is not good to know too much. Prison was boring, and my many years as a hairdresser, listening to the stories of other people's lives, made it almost painful to mind my own business.

I briefly became the official troubleshooter for the girls, and an unofficial counselor to a lot of the men. I think Boone was jealous of every moment my attention was not on him, and he did not want me to be a part of prison society. I was his exotic pet. We were paired birds in our cage and separated from the flock for my protection. Boone told me I was too good for that place, and I should not be a part of their world. He was successful at keeping others at bay while enjoying the respect and friendship of only a few, carefully chosen friends. I, on the other hand, am a social butterfly, and took too much pride when others came to me for guidance or information, often unaware it could lead to my being taken advantage of. There was little danger of that happening with Boone around. He was extremely protective.

I was due to go home in mid-January if I applied for, and was granted, my lost good time credits. I was terrified of the prospect of getting out. I had destroyed my life as I knew it. I had nothing to go back to. It was all gone. I was safe now. Boone took care of me and our needs were met.

I made our little cell so homey the men teased me and called me the Martha Stewart of Soledad. I had stopped taking anti-depressants soon after I moved in with Boone. I was drug-free and healthy. I was in love, and, as strange as it might seem to the free world, I was happy.

I thought about going back to Maine and starting over there, but I couldn't bear the thought of going home a loser. My pride would not allow me to depend on anyone else, and I despise a cold climate. Maine is too damn cold too damn often.

How would I pick up the pieces in California? How could I face everyone as an ex-convict? It made me sick to think about, so I tried not to. I was hoping someone would make all my decisions for me, like they did in prison, but I knew that, one more time, I was on my own and would have to sink or swim.

As Christmas approached, I thought of all the holidays Boone had spent alone in a cell. I watched the other men busying themselves with handmade cards and gifts to send home to their loved ones and I was sad at their meager offerings, but cheered by the spirit of giving being shown by some of the most selfish.

I hated prison food. Most of it was disgusting and I refused to eat it. Boone, on the other hand, was usually quite satisfied with what was served. He lived through earlier and less humane days of near starvation or food far worse than what I turned my nose up at, and now he had a kitchen job where he had access to plenty of food, good or not. I've never forgotten a story he told me of Old Folsom Prison; where the inmates were given apples too large to fit through the bars of their cells. He said he was so hungry he had to reach his hand out to hold the apple and press his face between the bars to eat it until it was small enough to pull inside. He told me he looked up and down the tier and observed dozens of disembodied hands holding disappearing apples and truly believed he was in Hell. For some reason I have never been able to get that image out of my head.

He casually mentioned to me that he looked forward to Christmas because The Salvation Army gifted each inmate with a bag of hard candy, a bag of nuts, and some fruit. I looked for sarcasm in his face, but saw only sincere gratitude at these meager gifts, and it was at once clear to me how seriously deprived of even the simplest human kindness he had been these past sixteen years. My heart shattered with compassion, and I was reminded with shame of how seriously spoiled I had become since my childhood, when I too looked forward excitedly to Friday afternoons when my mother came home with a bag of candy.

This was a defining moment because it was the moment I realized I would never be able to walk away from Boone. I could not be that person who claimed to love him forever only to abandon him. It's not how I'm made. I was consumed by a desire to give him all the things he had missed all those years, to give him hope when he had so little, to put a smile on his handsome face as often as I could, to protect him in the world outside these walls and fences the way he had protected me in his world.

I was determined to give him the closest thing to a Christmas he had seen in sixteen years.

An inmate is allowed to own so very little it makes gift buying a challenge. My resources were limited, but my imagination was not. I scavenged the building for pretty and shiny things to use to decorate our cell. I fashioned a small tree and wreath for our door, and hand painted paper to wrap the few gifts I'd bought or traded with other inmates. I hung stockings stuffed with candy and necessities from the commissary, and had it all ready when he came home from work.

When Boone walked into our cheerful little cell, he was moved to tears. It seemed so primitive to my spoiled eyes, but I knew it was the gesture itself that meant so much. In turn he gave me a beautifully hand-tooled wallet he spent countless hours creating that I still have today. He told me it was the best Christmas he had ever had.

It was the year 2000. I would be forty years old in May. I'd spent nearly four years in and out of institutional life in one form or another, and over ten years battling addiction.

It was easy for me to stay clean in prison. There were drugs everywhere, and they were easy to get, but I saw what they did to people who got involved in the prison drug life, and Boone was adamant in his dislike of drugs and the people who used them, and kept it away from us.

Boone and I laughed a lot. He loved to tease and play practical jokes. His boyish ways were a big part of his charm. He quickly learned what buttons to push to harass or provoke my ire, and amused himself often by pushing them. I confess to being gullible at times, making me a perfect victim for pranksters, but he was never cruel or unkind to me, and it made the days easier to laugh and smile, even if it was at my own expense.

It is a big mistake to believe most men in prison are telling the truth about who they are or why they are there. Never being a successful liar myself, I saw little reason to question a man's story unless given good reason. I was not there long enough to realize that time can change memories and people can rewrite their own history. They can be whoever they wish to be, and the story can be however they decide and there is no one to refute it. Unfortunately, many see themselves as victims of circumstance rather than choice, and avoid taking responsibility for their crimes.

I never saw that in Boone. In the few vague references he made to his crimes he seemed genuinely remorseful, and often said he got what he deserved, but did not give any details of why he believed that or why he was there. It bears mentioning again that it is a violation of the prison code to ask someone about their crimes. If they offer, it implies a great deal of trust and an expectation of reciprocated candor. If they don't offer, you don't ask.

I could have gone the rest of my life without knowing what Boone did to put him away for twenty years and of course I imagined it must have been something terrible. The time came when he felt I had to know. To recall and write this private and painful episode, with the knowledge that it may be read and I may be judged by many, or even the few closest to me, forces me to halt, my pen poised in thoughtful hesitation. The shattering of the idyllic fantasy I had with the man I'd grown deeply in love with, and the monumental decision I ultimately had to make of whether I could live with the truth, is something I'm doubtful few could understand.

I made the decision not to apply to get my good time credits back. I felt I could not leave him one minute sooner than I had to. I believed that life with him in prison was better than life outside without him. At the time, I would have gladly stayed with him four more years in our little cell, away from the world he had forgotten and I was afraid of.

As the days rushed by at breakneck speed, we clung

to each other in quiet desperation. We left each other's side only when forced to. My mind frantically grasped at potential scenarios that might prolong our time together. I could cause some trouble. I could disrespect a guard or break some rules to buy more time. But we both knew if I made trouble they would separate us as punishment and I would be doing time without him. They would punish me by taking what I valued most. That is the staff's only real means of control and they use it vigorously.

Boone said to me "Puppy, this is no place for you. You have to go home. Go out there and be a star and don't ever come back to this awful place. You are too good to be in a place like this and don't ever forget that."

An old friend offered me a room in his home upon my release, and I was grateful and relieved that I at least had a place to go and begin my journey back to civilization. As my time grew to its end, I could hardly bear to see the sadness in his eyes. He told me he had never felt such love as he felt for me, and I didn't doubt his sincerity. Boone had shyly declared his love for me months before, and to prove it he took the huge leap of telling his family of our relationship. Few men share with the outside world their private affairs behind those walls. It's a world that free people cannot understand, and a perfect example of things better left unsaid. My own mother was greatly relieved when I told her of the special man who looked after me, and she remained grateful to him until the day she died.

Boone grew quiet and distant. I assumed he was pulling away from me emotionally in preparation for my departure. He did not ask me to wait for him. He told me it was selfish to ask that of someone you love. It made me want to wait for him even more. Everyone seemed to put more distance from me as I got closer to my release. Boone said it was just the way it is. They know they will never see you again, and many are resentful it's not them leaving. He also told me it was a dangerous time in one's sentence, as an unsuspected enemy may try to exact revenge before you are beyond his reach forever.

I chattered nervously, and worried out loud about the obstacles that lay ahead in the free world, and Boone always looked at me sadly and said, "I believe in you, baby. You're going to be a star out there."

His withdrawal from me hurt and bewildered me. I re-assured him I would not abandon him. I would write, and he would call me, and when I finished parole I would visit, and when he walked out those gates in four years and four months I would be waiting on the other side. I meant it, but he didn't believe me. He had seen too many prom-ises left at the gate in his many years as an inmate to be-lieve I was really different, and his lifer friends chided both of us for thinking we would survive the separation. And he carried his secrets, the secrets that changed everything.

There was a group of Mexican gangsters in our build-ing that I despised. They were responsible for most of the drugs and violence in our building, and they sexually ha-rassed me whenever I was separated from Boone or the other whites. I didn't make an issue of it unless someone actually put his hands on me, because I knew it would cause race problems and put Boone in the position of defending my honor.

One morning, as I walked nonchalantly down the tier, I was grabbed violently by my shirt and dragged into a cell. It happened so fast and unexpectedly I had no time to defend myself. It was one of the Mexicans I despised. They called him Spanky. He was a huge and dangerous man and a heroin addict. He threw me against the wall of his cell and I saw stars when my head hit the concrete. I didn't know why he attacked me until he pushed his body against mine and I felt his hardness against my bel-ly and his breath hot against my throat. He brought his face down to mine and tried to kiss my mouth. I turned away and struggled for release but he outweighed me by at least one hundred pounds. He whispered fiercely, "C'mon baby, let me have some of that! I'll make you feel good."

I pushed him back enough to look him in the eyes and said, "If you dare to do this, I will tell every white man in here, and Boone will come after you. If you let me go now I won't tell anyone this happened." He relaxed his hold on me, but with his body still pressing me against the wall, he halfheartedly pleaded with me to submit until he realized I would not comply. It seemed to dawn on his drug-addled brain the enormity of what he was doing and the potential consequences. He stepped away, releasing me. As I turned to leave, he grabbed my arm and said, "Please, Pup, don't tell anyone I did this. I'm sorry, I just got too high and lost my head, Man. I didn't hurt you, did I?" I told him I would not tell anyone and I didn't.

I left his cell shaking with fear and fury and the full knowledge that the situation could have just as easily gone the other way. I had made it nearly to the end of my time without another rape in my life. Spanky never so much as looked at me for the remainder of my stay. That was not difficult, as we spent most of it on full lockdown.

Mario, a quiet heroin addict across the tier from us, was brutally stabbed to death, and I knew who was responsible. I think most everyone in the building did also. Mario owed a drug debt he couldn't pay. Debts of any kind in prison cannot be ignored, and if a debt is not paid something must be done or the dealer will lose his respect and power. The dealer will first go to the debtor's people and give them the chance to settle his debt for him. If he is a member of value, they may settle his debt. If he and his habit have become a burden to his people, he will be sacrificed. If he is a member of an opposing gang, there is a good chance he will be disposed of by his own people to keep peace between enemies. One person is rarely valuable enough to risk an all-out race war that could upset the entire population. I was not on the yard when Mario was murdered. Though I knew exactly who did it, I was glad I was not a witness.

I had seen and lived through enough violence in that prison and in my life. It depressed me to realize it was no longer affecting me the way it should have. I never wanted to become one of them. I never wanted to be someone who shrugged off the taking of a life or made a joke of suicidal despair. I had been on the yard many times when violence broke out. Any outbreak of violence or breach of security resulted in the yard shutting down. When the warning sirens wailed, all inmates were ordered face down on the ground. Anyone left standing would be shot by the tower guards. One never knew if they were warning shots or aimed to kill. I had been told they sometimes used rubber bullets or wood blocks instead of real bullets, but no one really knew, and the guards wouldn't say.

Boone kept me close to him on the yard. As my husband, it was his responsibility to protect me. In some race wars, the enemy will attempt to kill each other's "girls." On both sides of the law, punishment was publicly confirmed with taking something the enemy values.

I have lain face down for hours in the dirt of that yard while order was restored. Once order is restored, each inmate is individually strip-searched for weapons, then name and inmate number is recorded for future interrogation, and we are led back to our cells for lockdown. Lockdown is a dreaded punishment. The actions of a single inmate can lead to misery for the entire prison population. By punishing everyone, the staff hopes to force someone to tell what they know. Of course, this seldom works as being branded a snitch is the worst possible thing that could happen. Snitches spend their time in solitary confinement for their own safety and can never walk the yard again.

Once everyone is locked down, the interviews begin. Each inmate is taken to a private room where staff attempt to coerce information. The only inmates allowed out of their cells are inmates whose jobs are essential to the basic functioning of the prison. Clerks, kitchen workers, laundry, and a small crew to serve food to the cells are the only inmates moving in the building. The staff love lockdowns. With everyone safely locked away, they have almost nothing to do but sit around and get paid for it.

I knew who was responsible for Mario's murder. The very same group of Mexican gangsters I despised was also the primary drug dealers in the building. Their leader was a disgusting human being, even for a prison, and he rarely let me pass without a rude gesture or lewd comment. I never understood why he chose me among the homosexuals to harass. He referred to me as "Hollywood Bitch." He was physically repulsive and carried the attitude of a fourteen-year-old schoolyard bully. He wielded his power as a drug dealer mercilessly and behaved as if none of the rules applied to him. I truly wanted to see him go down. I wanted to snitch on him and watch them take him to solitary, but I could not take that risk so close to home. I could only hope that one of his many enemies hated him as much as I did.

Boone and I were not on total lockdown. He was a kitchen worker, and I was enlisted to help serve food. There were three of us for food service; a black, a Mexican, and a white, and each of us was expected to do the biddings of our fellow race that they could not do for themselves. I spent all my time running from one white cell to another, delivering messages, cigarettes and whatnots until I nearly begged to be locked up again. The building was still on lockdown when I paroled.

One morning, a few weeks before I was due to parole,

Boone said to me quite gravely, "Pup, there's something I have to tell you."

I hate it when someone tells you that, because it's never something good. He could not look at me, and I felt my chest constrict in panic. He said, "I never thought I would have to tell you this. I never dreamed we would fall in love. I thought we would have this time together, you would leave and forget about me and never have to know the truth about why I am here. When you know the truth about me, you will not love me anymore, and I will understand because you are a good person."

I didn't want to know the truth if it meant I couldn't love him. I didn't want anything to change the way I felt, but there was no turning back now. It was eating at him. Apparently, this was the cause of his recent withdrawal from me.

I told him I couldn't believe he could tell me anything that would change how I felt about him. Just tell me and I will deal with it. I don't know what I expected. I knew it wasn't going to be easy, but I was genuinely dumbfounded and stricken when he said, "Puppy, I am in prison for rape."

I can't say I immediately comprehended what he was saying to me. My soul scorched with those words and my stomach pitched and rolled with nausea. I knew there were men all around me that had committed rape and crimes far worse, after all this was a prison, but not my sweet, gentle Boone. I had wondered and imagined him as a young man with a quick temper, robbing a bank or even killing a bad guy in a drug deal, but I had never imagined the sweet man I fell in love with hurting someone innocent, especially in sexual violence. I could see he was in genuine distress telling me this. He kept his eyes averted and did not try to offer me physical comfort. I felt alone and bewildered. I had a million questions spinning through my head and no courage to ask them. He said, "Pup, I had to tell you. It's been killing me. I love you so much and you deserve to know the truth."

He was due to leave for his kitchen job for the next six hours. He went to his locker and pulled out an inch-thick folder and handed it to me. "These are the court documents that show everything I did that put me away. I will understand if you want to leave and never speak to me again, but please know that it was all a very long time ago, and I am not that person anymore." His eyes welled with tears when he turned and left our cell. I was left alone with the pages of proof that no matter who you are or where you are, you never really know someone the way you think you do.

I sat and stared at that folder for hours before I picked it up and began to read. I already knew more than I wanted to, and now I had to know the rest. With each page my heart grew heavier, and when I finished I felt the weight of the world pressing me down onto the mattress of the bunk where I lay immobilized until he returned.

I had looked in the face of Charles Ng, one of the most notorious serial killers in California history. I had stood only a few feet away from a man who kept dead women in a U-Haul freezer and had sex with their corpses. I had served meals to a man who smothered his three small children to punish his wife for divorcing him. I had eaten, showered, and slept beside the worst of men these past few years, but I did not love them, and I didn't care what happened to them. This was personal. This hurt me.

Returning from his kitchen job, he entered our little home obviously distressed in anticipation of what would happen next. I felt sympathy for what I imagined it must be like to divulge such horrific news to someone you love and try to prepare yourself for their reaction.

He sat on the edge of the bunk I lay curled on and

asked, "Did you read it?" I whispered. "Yes, I did." He sighed heavily and said, "Part of me hoped you wouldn't. That you loved me enough that it wouldn't matter."

I said "How could it not matter?" When I looked at him I still saw the man I loved this past year and promised my life to. I was so conflicted and confused. I didn't want to know any of it, but I didn't ever want anyone else to tell me something I should have known already. My response was denial, and then an attempt to make excuses for him with what I knew of his violent childhood. He did not allow me either avenue of solace. I did respect that he took full responsibility for his actions and did not deny the enormity of his crimes or attempt to place blame elsewhere.

He said "Puppy, don't try to make excuses for me. It was not my parents' fault or anyone else's. I don't know why I did what I did, but I knew the difference between right and wrong and at the time I didn't care. I paid with twenty years of my life and lost everything and everyone I loved, and I deserved it all. As you told me the stories of your childhood and life, and I listened and saw what men like me did to hurt you, it broke my heart and filled me with shame, and I knew that I had to tell you and risk losing you forever and set you free to move on without me."

Maybe that's exactly what I should have done. But I couldn't. I was in too deep.

I asked him why he didn't tell me sooner. Why did he let me fall in love? I will never forget what he said. It is burned into the tender reaches of my heart.

With downcast eyes he said, "I am sorry Pup. I wanted you and I wanted you to love me. I wanted to know what it felt like to be a normal person and to be loved. If you never speak to me again, I will always love you and be grateful to you for giving me that. You are the most beautiful and amazing person I have ever met, and I will never forget you or our time together. I have had to hide and lie for sixteen years to survive in these places and God will probably kill me before I am ever freed for what I did, but for just this one piece in time, it was wonderful to feel like a real human being and not a monster."

What could I say in the face of this declaration? Was this what they call a monster? For the past year he was the love I had only hoped for and dreamed of. He loved me when I had nothing to offer but myself, and he protected and cherished me in the darkest hours of my life. He was generous to those in need, defended the weaker inmates, and gentle to the stray cats on the prison yard. He was liked and respected by the staff and other inmates. This could not possibly be the same man I read about in those papers.

My head and heart waged war on each other, and there has barely been a ceasefire in the ten years since.

I had questions. He answered them with obvious discomfort and reluctance, never giving more information than I specifically asked for. I was disillusioned, confused, and a little angry.

There were six victims. They ranged in age from eight- to seventeen-years-old, all female, and all strangers to him. They were randomly selected, stalked, and forcibly sexually assaulted. His rampage lasted two years before he was stopped.

I asked him why he did it.

He said, "I don't know why. I had the impulses and thoughts for a long time before I acted on them. I felt it building up in me until I couldn't control it anymore. After the first one, it got easier. I became someone else, someone that didn't care. I knew my life was over. I knew it was just a matter of time before I was caught. I imagined I would force the cops to kill me when they came for me. I've asked myself every one of these questions over and over for sixteen years. Pup, I was sick. That's the only answer. Don't try to make sense of insanity; it will only drive you crazy too. Please believe me when I tell you that I am not that person anymore. Time and prison has changed me. I would never hurt anyone again."

He lay on his bunk, depressed and dejected. He told me he was haunted by the faces and voices of the people he had harmed, and he had never had anyone he could trust enough to talk about it with. He would have been killed in those prisons, if the other inmates knew. He felt he had never had a real friend because his secrets prohibited allowing anyone too close. He had contemplated suicide many times and, until he met me, decided he would kill himself before his release rather than face the world alone.

Perhaps I was wrong to feel compassion for him, but there it was, rising in me as I imagined the loneliness and shame he carried for sixteen years in silence and isolation.

I lay beside him on his bunk, put my arms around him and lay my head on his chest. He stiffened and said, "How can you stand to even touch me now, knowing what I am?"

I chose my words carefully. "None of us is simply the sum of our mistakes, Boone. If that were true there would be no hope for the human race. I hate what you did, but I still love you and what we have together. I am struggling to put it all together so it makes some sense to me, and we will get through this somehow."

What I did not say aloud was the questions screaming silently in my head. Why? Why is this happening to me? How could I fall in love with the kind of man that took away my childhood? What am I supposed to learn from this? What am I supposed to do with all this?

I remembered Boone's tears of sympathy when I told him of the theft of my innocence by Roger, and I wondered now what it felt like for him to see and hear the face and heart of a victim up close. I wondered if it was part of my destiny, or my human experience, to see and love the very human side of someone I had always imagined as less than human. I don't know. Maybe God wasn't there in that prison at all, and it was just another example of my uncanny tendency to draw to me the most damaged of men.

Our last days together were some of the most painful of my life. My thoughts and feelings convoluted and contradicted each other to where I felt I might go mad. Boone had no idea how much his revelations changed my vision of the future. It had nothing to do with whether I still loved him or not, or whether I could still keep my promise to wait for him. Everything changed because now I knew we could never put the past behind us and have a new life. Now I knew he would be a registered sex offender for the rest of his life, and they never get to put the past behind them. It's not how it works for guys like him. Things had become progressively worse, and the laws, even for a man that had done his time, were harsh and unforgiving. The politicians and the media bred hysteria for votes and ratings, and sex offenders became the new lepers of our society.

Not for a moment do I mean to suggest that necessary safety measures to protect the innocent are somehow unfair to the guilty, but hysteria rarely breeds progressive or positive results, and society seems to ignore reasoning with these particular criminals.

Boone was too disconnected from the reality of the outside world to understand what I knew, that he would never finish doing his time, and on the other side of those walls did not lay the freedom he dreamed of, but an entirely new kind of punishment, a public one. There would be no more hiding as he had done for sixteen years. There would be rejection, degradation, humiliation and judgment at every turn. I kept these thoughts to myself. He had four more years to go and a lot could happen in four years. I was sad to be leaving him behind, and frightened to death of going back out to the world and rebuilding a life. Prison had become easy, and I suspected it would be a long time before anything was easy again.

The night before I left, we wrapped up in each other's arms and encouraged each other with promises. Boone told me to go out there and make him proud. He told me to enjoy my life and my freedom and don't ever come back to this awful place. He told me, "You are the single greatest love of my life, and I will never forget you. Don't wait for me, Baby, just live your life, and if they ever let me out of here alive, I'll come looking for you, and if you still want me I will never let you go again. I will write you every day and I will always be your greatest fan. All I ask is that you don't forget me."

He did write me every day and I did not forget him.

We did not sleep that night. As the morning light crept between the bars of our tiny window, I was stricken with grief and panic. There was no joy in having finished my time, no relief in having made it out of that place alive, and no excitement for what lay ahead for me. There was only loss and fear.

In the silence of the dawn, the sound of our cell door unlocking was like a gunshot to my heart. I sobbed, brokenhearted, in his arms, until he whispered in my ear, "Go Puppy, and don't look back."

But I did. I got to the open door and I looked back for one last look at him. And his image stayed with me for all the time we were apart. My big, handsome, muscled convict, stood at the back of our dimly lit cell, his face wet with tears. He said "Don't forget me." As the cell door closed behind me I heard a muffled sob. It would be over two years before I saw him again.

A Handout

What do you do
in a world gone askew
and all that you knew
disappeared in a few
moments of time

What a crime
to be dispossessed
when you once rode the crest
on a wave of success
and plunged into Hell
Now they're ringing the bell
chiming your time is near
and all you hold dear
is soon to be history

Was my life a mystery
or a novel of fiction
that saw no restrictions
save what I held back
because what I lacked
in courage or nerve
I'm now being served
a cold meal of the truth

It's stuck in my mouth
so no words can come out
This unpalatable meal
that's begun to congeal
digests to my soul

Now I'm on the dole
for a handout of hope
on this slippery slope
as I blindly grope
to stand disengaged
to quell my old rage
and step from this cage
and live this new age and new life.

E.M.

Chapter Ten
Princess Jenny

In release they gave me the clothes my friend Sue sent me to go home in, and searched my possessions to ensure I was taking nothing that belonged to the state. I found that amusing to the point of absurdity. What would I take? The garbage they called food? The rags I was forced to wear, or perhaps the soap or toilet paper that dried and peeled my skin like sandpaper? All I had were the few things Boone had given me as tokens of love and remembrance. I owned nothing else.

I was transported in a van with other men being released to the nearest bus station. My bus ticket was purchased out of the $200 "gate money" given to every man upon release and I was on my way to Orange County with instructions to report to my parole officer within twenty-four hours.

It was finished. I was free, or almost free. I still had three years of parole supervision ahead of me, and that is no easy task. The failure rate is notoriously high, and only a very few make it through without a violation and a return to prison. I walked out of there with the utmost confidence I would be one of those few.

I paroled on April 13th of the year 2000. I would be forty years old in three weeks, and I had nothing left to show for it. I had been a winner and I had been a loser, and I liked being a winner much more. There was no time left to be afraid and no patience for my own weaknesses. I knew as long as I stayed clean I could rebuild a life, I could succeed, and I could be happy again.

An old friend gave me a place in his home as long as I needed it. He met me at the bus station and took me to my new home. It was nice to see a familiar face, and to this day I remain grateful for his kindness. Living in his home for the next year was a challenge to my resolve to stay clean. He was a using drug addict, but I didn't have any other options. I was broke and homeless and had burned a lot of bridges. In all fairness to him, he did his best to respect my position and kept his drugs out of my sight. But I knew they were there, and all I had to do was ask. He gave me a place to start over, and staying clean was my problem, not his. I was over that life, and watching him and his friends made it easier. They were where I had already been, and I knew where they were going. It didn't look fun to me anymore. It looked sad, desperate, and lonely. It looked like prison, but without a release date.

My mother was the first person I called. She cried with relief and happiness that I was free and safe. I promised her she had seen the last of my troubles, I would come home to see her soon, and I would call often. Of course, I humbled myself to the inevitable lecture I knew was coming, and I was patient with her mistrust and grateful she loved me enough to still care. There were only a handful of people I was ready to call and let know I had returned to the free world. I carried a great deal of shame, but my dignity did not allow me excess humility. Besides my mother, there was Tina, Rod, Jeff, Crystal and Sue. Those were all the people I loved most and the first ones I called. But even then, when I should have been rejoicing, the one person I longed for the most was out of my reach, on lockdown at Soledad State Prison. I had four years and two months to figure out whether I had a future with Boone, but for now I missed him terribly, and the security I felt when I was with him.

I had forgotten the world was so big and busy and loud. I felt anxious and overwhelmed, and paralyzed by the smallest decisions. I had forgotten how to make decisions on my own.

I called my friend Jeff. Jeff was – and is – a near perfect example of the happy, well-adjusted, clean and sober addict/alcoholic, and I treasured his friendship and guidance in the sober world. I asked him to take me to a meeting. I needed to connect with people who understood who I was and what I'd been through. There was no treatment for addicts in prison, and there was a two-to-three year waiting list just to get into a twelve-step meeting. I needed to stay clean above all else, if I was going to stay out of prison and rebuild my life. I saw many familiar and welcoming faces in that room, and I knew I was exactly where I was supposed to be.

I reported to the parole department and met my assigned officer. She was cold, businesslike, and threatening. She opened my file and read my criminal record to me. When she finished and closed my file, I looked directly into her eyes and asked, "Is that all you have?"

She said, "What do you mean?"

"Is that all you have about me in your folder? The last four years? Where's the other thirty-six? You hold my freedom, my future, the power to put me back in prison at will, and all you know about me is the worst things I've done. There is a lot more to me than the mistakes I've made. I was a good businessman and member of my community. I'm a brother, a son, and a friend to many. I wasn't always a drug addict. If your job is to mete out justice, and you hold my freedom in your hands, I think it is only fair that you know more about me than just my failures."

She was obviously surprised at my assertive elocution, and her attitude of bored indifference visibly changed to one of marked interest. I assured her I was well aware of what was expected of me and what her position was, and that I had no intention of making her job difficult or giving her any reason to put me back in prison. It was the beginning of a mutually respectful and cooperative relationship.

I explained to my new roommate the rules I had to live by. The parole officer could enter our home at will, and would have access to my room and the common areas we shared, but not his private quarters. So anything that could put me back in prison had to be kept in his room. I felt my presence might be an imposition on his lifestyle, but he didn't make me feel that way, and was respectful of the guidelines and saw to it that his party friends were too. He often told me he respected what I was doing with my life now and my commitment to stay clean, but he was just not ready for that commitment himself.

Within days of my release, I got a surprise call from my older brother Norm. He wanted to know what he could do to help me. Norm and I had had a controversial relationship for many years that resulted in an occasional call and a polite distance on my rare visits home. I loved all my siblings, but lived so far away for so long I didn't really feel like a part of the family. Norm's religion prohibited the acceptance of the gay lifestyle, and I had an aversion to religion in general and resented what I felt was judgment on his part. He was going through some difficult challenges in his own life. His marriage was ending, and he was straying from two decades of stringent church life. He reached out to me in my time of need, with no preaching lectures or judgment, and I was moved and grateful for my brother's love and support. Of course my

pride denied I was in need, and I insisted I was fine without help, but he knew better and insisted I accept it.

I needed a car. Any dependable car would do. Orange County is difficult to get around in without a car,
and I had a lot to do. I found a little car at an impound
yard for $1,000, and Norm bought it for me. I promised to
pay him back as soon as I got on my feet, but he insisted
it was a gift, not a loan. He said "You have always helped
anyone you could when they needed it. It's your turn to
let someone help you."

I remember my throat closing up and fighting back
tears at his much-needed reminder that I was a good
person before I became a loser, and someone remembered it. Even better, it was a whole new beginning and
opportunity for a real relationship with my big brother. For
the ten years since, we have always been there for each
other, and I count him among my closest friends. On the
outside, we are as different as night and day. But on the
inside, where it counts, we are kindred spirits and both
indelibly linked as the sons of a woman unfailingly kind
and dependable, who encouraged and sometimes demanded those qualities in her children. I longed to see
my mother. She could make everything all right just by
being herself and my seeing her in her place in my childhood home.

The prison had changed me. I didn't realize how much
until I left it. I was humbled, but stronger. Stripped to my
core self, I realigned my priorities. I felt hideously real. Instead of seeing myself as someone who lost everything, I
started to see myself as someone with an opportunity to
start over with a clean slate at forty years old. I could reinvent myself as someone better, and do it right this time.
I reached for the boy and man who had bent without
breaking a thousand times before and set a plan of action. My priorities were first, to stay clean, and second, to
get a job.

Just my second day out, I got my first letter from Boone. He must have written and sent it before I left as nothing moves that quickly in a prison. All his thoughts and feelings about my leaving, and what our time together meant to him, were poured into a beautiful love letter. A few days later another came. They were still on lockdown. He was depressed with my leaving and having a hard time getting through it. I knew the lockdown made it worse. He couldn't stay busy with his sports and friends, and there were just too many hours to think.

I decided to do something I should have done before I left that prison. I snitched on Mario's murderer. I wasn't in prison anymore and I didn't have to observe their warped code of conduct now. Mario's life was worth nothing more than a handful of drugs to this bastard, and everyone else was paying the price to protect themselves from retaliation. I wrote an anonymous letter directly to a staff member of the building, telling everything I knew. I would not divulge my name, or how I knew, but gave them the lead they needed to investigate the murder and remove the culprit from his position of power and destruction. I told no one what I had done, but felt quite good about it. I felt even better when, a few days later, I got my first call from Boone. The lockdown was over. The killer was taken away to solitary confinement, and the rest of the men could go back to their routines.

Boone seemed amused and loaded with innuendo while telling me how the lockdown ended, and said "I wonder how they found him, Puppy?"

Equally amused, I responded with, "Hmmm, I really couldn't tell you, Boone."

It was my gift to the good guys I knew in that building and my middle finger to the ones who made it so much worse than it had to be for everyone else. I have seen the face of evil up close too many times to pretend it isn't there in the hearts of some men, and I draw courage from confronting it. It gave me the opportunity to do something good and right and to confirm my status as a free man, no longer obliged to stand aside and let cruelty go unpunished.

The things I saw in those prisons made me feel damaged. It was a stain on my soul that wouldn't wash off. I would feel haunted for years to come, and even now, a decade later, images of violence and despair flash through my mind unbidden. It was only when I emerged into the free world that the full impact of the experience came to rest on my conscience.

I needed to do something meaningful with myself, something to make me feel good about me again. Too many years of ugliness had built layers of self-hate to weigh me down. In my heart, despite my misgivings for the nature of Boone's crimes, and all the obstacles promised because of them, I knew I would wait for him and work to create a safe place for him to come home to. I knew that if getting out was this hard for me, it would be a hundredfold for him, and I could not let him go through it alone.

My friend Sue had somehow rescued a few boxes of my possessions. Some clothes, photographs, and – most valuable – the tools of my trade and client files. I didn't want to call my clients and ask them to give me yet another chance to rebuild my business. I was just too embarrassed to face them. Many had been with me nearly twenty years and seen me through a lot of madness. Being outrageous was nearly my signature, being a criminal was a completely different pill to swallow. I took a job in what I have always referred to disdainfully as a "drive-through salon." It was so far beneath any job I had even considered in my twenty years as a hairdresser, but it was probably equal to my self-esteem at the time, and I was eager to be employed and get my feet wet in the salon environment again.

I went to twelve-step meetings four and five nights a week, and spent hours in my room writing letters to Boone. I bought my clothes in thrift stores and lived frugally and quietly.

My roommate and his buddies partied just outside my door, but I was a thousand miles away from them and did not struggle with temptation to join them. I had no place else to go and no money to go there, so I accepted the situation as bearable and temporary. I had a place to live, a car, a job I hated, and a handful of people who cared about me. I guess you can call that a life, or at least a start on one.

I received a letter from my friend Chris, from Soledad, informing me that Boone had been taken to the infirmary for acute depression. I didn't expect him to take my departure as hard as he did. I imagined he was used to goodbyes, but I have learned that is one thing one never gets used to, and the older you get, the harder it gets. I worried until I heard from him a week later. He was on anti-depressants and had applied for a transfer out of Soledad. He told me he couldn't bear our cell anymore without me and thought a change of scenery might help. I encouraged him the best I could, and he did the same for me.

I was a man who prayed only in crisis and without conviction. I was always told God did not love people like me, and I sure didn't love myself. I proved that over and over. If there was ever a time to see things differently, it was now. More than once I was driven to my knees in desperate prayer in search of peace and guidance. The twelve-step groups taught me I did not need a God of religion, but a higher power of spirituality that I could turn to with the things I could not handle alone. The very act of admitting myself powerless over everything, except myself, empowered me. I was able to let it go. I couldn't change a damn thing that had happened, only what might from then on. Who I used to be, who I thought I was, and the life I used to have were just ghosts now. The past had meaning only for the experience of teaching me, and the people who knew me, how to completely fuck up a perfectly promising life.

I decided to take all the free time a penniless man has, all the free thought and emotion my circumstances provided, and all that free brain matter previously suppressed with substance abuse, and get some education.

I had to get another job, too. After two weeks of drive-through haircutting for a pittance of what I was accustomed to, my confidence returned enough for me to take another look at the help wanted ads. I found a salon in the general vicinity of my old clientele that was looking for a stylist. When I interviewed with the owner, Sue, I told her everything about myself and my past, leaving nothing out. Sue is a true Christian woman who seized an opportunity to practice what she preached by forgiving me my transgressions, respecting my candor, and hiring me.

I swallowed my pride and began calling my old clients to let them know I was back in business. I was touched with the support I received from the majority, and graceful with the few unforgiving. Most were happy I was back and eager to get back in my chair. The positive feedback kicked me into high gear, and I was on my way back in business. Word spread quickly that I was back and clean. My books began filling with appointments, and I felt that old fire of confidence ignite. The one place I was always confident and in control was behind the chair with a pair of scissors in my hand. The salon was my stage, and I was the star of the show.

I had been speaking to Boone's mother on the phone. I suspect he asked her to check on me. His parents were considering a visit from South Carolina to visit their son and expressed interest in meeting me. She seemed a very sweet but sad woman who loved her son very much. She appeared very religious, provoking my curiosity of how she reconciled those beliefs with my relationship with her son. She didn't. She chose to see me as his friend, not his lover.

It was troubling to discover that nearly all Boone's family members – his parents, brother, ex-wife and daughters – did not speak or associate with each other or with him. As time went on, I became tangled in a family web that I have only now extricated myself to a point of manageability.

Though my letters, phone calls and plans for the future with Boone were a daily part of my life, I was able to set them apart from focusing on what I needed to do for myself. Yet I never quite lost the feeling that I was doing it all for him, and that he was my reason to go on. If I let him go, my reason for living would go with him.

The knowledge of his past, and the complications that came with it, weighed heavily on my mind, but I told myself I had four years to sort it out, one day at a time. Boone wrote to me every day. His devotion was unwavering. I wondered would he find another man to fill my place in his life and in his cell, but he always reassured me he had no interest in replacing me. He said if I could wait four years for him, he could do the same for me. A part of me hoped he wouldn't.

I knew my friends in the free world didn't approve of my continued attachment to a man in prison and thought I should move on and leave him behind. They couldn't possibly understand the bond between us. Even I didn't really understand it. I understand that love doesn't make a damn bit of sense sometimes.

The next year was a whirlwind of activity for me. Work, meetings, and establishing myself as a productive member of society filled most of my time. With what was left I wrote letters to Boone and immersed myself in books. There were things I needed to know. The man I was in love with was a convicted rapist. There were multiple victims and they were all young girls. He was married with children when he committed these crimes, and had a successful career in the Navy. By all accounts, he was a good husband, father and coworker. It made no sense to me, and that he had now committed himself to a gay relationship made less. I needed to find some answers to the many questions plaguing me or I would never be able to keep my promise to stand by him with confidence and security. Was he mentally ill? Was he a pedophile? Was his homosexuality just a product of long-term incarceration? Would I ever be able to trust him? Was he cured of the problems that led to his crimes?

I knew he was uncomfortable with my inquiries and I feared he only told me what I wanted to hear. I bought every book I could find on the subject and searched their pages for comfort, understanding, and peace of mind. I used the internet to study laws governing sex offenders and mental health sites concerning evaluations and treatments. As I educated myself, it helped to allay my fears somewhat, but far from entirely. Knowledge is power, but all the knowledge in the world can't give you guarantees. All I knew was, the longer I was away from him, the more I missed his companionship.

Drug and prison reform became passions for me. My experiences had made me more conscious of the masses of people out there who had no voice and were not as capable as I in successfully overcoming their demons and obstacles. I joined groups of like-minded others who felt California's prison system had grown wildly out of control and was dismally unsuccessful at rehabilitation, and who were working for change. I volunteered time, energy, and personal experience to speak at colleges, twelve-step groups, and public forums, sharing my story and an insider's view of life as a drug addict and a convict.

Time was flying by. I was already wondering how much longer I could stand my living conditions. My roommate's drug problem was not getting any better, and I was getting increasingly uncomfortable living among drug users. He and his friends were becoming less respectful of my boundaries, but I didn't feel I could complain to him in his own home, and he was there for me when I was destitute. I just stayed away as much as possible.

Boone's parents decided to come to California to visit him and to meet me. They hadn't seen their son in five years. Their plan was to stay a month in California. I was apprehensive to say the least, but curious to know more about him and his background. Perhaps I would find some answers through them.

A few days before their arrival I received a call from a girl claiming to be Boone's daughter Maggie.

I was completely blindsided by this turn of events. He had had no contact with his daughters since going to prison, and Maggie was barely two years old when he was taken away. When her mother remarried, she coerced Boone into allowing her new husband to adopt the girls and subsequently forbade him any further contact. He agreed it was best for them to be adopted but told me he never lost hope that someday he would see them again. He seemed to truly love his five years of fatherhood before he destroyed it all, and often told me bittersweet stories of his little girls.

Maggie told me Boone's parents gave her my number as a means to contact him.

Her mother and stepfather had divorced, and she was eighteen years old. She had spent her short life wondering about her father and was determined to meet him. The second shock came when she told me she was already in California and less than an hour away from me. She had taken her mother's car, talked some boy into coming with her, and had driven across the country from

Florida. She refused to go back until she had met her father. I was impressed by her guts and determination and
agreed to do anything I could to make it happen. I invited her to come see me. As far as I knew she thought
me only a friend to her father and nothing more. I was
correct in my assumption that her grandparents did not
offer her any details.

Boone and I had worked out a call schedule and he
was due to call that evening. I was excited to be a part of
the reunion and to give him something of such immense
value. I wasn't sure how I would handle the nature of our
relationship should the subject arise, and decided I would
just have to feel my way through it. I was surprisingly nervous awaiting her arrival.

When I saw Maggie for the first time, I was amazed at
the resemblance to her father. There could be no question as to paternity with this girl. She was a mirror image
of Boone.

Her friend was a quiet and polite young man. His name
escapes me now. He chatted with my roommate while
Maggie and I got to know each other. When I told her
that her father would be calling later and she could talk
to him, she was terrified and excited at the same time.
She said, "What will I say? I've waited my whole life for
this. Do you think he even wants to talk to me?"

It broke my heart to see this young girl so nervous to
talk to her own father and to wonder if he even wanted
to talk to her. I did my best to reassure her that he had
never forgotten his girls and it was circumstances, not desire, that kept him from them. As we talked, I told her of
the man I knew and lived with and she told me of the
monster she had only heard about in the rare moments
he was mentioned at all. It was impossible for me to hide
my feelings for him and I didn't try. She was not asking but
making a statement when she said, "You and my father
are more than friends, aren't you?"

I never expected to be put in the position to tell one of his daughters of his private affairs, but I also knew he would never expect me to lie either.

She saw my discomfort and quickly put me at ease. She said, "It's okay. I'm glad he has someone to love him. I always thought he must be so lonely and felt bad for him. My sisters and I talked about him and imagined what he was like, what he looked like, and what we would say if we ever saw him. I never really thought about him having a boyfriend in prison, but it makes sense after all that time that he would. I have lots of gay friends, and it doesn't bother me at all."

I liked her immediately.

Her family was furious with her for this trek across the country to meet her father, but she felt it was something she had to do. They spent sixteen years hating him, and felt betrayed that Maggie had any interest in him at all. They had loved, trusted and accepted him into their family, and he had devastated them all with his shocking crimes.

Maggie shared with me the years of growing up with an abusive stepfather, and I knew Boone would be very sad to know he had given up his girls to a man who did not give them the happy life he envisioned when he signed them away. She wanted a father, and I wanted to give her one. My own father never cared about me and I understood the loss. And I wanted to give Boone back his child.

Not long ago I was accused of selfish motives when I orchestrated reconciliations with the people of Boone's past, and it's possible there is some truth to that. In some way, I suppose, I wanted to be a hero to all of them. I wanted something nice to come out of so much pain and ugliness. I wanted to be the good person who fixed something broken. I suppose I wanted to be recognized for all I had done and was willing to do because I loved him.

Another of his daughters accused me of attempting to bind him to me by establishing relationships with them. I felt that unfair as each of them sought me out and initiated contact. I never imagined I would have contact with them before he did. As I delved deeper into the still raw and bloody wounds of his past, I came to regret forming relationships with most of the people from his past.

But I had no regrets that night. That night, when Boone called, I felt I was part of something heart-wrenchingly beautiful, and I hoped it was the beginning of the healing of old and great wounds that shredded a family for nearly two decades. But I was wrong. You can heal a wound, but you can't remove the scar, and some things can't be fixed.

When the phone rang and the operator said I had a collect call from a California state prison, I nodded to Maggie. She said, "I am so nervous! I thought this day would never come."

Prison calls are limited to fifteen minutes, so I wasted no time in launching into the day's events. "Boone, you are never going to believe who is sitting here with me waiting to talk to you."

I went straight into the story of how a young woman claiming to be his daughter Maggie contacted me wanting to meet her father, and she was at that very moment in the room with me waiting to talk to him. He was silent while I talked, but when he spoke it was in a voice choked with emotion and disbelief. He said, "Puppy, I feel like I'm in a dream. This can't really be happening. How could this be real? I'm waiting for the punch line of a cruel joke."

I said, "It's no joke and no dream, Honey. I'm going to hand the phone to her now. She's been waiting a long time to talk to you."

I handed Maggie the phone and stepped away. I should have left the room, but I was mesmerized by the unfolding drama and sat silently weeping as I listened to a young girl talking to her long-lost Daddy for the first time.

Of course, she wanted to see him in the flesh, and I knew there would be obstacles to overcome before that could happen. One cannot simply show up at a prison and expect visitation.

She handed me the phone after tearful goodbyes, and I reassured him I would do my best to help her visit him. He was delirious with joy, and I was happy to have been a part of it. We planned our next call before being abruptly disconnected.

I had well over two years to go before I could apply to visit, if I had to complete my three-year parole. I knew it usually took at least thirty days to get approved for visits, but I also knew there were exceptions in emergencies and special conditions. I felt this warranted special consideration, and promptly started making calls to people I knew in the system. Boone's parents would arrive in a few days, and I hoped for Maggie to visit along with them.

My life was already slightly tilted with Maggie's unexpected arrival, and it would be even more so when his parents arrived. They had not seen their granddaughter in many years either.

Maggie and I hit it off immediately, and remain close to this day. She is a strong, determined young woman, with a soft and loyal heart. Slightly tomboyish, but pretty, she is unreasonably insecure about her looks. So I set out to get her approved to meet her father and to use my professional skills to make her look and feel pretty for the occasion. We swapped stories of our lives, our families, our dreams and our losses. She told me about her sisters, and what it was like growing up with a father in prison and the shameful knowledge of why he was there, and the nagging curiosity and desire to meet him. She claimed her two sisters had no such desire. To a lesser extent, I had a father I was very much ashamed of and wished to be accepted and loved by, but I had let go of those dreams and hers were just beginning. Maggie and I understood each other.

Two days later we picked her grandparents up at the airport.

Prior to meeting Boone's parents, I had absolutely no exposure to Southerners or their culture. I thought these two characters straight out of a Tennessee Williams' play, he the dominant, self-important patriarch, and she the demure, fragile southern belle. They were out of their element in Southern California, and I was at a complete loss as to what to do with this sudden invasion of strangers in my life. Boone and I were both so isolated from our families, and I did not expect to have to deal with them without him to guide and protect me. They were nice to me, though I knew from the beginning that his father's personality promised imminent challenges.

They were happy to see their granddaughter, but Maggie seemed a bit uncomfortable. It was much later I learned the history of conflict that led to estrangement from Boone's children and former wife.

I was impressed by his mother's delicate beauty and sweet nature. By contrast, his father was a hulking man, though you could see he was once handsome. He had an abrasive habit of dominating every conversation and saying the wrong thing at the wrong time. They seemed a poorly matched couple to me at the time. Later I learned they were not at all supportive of their son's sudden declaration of love for another man, and I wondered why they bothered to meet me at all. I suppose they believed I was simply a result of his long-term incarceration, as many did, and I came to wonder myself, though Boone continually reassured me otherwise. I've wondered if they were just happy to have another person they could share the secrets of their son with. Later, I learned they had told no one the truth of their son's whereabouts or shameful past. It's possible they were simply curious.

Within a few days, I managed to get Maggie approved to visit. Boone's parents stayed at a nearby motel, and Maggie and her friend stayed with them. They planned a weekend trip to make the five-hour drive to Soledad and, though I was not allowed to visit, I went along and spent the entire day in a motel room feeling left out and resentful. I was happy for Boone but sorry for myself. I imagined Boone overwhelmed with emotion at the sight of his daughter for the first time since she was two years old, and I was eager to hear all the details when they returned. She was surprised her father was not the brute she had imagined, but a soft-spoken, well-mannered, handsome man. I was pleased it all seemed to go well. Her family was pressuring her to come home, and I couldn't offer her a place to stay. She had done what she set out to do and connected with her father. They began and maintained a relationship through the mail until his release.

The time raced by and Boone's parents and daughter returned to the Southeast, and I returned to my routine of work, twelve-step meetings, and friends.

After a year of living in a drug-infested environment, I was ready to move on. I wasn't tempted to get loaded. It just depressed me to be in such close proximity to that lifestyle, and I feared my roommate would be careless and get me in trouble with my parole officer.

There was an adorable little gingerbread-style cottage for rent close to my job and within my budget. The landlords were an elderly couple, both retired police officers. The cottage was secluded behind their home with a shared yard and was once the home of his mother. I loved that little house, and I loved them. My good friend Susie lived there only a short time before a brain aneurysm killed her at forty-four years old. We were not friends a long time, but we grew close quickly. She worked part-time as a receptionist in the salon I worked in, and we spent a lot of time together. Susie was a good person and fun to be with. She had an undependable car, and I often picked her up for work in the mornings.

One morning, she complained of an excruciating headache and told me she could not work that day. The following day she felt better, and I picked her up for work. On our drive she told me about this unusual headache that almost drove her to call an ambulance. She looked worn out but was her usual cheery self. She had a date that night, and pleaded with me to straighten her unruly hair for the date. I squeezed her in between two afternoon appointments, and we chattered and laughed while I worked. When I finished, she stood, took several steps away from the chair and crumpled to the floor. I thought she had either tripped and fallen or fainted. When she didn't move, I rushed to her and knelt at her side. When I saw her face, I knew something was horribly wrong, and I screamed for someone to call an ambulance. Her face was purple and grossly disfigured with swelling. Her tongue protruded and her lungs rattled in aspiration. I noticed she had lost control of her bladder and thought how embarrassed she would be when she realized she had wet her pants in public. I thought she was having some type of seizure, but it wasn't subsiding. I sat on the floor and placed her head in my lap and stroked her hair, softly encouraging her to hang on, help was on the way.

I followed the ambulance to the hospital, her purse and shoes with me, thinking she would need those to come home, but she was pronounced brain dead from a massive hemorrhage when I got there. I gave the hospital all the information I could on her next of kin.

It was surreal to watch someone go from very much

alive to dead within minutes without an in-between. I had seen countless young people die in the '80s and '90s, but it was a process, and usually a long one. Susie and I saw each other nearly every day. We talked about our dreams and futures. We were only two years apart in age. And then she was just gone without warning, a life wiped out by a simple bubble in her head. It was so unreasonable. I was shocked and rattled to my core at this cruel display of life's fragility and unfairness. The image of her dying with her head on my lap is one I have been unable to completely erase, but I took great solace in the doctors' assurance that her death was painless and she never saw it coming. Perhaps it was not such a bad way to go.

I cleaned out the little cottage and made it my own. It was the first time in about five years that I had a place of my own. It had a small yard for me to grow flowers. It was quiet and private and loaded with cottage charm. I painted and decorated and planted flowers and made it mine. My landlords were thrilled with the transformation and thrilled to have a tenant who took pride in his home. They were kind and supportive when I shared my past with them. I have never kept my past a secret. I don't think it's fair to keep secrets from the people in your life who could be affected adversely. Secrets breed shame, and shame is destructive to self-esteem. Secrets also breed mistrust, and it is important to me to be trusted by the people with whom I engage.

I had a good job and my own little place in the world again. I was living a life I could be proud of.

It was time to go home and see my mother. I hadn't seen her in six years. In that six years she had fought and won two battles with cancer, and now she was having more problems with her health. I had not seen my niece Jenny since before she emerged from the coma, but we spoke often on the phone. She could speak with difficulty, and she had limited use of one hand, but could do little else from the confines of her wheelchair. I was not at all prepared for what I would feel when I saw each of them.

Parole allowed me to leave the state for a three-leg trip to South Carolina to visit Boone's parents and on to Maine for a week with my family before reporting back to California in ten days.

Boone's parents were gracious hosts and showed me around the quaint little Southern town he was raised in. I left having learned more about where he came from, but not much more about who he was. I don't believe his parents knew much more about him than anyone else, and it is not the Southern way to display painful or private affairs. I also left believing it would be a cold day in hell before I would ever live in Georgetown, South Carolina.

I was learning to love being free again. The fear left me, and my obsession to destroy myself with substance abuse was lifted. I felt enthusiastic, confident, and hopeful. I had wasted a lot of precious time heading in the wrong direction and I had the unfamiliar but delightful feeling I was heading in the right one. I felt I was finally evolving into a man of good character through the age-old methods of perseverance and hardship. My heart was not the worse for wear. It was intact and passionate, still vulnerable and naive at times, and ready to face the painful realities and ravages of time, long hidden behind the gauzy veil of narcotics.

Throughout the years, every time I came home, my mother waited on the front porch to be the first to greet me. She never failed to have a smile as wide as the line of old maple trees along the front of my childhood home. When she smiled like that, I could not remember a single bad moment in my childhood. I saw the only thing I ever asked of her since I was a boy: that she see me, accept me, and love me for who I am. I saw all that in her smile and felt it in her embrace. Finally, at forty years old, I had come home.

What I saw next clutched my heart with fear. She was old. It was my grandmother Fannie standing on that front porch twenty-five years ago. She stood with one hand shielding her eyes from the sun and the other resting on her lower back. The sun glinted off the frames of her glasses and the silver white of her hair. She laughed and waved but did not run down the stairs of the porch to greet me as she always had. She steadied herself against the porch rail as if she were frail. Her face was cut with deep lines, and her spine curved forward.

It was only six years. How did she get so old in just six years? This was not the mother I left when I disappeared from her world. I felt panic and shame that I didn't know or understand this was happening to my mother, while I was acting the fool and only thinking of myself. And the last time I saw her I was so drugged out of reality that I let her think I had AIDS! We both cried our hearts out at what we imagined the other had been through.

I said, "I'm so sorry, Ma. I'm so sorry. You must be so ashamed of me and my foolishness."

She grabbed my hand and pulled me to the porch swing. I curled up beside her and made myself small. I rested my head against her chest and she stroked my head just the way she did when I was a little boy, and said, "Now you just stop that right now. You got nuthin' to be ashamed of. You are a good boy and you always have been. I'm proud of you. You made your mistakes just like everybody else, and you just get right back up and keep fightin'. You're tough, just like your ole Ma."

She didn't look so tough anymore. This woman was worn down, quieter.

She took my hand and said "Well, Honey, I may as well tell ya. They told me I have the old timer's disease. My brain ain't workin' right no more."

So that was it: diagnosed with Alzheimer's disease at only sixty-five. Her father was even younger when he began to suffer dementia, so it was easy to imagine she inherited it. I recall her saying she sure hoped she didn't end up like her Daddy. Yet something didn't fit in the picture for me, and from the beginning I never believed she had Alzheimer's disease. Within a short time my siblings began to arrive, and Ma's little house filled with the boisterous chatter of our clan.

Something had happened in the years I was away. Perhaps it was my fall from grace, perhaps it was just the passage of time. We were all grown now and either in or approaching middle age. All my siblings were parents and some grandparents. There were small children vying for my attention, and I had no idea who they belonged to. There were tiny babies to cuddle and admire their beauty. I felt a part of it all for the first time in my life. The prodigal son had returned once more. But this time not just as a visitor, but as a full-fledged member of the ever-expanding private club of my family. All the old hurt fell away like dropping a cloak of thorns. They welcomed me back to the fold, not as the exotic traveler dropping in for a visit, but as one of them. I was finally ready to accept my place among them.

And there she was in the middle of it all, our mother, Lottie Jane, queen of the country bumpkins, with a smile of satisfaction and pride, watching her life's work and their offspring laughing and loving each other, and smothering her with only a fraction of what we all knew she deserved, and she was happy. That might very well be the first time in my life I understood what real success is, watching my mother watching us. We were her purpose, and she felt she had done a good job. I understood her now, and I admired her beyond anyone else in the world.

The last to arrive was my beloved Tina and Jenny.

Ma tried, but it would have been impossible for anyone to prepare me for Jen's condition. When Tina wheeled in my beautiful little princess, almost twenty-two years old now, she looked up at me with those huge blue eyes from another world, and I was wracked with anguish. It seemed she represented the past ten years of my life. Her accident, Robert's death, Susie's death, drug addiction and prison, and some more tragic news that my sweet little godson Jaime was a drug addict doing eight years in an Arizona prison. It all seemed so unfair, so wrong. I couldn't hold back my tears as I bent to embrace her in that awful chair. She worried she had somehow upset me, and I quickly reassured her I was just overcome to see her. The little girl I loved so much from the day she was born was gone. The damage to her brain had changed her completely. All the hope and promise in watching that pretty little girl grow into a beautiful woman was gone, too.

Her short-term memory destroyed, she repeated herself over and over. The filtering system in our brain that recognizes right from wrong was also destroyed. Her temperament was unpredictable. She could swing from a sweet young lady to a vicious and vulgar child without warning or reason. Six years had passed, and though she had come a long way from the girl who could not hold up her head or breathe on her own, it was evident this was about as good as it would get, and she would never have a normal life again.

After overhearing my mother discussing her recent diagnoses, she comforted my mother with the comment, "It's okay, Grammie, you're not alone. I have a fucked-up brain, too."

Jen could lighten a mood with her unfiltered honesty, along with embarrassing the hell out of everyone. We had one of those moments during a visit to a crowded Chinese restaurant. Ten of us sat at a round table eating and chatting when, for no apparent reason other than the thought popped into her mind, Jen shouted at my mother, "Grammie, do you still give Grampa blow jobs?"

The entire restaurant went silent, and my mortified mother burst into tears. Tina quickly admonished Jen, and it was evident she had absolutely no idea she was being inappropriate. I started to giggle at the look on Ma's face and everyone else was suppressing grins. So I looked at my mother and said, "Well, aren't you going to answer her?"

That broke the tension and we all started laughing. Ma looked at me and said, "No, I will not, and it's nobody's goddamned business what I do anyway!"

Now that was the mother I knew! My mother never backed down from a rousing conversation, and she appreciated the ridiculous and laughed the loudest.

People were generally either uncomfortable or compassionate in Jen's presence, and she was thankfully oblivious to most stares. Later she became more aware of people's reactions to her, and was particularly annoyed if she was spoken to like a child. She would get straight to the point and say, "I'm not fucking retarded, you know. I have a head injury, and it's not the same thing."

Secretly, I enjoyed the discomfort of the rude and ignorant. I had more than my share of those types in my own life but never had the luxury of a head injury as an excuse to always say what I was thinking.

A few days later, Tina and I pushed Jen down a sidewalk window shopping. A girl lingered on the sidewalk near us. She glanced at Jen distastefully, and seemed annoyed the wheelchair was blocking her path. She wore size eight cut-off jean shorts on her size twelve body, a halter top that revealed most of her pendulous sagging breasts, and topped it off with a mass of dry, home-dyed, canary yellow hair with a good two inches of black roots. It has never ceased to amaze me what some people think is attractive and are willing to subject the public to, but in some cases, judging a book by its cover is hard to avoid.

Very sweetly, Jenny said to her, "Hello. Do you want to know something?"

Again I saw that fleeting look of distaste pass over her doughy face as she leaned over and said, "Sure."

As innocent as any small child, Jen said, "You shouldn't wear that outfit. It makes you look like a whore."

Tina immediately moved to apologize and make excuses for Jen, but the girl stomped away, cursing us loudly.

Jen realized she had said something wrong and grew distressed. I thought it was funny as hell and the absolute truth. I told her, "Don't worry about it, Honey. She did look like a whore, and a cheap one at that."

It was time for me to go back to California. Though it had been a painful visit in many ways, it was the best I'd ever had up to that point, and it made me happy and stronger and determined to go home as often as possible. Time was not on my mother's side anymore, and I wanted as much of her as I could get in the time we had left. I hated to leave her. Everett did his best to look after her, but he was used to being the one taken care of, and was sometimes impatient with her infirmities. I knew my sisters would help take care of her, but I couldn't help but feel guilty that I was always leaving to go live my life when she had given us all of hers. I never felt like I did my share.

We said goodbye on the front porch. I told her I loved her, and if she needed me for anything I would be on the first plane back. She held my face in her hands and said, "When you were a little boy, you stayed so close to me all the time, and now you are always the farthest away. I just hope I know who you are when I see you again." She kissed me all over my face, and I sniffled all the way to the airport.

My plane rides back to California were always spent in quiet reflection. I replayed the sweetest moments of my visit home during my journey to the other side of the country. I thought of my siblings and their lives. Of my mother and stepfather, and the father I never saw. I always wondered how come I was the one who lived outside their world. What twist of fate sent me so far away and kept them all there?

As I approached the bright lights of the big city, I was comforted with the knowledge that they were all still there, somewhat battle-scarred, too, in their own ways, but all still standing like those big old maple trees in front of our house.

Princess Jenny

Oh my little princess, I wonder of your thoughts
I weep rivers for your lonely life
in the tower where you're caught.

Oh my lovely lady, we must wield a sword to fight
the dragons that come to chase you
in the terror of the night.

Oh my broken beauty, in the prison of your chair
alas, I am no shining knight
that rescues maidens fair

I am but a humble servant, knelt before your throne of steel
who is chased by dragons also,
and understand the way you feel.

E.M.

Chapter Eleven
Hollow

The next year passed quickly. I hardly remember it except for the steady climb upward, and the gathering of all the best people from my past back into my life.

I completed my second year of parole without incident and was released a year early for exemplary conduct. Now I was really free. No more pissing in a cup in front of a stranger. No more asking permission to leave town. And no one could enter my home without an invitation. I could now apply for visits to Boone.

Boone had transferred out of Soledad to Avenal State Prison. Avenal was a bit closer but still almost five hours away.

Prior to Soledad, he had worked in Prison Industries Mill and Cabinet vocation. As his release date grew closer, he wanted to be better prepared for the job market, so he enrolled in a vocational training program for Heating, Ventilation and Air Conditioning, and got his certification before returning to Mill and Cabinet to do what he loved. He started going to church and enrolled in a Life Skills class. I was proud of him, and encouraged that he was taking advantage of what little opportunities the prison offered to better him for the outside world. The majority of the men I met in prison did nothing to better themselves while incarcerated, and the system didn't force them to.

I decided to go back to school. I was a high school dropout. Other than beauty school, I had never expanded my formal education. I was insecure about my lack of formal education, even though it had never stood in the way of anything I wanted to do. I wasn't interested in a degree or changing careers, I just wanted to set some new goals and challenge myself. All of the essentials in my life were secured, and free time on my hands had always proven unhealthy for me. Boredom is the enemy of the addict personality.

My application to visit Boone was denied.

I had a feeling the department of corrections was not going to make it easy on me, but they underestimated my tenacity. They had no legal or justifiable reason to deny me visits. I had paid my debt to the law and was supposed to be an equal member of society again, and I expected and demanded to be treated as such. I read in detail every rule and law governing visiting procedures and found none justifying their denial. They attempted to use my prior criminal history, citing me as a threat to security, and I counterattacked with dozens of examples of heterosexual couples in identical situations who had not been denied visitation. Therefore my only conclusion was to assume we were being treated differently because we were a same-sex couple, and I threatened the state with a lawsuit based on discrimination.

The California Department of Corrections is an arrogant and powerful entity. They are accustomed to dealing with the least educated, least powerful members of the public: those who do not have the means or the confidence to oppose or challenge them. I had both, and over the next few months I used every resource at my disposal to challenge their decision until they capitulated and reversed it. It was no small feat to win a battle with the CDC, and I took enormous satisfaction in my victory. I'd spent too long under the rule of people who did not give a damn about me, and I refused to be bullied or disenfranchised anymore. I was a free man, and I demanded to be treated like one.

The friends and families of inmates are treated only a fraction better than the inmates, and it seems the officers go to great lengths to make visitation as difficult and unpleasant as possible. Their judgments are obvious, with thinly concealed contempt, and their pettiness is exasperating. I knew I would be closely observed, and I rose above their pettiness with a little imperious contempt of my own. I dressed elegantly, I spoke to them concisely and only when necessary, and I made it a point to appear as bored and dismissive as they did, so that they might know what it feels like to be treated like pestilence.

I was nervous and excited to see Boone again. I needed to look in his eyes and see if all those dreams and promises were still alive there. I needed to see if the butterflies would still flutter in my stomach at the sight of him. I wondered if I would feel different after two-and-a-half years apart, after successfully building a life in the free world.

I wish I had felt nothing. I wish it was all gone when I saw him again. It would have made life so much easier if I could have walked away. But it was all still there, in his eyes and in my heart. The moment I saw him enter the visiting room, I knew it wasn't over. We were just beginning a new phase of our relationship, halfway between prison and the free world. Sitting across a table from him, prohibited from touching, was torture, but better than not seeing him at all. I was allowed to visit Saturdays and Sundays. I made the trip at least once a month and often twice. We both felt good about what we were doing with ourselves, and confirmed our commitment to each other.

In less than two years he would be free, and there was much to do before then.

Every minute not sleeping, I was on the move. Work, meetings, speaking engagements for prison and drug reform, writing and visiting Boone, tending to my little house and garden, classes and studying, I honestly do not know how I did it all and enjoyed it too. It was great. It was life happening. I was not slipping back, and I was not standing still. I was moving forward.

As Boone's release grew closer, it was only going to get more challenging. The social and political atmosphere for sex offenders was getting increasingly hostile, and I needed to put some heavy thought to what lay ahead for us. Abandoning him was always an option, but not one I seriously considered. His crimes were so far in the past and he gave me many opportunities to opt out of the relationship, as I did him, but I couldn't let him go. He needed me, and I needed to be needed.

In the back of my mind always lived the question of whether he was really gay or just the product of two decades in an all-male world. He had been married, which in itself is not terribly unusual for men in our age group, but more perplexing to me was his crime of sexual assault against females. Did he hate women? Is he bisexual? Bisexuality remains somewhat of a mystery to me. I'm about as gay as it gets.

When I shared my fears with him, he unfailingly reassured me he was comfortable and content in a gay relationship, and I was needlessly harassing myself with doubting his commitment or devotion.

When you love a convicted sex offender you must move through, and live in, a world that hates them.

They have partners and wives, parents and children, and those loved ones must bear it in silence while people openly express hate and disgust for someone you love.

Your shame doubles, first for that loved one's crimes, and second for not defending them.

But how does one defend the indefensible? One doesn't.

We can't help who we love. I learned to live with my choice by never defending the crime but always defending the love and the human being I knew and believed would never harm anyone again.

Each time a released offender committed a new crime, he brought the hammer down harder on all the rest. The media and the politicians love a good horror story to exploit for their viewers and voters. Each time a sex offender made the national news, the lawmakers had to rush to create a newer and harsher law to placate the voters, knowing it wouldn't change a thing.

People have been killing, maiming, raping and robbing each other since Cain slew Abel, and we can execute or incarcerate at every opportunity, and there will always be another being born or bred to take his place. If a society cannot address and treat the cause of the problem, it will never overcome it, and, though prisons are necessary, I see them as a Band-Aid on a brain tumor; particularly for sex offenders.

A relatively new law came to my attention that was reasonable in theory but, like many laws, had the potential of manipulating justice detrimentally. Unfortunately, unlike other laws, new laws governing sex offenders were grandfathered to affect those who had already been sentenced or done their time. I felt those laws unfair, particularly for offenders who plea-bargained for their sentences. When the court offers a confirmed punishment for a confessed crime, it cannot change or give additional punishment once sentencing is passed. Sex offender laws do in fact continue to increase punishment for those already sentenced, and often released, even though they have committed no new crime. Essentially the courts

have reneged on their bargain, and under most circumstances the new laws would not survive the challenge of
protection against double jeopardy. The Supreme Court
has suspended that protection with sex offenders.

Until I met Boone, I knew very little and cared even less
about sex offenders or whether they were fairly treated. I
was about to learn far more than I ever wanted to.

A new law passed giving the states the power to evaluate paroling sex offenders with a sexually violent predator status to determine if they remained a menace to
society. If so determined, rather than be released upon
completion of their sentence, the state could remand
them to a state mental health care facility for an indeter-
minate length of time. This most likely translates to forever.
I feel the law is unreasonable in some aspects and not in
others.

My most impassioned argument asks the states why
these offenders must wait until their sentence is completed before they are considered for mental health evaluation and treatment. To keep a man caged for years
on end, believing he will be set free after completing a
determined sentence and failing to assess, recognize, or
treat any potential mental illness, only to pull the rug out
from under him six months before his release date, con-
stitutes not only cruel and unusual punishment but a blatant manipulation of sentencing laws. Though the state is
required to hire independent assessors in addition to their
own, one wonders how independent someone can be
from the organization paying for their services.

After serving twenty years, Boone was informed of his
impending psychological evaluations less than six months
before his release date. In the twenty years prior he was
never given a psychological evaluation and never offered or encouraged therapy for the issues that led to his
crimes. I found that a blatant disregard for the welfare of
the inmate and the safety of society.

He was absolutely sure they would find a way to block his release and keep him forever. His hope, along with our plans and dreams, began to disintegrate. I felt so scared of possibly having to let go of him, and angry at all I waited and worked for being threatened in the last stretch of the race. I immediately hit the books, internet, and phone, to find out as much as I could about this law and how it could affect us.

There was already the issue of where we would live. The state required a parolee returned to the county of their conviction. Boone was in northern California at the time of conviction. They would dump him in the street of the community in which he had committed his crimes, after twenty years in prison, without any means of survival or support, and a yoke of new laws that would make it nearly impossible to build a new life if they let him out at all. I couldn't let that happen to him.

They wouldn't let him transfer to live with me. Parolees can only transfer out of their county or state to a spouse or immediate family member, and they must be accepted by the county or state requested. No one wants someone else's parolees added to their case load, especially not a sex offender. Our prospects were bleak.

I would have to move. I would have to leave the life I'd rebuilt and build another one if I wanted to be with him. It wasn't an easy choice but I made it over time and with much thought. I had saved a lot of money living beneath my taste level and means, and this was why I did it. I would do whatever I had to do and live wherever necessary to follow my heart, and he was my heart. Every visit we had was another link in the chain that bound me to him. Every love letter he wrote me I read again and again, looking for clues that indicated I was doing the wrong thing, or validation that I was doing what was right. I wondered aloud to him if we could transcend the troubles and time to grow old together. I wondered if he only loved me because I was all he had. I warned him that life in the free world had thirty-one flavors, and I was only one. I begged him to set me free, if he had any doubts at all that he could be in it for the long run ahead of us. To all of my wondering, he promised me his love and devotion for eternity, and I believed him.

The only solution left was to get him transferred to his hometown in South Carolina. His parents were there, we could find a place to live away from other people who might feel threatened by his past, and I would have to move to one of the last places on earth I wanted to live and start over one more time.

But he would be safe there. He would never be safe in California and could not survive on his own anywhere. He thought he could, but he was so out of touch with what the world was like for someone like him, and it was only getting worse.

Outside of work, my life was consumed with securing Boone's freedom and safety. I contacted all the key people in both states, and, with his mother's help on the east coast, got all the wheels turning for his transfer to South Carolina.

In my persistent study of the laws, I found Boone did not meet the stringent criteria to designate him a sexually violent predator, and the state could not cite the law to block his release. I assumed they knew this and didn't understand why they continued their evaluations, unless they planned to circumvent the law, or were simply going through the motions to protect themselves, in the event he proved to be a continued menace to society and they would be held accountable.

Regardless, Boone was convinced his parole would be blocked somehow, and I had to behave and prepare as if it wouldn't. I had to be ready the day he walked out those gates.

I relied on his mother to work with the parole department in South Carolina. I believe his father had to be coerced into helping. I figured out rather soon that his father did what he had to do to placate his mother. He didn't want his life interrupted, especially by his convict son and his gay lover, and he and Boone had always had a volatile relationship. He maintained the illusion that he had a reputation that would be damaged by his son's past being made public, and they belonged to a notoriously anti-gay church. I was horrified to learn they belonged to the very diocese that had led a national debate and split of the Episcopalian church over the ordination of an openly gay bishop in New England. I certainly sympathized with his parents in some ways, but resented them in others. Recently his mother, in reference to this book, said to me, "I hope you'll be nice."

After giving her statement some thought, I concluded you can be nice or you can be truthful, but sometimes you can't be both.

From what I knew of his youth, his father was not so different from my own. Booze, women, physical and emotional abuse blighted Boone's childhood. As do many of his generation, his father carried the same arrogant refusal to acknowledge wrongdoing, and the need to have absolute control of everyone around him, as my father did. It was all there. He was my father with a southern accent.

I had no intention of leaving California immediately upon Boone's release. I needed the income, and needed to have him in a safe and secure place before I could leave the security I established since my own release. I needed to see that he could make the transition, live by the conditions imposed on him and, most of all, to see what the outside world had to offer and still choose to be with me.

In the eleventh hour, his transfer was approved. We were all amazed South Carolina was willing to accept him. I honestly didn't think it was going to happen at that point, and, when it did, I was seized with terror at the prospect of moving and starting over again.

A week before his release, for reasons no one cared to explain, they put him in solitary confinement.

He was not allowed to use the phone and had no idea his transfer was approved or what was happening on the outside concerning his release. I know it was torture for him, and I thought it was a cruel thing to do to a man in the last week of a twenty-year-and-four-month sentence.

I purchased tickets for both of us to fly to South Carolina the day of his release. My old friend Crystal flew to Northern California with me the night before so I could be there to greet him as promised. I hardly got a wink of sleep that night, and neither did he. I was disappointed in the morning when parole would not let me go to the prison and be there to see him walk out those gates. They made me wait at the parole office, while an agent picked him up. When he walked into the parole office and I saw him for the first time in the free world, I was overcome with a myriad of conflicting and powerful emotions. Relief, joy, triumph, love, and fear are the ones I can find words for.

I could see in his face that stress overwhelmed any joy he might have had at the experience of leaving prison after twenty years. He was thinner than I had ever seen him, his face lined with worry.

Who could blame him? Kept isolated for the last week with no means of communicating with the outside, deprived of even the most meager of his possessions, and starved to the point where he grabbed discarded food from garbage cans on the way to the shower, Avenal State Prison made it a point to make the last week of his stay one of the worst of his entire incarceration.

The parole agent who picked him up was a very

nice man, and they were not always easy to find in his profession. He worked tirelessly on our behalf for months to get everything arranged for Boone's release and transfer. I'm sure he was more than happy to remove Boone from his case load and responsibility. A high-control sex offender's supervision is a lot of responsibility for an agent, and if something goes wrong, has the potential for the sort of negative publicity the department abhors.

Our first task was the Department of Motor Vehicles. Boone needed an identification card to board a plane. The agent called ahead to explain our situation, and we were in and out of there in record time, identification card in hand.

We killed some time in a Chinese restaurant. Just the simple act of choosing from a menu was so foreign to Boone, he was paralyzed with indecision. I ordered for him and watched him eat like a man starving. During the meal he was fascinated by all the people around us, but not nearly as much as by my cell phone. He had never seen one. Even the agent was moved, watching a man imprisoned over twenty years look at the world for the first time. He confessed he had never before met anyone who had done that much consecutive time. I hadn't realized what a rare case this was until he said that. He was required to stay with Boone until he boarded the plane.

We said our goodbyes to my friend Crystal as she boarded a plane home, and our heartfelt thanks to the agent for his help. We boarded and buckled up, exhausted but wired with tension, and headed for a new life in Boone's home town. I took a month off from work to get him settled in South Carolina.

It was June of 2004.

I was dead set against moving to the South, but when all our options were removed, I wanted to be with Boone, and it was the best place for him to be. We could not stay in Orange County anyway, and life in South Carolina was far more affordable for two middle-aged ex-convicts to try to build a life.

Boone's father set us up temporarily in a week-to-week studio apartment on the outskirts of town, where he was not close enough to anyone who might oppose his presence. The Sunset Lodge was once a famous old whorehouse, now just a rundown stretch of cinderblock studio apartments mostly inhabited by cheating husbands and people in transition. It wasn't what I was used to, but it was a step up from a prison cell, and it would suffice until I could find something better.

His reunion with his mother was tearful and precious to behold. He told me often that until I came along, his mother was the only one that did not abandon him. His father, obviously uncomfortable with displays of emotion, held back, except to incessantly share with us his favorite topic, how much our situation might possibly cost him. I have rarely met anyone so obsessed with money and so willing to discuss it at the most inappropriate of times. I got the feeling right away that he resented anything he did on our behalf, and every dime pried from his tight, stingy fist was recorded somewhere to be used against us at a later date.

From the time I left prison, I supported Boone financially, even when I had little for myself. I saw to it he had anything extra allowed an inmate, to make him comfortable and to show my devotion. I always felt a little guilty leaving him behind, and it made me feel better to do for him. When he walked out of that prison he had a full wardrobe even most established free men would envy. I paid his parole costs, required counseling fees, and anything else he needed, because he was my partner. I loved him, and I couldn't bear to hear his father complain about spending money. It made Boone feel ashamed and helpless, and I was sure he had plenty of that without his father adding to it.

We are proud men, accustomed to going without, and though his mother would starve to feed her son, his father controlled their money, and his incessant fretting and nagging set us both on edge from the beginning. I did my best to be patient, but it wasn't long before my naturally confrontational personality surfaced for combat and set the standard for my relationship with his father from then forward.

Our first night together, alone in our little apartment, is still clear as water in my memory. We had made it to the free world together. There is little in this world as exquisite as obtaining something you have worked hard and waited long for.

I laughed when, every five minutes, he jumped up to gaze with wonder at our fully stocked refrigerator, trying to decide what to eat next. Not because he was hungry, but just because he could. For twenty years he was not able to choose what he ate.

He was puzzled by the television remote control, the cordless phone and the microwave oven. Technology had changed a lot in the time he was gone, and he was endlessly fascinated and intimidated by all the gadgets he didn't understand.

We rolled around on the queen-sized bed and made love for the first time without having to keep a look out for the guards. We rediscovered each other's bodies with wild abandon. We couldn't stop touching each other, we needed constant reassurance it was real, and not just more of the seemingly endless fantasy we had lived for so long. We ate too much, and talked over each other. He modeled his new clothes for me, and I was pleased with how handsome he looked in street clothes.

Every time he heard a car drive past the apartment, he froze. He was sure the police would come to tell him it was all a mistake, and they were taking him back to prison.

I didn't mind the cinderblock studio. It reminded me of our little cell at Soledad. All that mattered that night, as we lay in each other's arms, was we had made a dream come true. We kept a promise alive for four years against the odds. We were free and we were together. If I could have frozen us in that moment, or gone to sleep never to wake, life would have been perfect. But the world came to greet us with all its anger and judgment, pressure and poison, and everything I tried to warn Boone of back in Soledad came to pass.

Our first visit to his parents' home was not a happy prance through childhood memories. He pointed out to me the bathroom where he'd found his mother after she had cut her wrists when he was six years old, and the window his father put him through in a drunken rage when Boone was an adolescent. He told me it was a house of ghosts he hoped to never see again. I wondered if we would not have been better off battling the ire of strangers in California than the demons of a bitter childhood that were waiting there for his return. He could tell me the things he felt returning to that house, but he couldn't tell his parents.

His mother cooked and fussed over us and his father lectured and complained, simultaneously making us feel both loved and burdensome.

He reported to parole, where they informed us he would be electronically monitored with an ankle bracelet and could not go more than one hundred feet away from our house without permission. He would not be allowed to get a job or drive a car until parole decided. He was basically under house arrest.

It was starting. All the realities of life for a sex offender didn't give us twenty-four hours of freedom before tearing a gaping hole in the dream. Boone was graceful through it all. He was used to rules and restrictions. He felt bad for what everyone else was going through on his behalf, and didn't ever complain.

Again we got lucky with a really good parole agent. She was a really nice woman, intent on doing her job well. She recognized the extraordinary circumstances and pressure we were under, and did her best to reassure us we would all get through these initial difficulties. I realized that she too was under a great deal of pressure. She told us she had never handled a case quite like his, and there was no room for mistakes for either of them.

In less than a week we were thrown out of the Sunset Lodge.

Boone's father had lied to the manager about who was living there. When they found out, we were told to leave. I was never sure if it was the sex offender issue or the lie that got us thrown out, but either way you know you're not too popular when you get thrown out of a run-down old whorehouse.

Now was the time to panic. We had no place to go. His parents lived too close to an elementary school, which was forbidden to a sex offender, and I would have rather gouged out my eyes than live with his father. I had to be back in California in less than three weeks, and Boone didn't have a place to live. The parole department gave him thirty days to find an acceptable residence, or they would revoke the transfer and he would be shipped back to California. It was decided during that thirty days he would be allowed to stay at his parents' home but was essentially under house arrest: so much for the concept of freedom.

Within days the neighborhood he was born and raised in got wind of his presence, and all my fears were realized.

Reporters called and showed up at the door, and a group of those fine Christian folk plastered the streets with his photo. When his face made the front page of the local newspaper, his parents received many calls of sympathy and support from friends and people who'd known Boone as a boy, but his mother was mortified and hurt by the vicious statements made by some of her neighbors. None of the supporters were quoted in the newspaper. Only the voices of hate were heard. Boone gave a statement announcing that he understood the public's concern and asked only that he be allowed to prove he was no longer a menace to society. I was proud of the way he handled the situation.

His father and I embarked on a desperate mission to find him a home. After the news coverage it was doubtful anyone would be willing to rent to us, and we had to find a place where no children lived or gathered, and not near a school, park, playground, daycare or church.

His mother threatened to pack up and move to California if her son was forced to leave. She had waited two decades to be with her son and refused to lose him again. I admired her determination and began to see glimpses of steel beneath the surface of the fragile southern belle persona.

I have learned the ways of southern ladies this past decade. They are geniuses of manipulation. I say this with admiration and respect. They make an art of controlling their men, while allowing the men to feel and appear in control. They do not emasculate their men with humiliating browbeating. They use subtle displeasure and frigid deprivation. A wayward southern gentleman will most assuredly be deprived of affection, servitude and sustenance should his wife be unhappy. Of course I only refer to the more refined and sophisticated of southern women. White trash is the same no matter what part of the country you're in. They just nag, bitch and threaten until their husbands knock them out or move to the Sunset Lodge.

Boone's mother dug her heels in and let his father know in no uncertain terms that she would not stand for her son to be sent away. His father grew frantic he might lose his chief cook, maid and companion. The stress was difficult, and I felt sorry for both of them. Their life had grown sedate over the years, and Boone's mother had many health problems. Though they had a tumultuous marriage, they had aged past most of it and settled in to a comfortable, if dysfunctional, way of life, and we had most assuredly come to create a tidal wave in their relatively calm waters.

Their son was simply their son. There were few choices there.

I, on the other hand, am a horse of a multitude of colors, and I suppose I can be a wee bit overwhelming to those less traveled. I chuckle to think what my staid southern townsfolk must have thought when this tattooed, bejeweled, loud-mouthed, gay Yankee came to town. The South is unreasonably concerned with public image, regardless of what may be going on privately, and my very nature violates southern tradition.

I found the town generally charming and beautiful. I still do, and because I was originally a small town boy, I wasn't ignorant of the natural curiosity when a colorful stranger comes to town. This was to be my new home, and though I had no intention of altering myself to please the community, I assessed my surroundings to look for my niche.

After being denied several potential residences by the parole department, Boone's father and I stumbled on an empty house sitting by itself on the outskirts of town. It was perfect. It did not appear to be for sale nor had it been inhabited in quite some time.

To this particular issue I would cease my sharp criticism of his father's annoying peculiarities and give credit where it's due.

Once the parole department approved the location as acceptable, his father tracked down the owners to inquire of their intentions with the property. They were in the process of upgrading to sell, and his father made a cash offer for a quick private sale. I donated a large portion of the money I'd saved toward our home. We had no time to deal with banks and paperwork. They accepted the offer, and we had a safe place for Boone to live. He was barely a week away from revocation of his transfer.

The house inevitably became a point of contention in a power struggle between his father and me, but at the time it was a gesture on his part I was grateful for. Parting with a chunk of money of that proportion was like driving a knife through his heart, and he even confessed to extreme nausea when he wrote the check. Later, he devised a scheme to recoup and even profit off the investment, at my expense, but I applaud his business acumen, if not his ethics and honesty. I was simultaneously amused and annoyed to hear him bragging that he "bought us a house" but leave out the part where he held the mortgage at a very profitable interest rate. Today I carry an interest rate half of the one his self-described "generous" father imposed on us.

I left South Carolina with a great sense of relief mixed with sadness that we would be apart again. My lover was safe, and the furor over his presence died quickly after he moved to the new house. Electronic monitoring kept him house bound, so his parents closed up their home and moved into the new house to look after him until I could make the permanent move.

I was disappointed that circumstances did not allow much room for the sweet and romantic fantasies I had for us when he got home. There was a lot of stress and ugliness, but neither was it the nightmare it could have been, or most certainly would have been, had he paroled to the brutal streets of California.

I was sad to leave him yet again, but I still had a life in California that would take a while to dismantle.

I was making very good money and I had just handed over a large amount of it to his father for the house and took on most of Boone's expenses to save us the humiliation of his father's complaints.

South Carolina does not pay for the care of criminals in any way once released. The cost of parole visits, monitoring, and mandatory counseling all fell to my hands, and I was happy to do whatever necessary to secure Boone's freedom. His parents fed him well and saw to it he met all his responsibilities, and I was grateful they were there to do what I could not. He had no one else.

I know it was lonely for him. Prison is very social, and he missed his friends of many years and the predictability of his days. He was a pariah out here, and just one of the guys in there. He was still caged in many ways, but without his peers, and no one that could begin to relate to how difficult and frightening the transition is.

We spoke every day, twice a day, on the phone. He kept himself insanely busy clearing our wooded lot and working to improve our home. The house had not had a single thing done to improve it since being built in 1970, and he knew how much I hated the old wallpaper and shag carpeting. Each time I visited, he proudly showed me his improvements in an effort to please me and coerce me into moving sooner. I returned as often as possible and made four visits before the final move, February 1st of 2005.

I prolonged the move further than my original plan. I wanted to be with him, but was scared to give up my life. He knew, and it made him sad. And that made me sad. I had kept every promise I made over the last five years, and I would keep this one too. I just needed a little more time.

On my first visit to what was to be our new home, I experienced a disturbing observation. The first time I entered the room Boone chose for himself I wondered why he chose the smallest of the three. I had left for California prior to the final purchase and hadn't been inside the house. When I entered his room, it was strangely familiar. My heart was wrenched with sadness when I realized it was familiar because he had replicated his prison cell. The room was set up in nearly every detail as the little cell we fell in love in and he lived in for many years. It was a haunting glimpse of his inner psyche. As I took it all in I felt a profound sense of foreboding. Taking the man out of prison was going to prove far easier than taking the prison out of the man.

I know from my own experience that prison changes you forever, but I had a life before prison that I easily slipped back to. For Boone it had been too long, and everything was foreign to him. He had only a limited confidence in himself and in the things he learned to do in a controlled environment. Everything else scared the hell out of him, and he found comfort in returning to the little room that felt like his cell. He even locked himself in.

Parole still would not let him look for a job, and he was going a bit stir crazy at home with his parents day in and day out. I feared he would cut down every living thing on our property just to keep himself busy. We managed to set up a small gym in the house and that helped. Keeping his body beautiful was more than a routine, it was an obsession. He worked out with a fury and a discipline I have seen in few people then or since. I often joked I would be in big trouble if I needed to go to the emergency room in the middle of his workout. When he worked out, the rest of the world ceased to exist.

We looked forward to the day he'd earned enough trust from parole to experience some actual freedom. When you love someone who's doing time, you're doing time with them, and I hated all the restrictions he had. I understood them, but I hated them anyway. His restrictions were far worse than anything I had experienced when on parole, but then, in all fairness, so were his crimes.

In September of 2004, I visited South Carolina again on my way to Maine to surprise my mother on her seventieth birthday. I threatened both my sisters with slow painful deaths if they revealed my surprise visit to our mother. Both are notoriously bad at keeping secrets, but this time they managed it.

A party was in full swing on the front lawn when we pulled up in Tina's van, but Ma didn't know the party was for her until I slid back the door of the van and popped out shouting, "Happy Birthday!"

There are some moments in my life of perfect heartwarming beauty. I wish they would have been recorded and kept to relive again when I am low, and that was one of them.

Ma peered at me from a distance and I heard her say, "Who's that? That looks just like Ernie? Is that my Ernie? Oh my God it is!"

She hobbled toward me, using a cane, laughing and crying at the same time. I hugged her small frame; she seemed to get smaller every time I saw her.

"What are you doing here? How come nobody told me you were coming?" she cried.

Family and friends all stood around beaming with pleasure at pulling off the surprise, and someone opened the garage door to reveal the decorations, gifts, and a cake flaming with seventy candles.

"I came for your birthday, Ma. That's why we're all here."

It was never easy to surprise Ma. If she thought anyone had a secret, she would pick them bloody and promise not to tell until they gave it up. She couldn't stand not to know everything. I think I have a bit of that trait in myself.

But this time nobody gave it up, and she was genuinely surprised.

When she saw the cake and everyone sang the birthday song, it brought on a fresh flood of tears. I remember her saying, "This is for me? All this is for me? Oh, it's too much, it's just too much. I have to sit down."

It struck me as sad that this woman who gave everything she had to the people she loved was overwhelmed to get anything back. That was my Ma. She never expected anything and was grateful for everything she got.

I had arranged to be there only a few days, and Ma said the same thing no matter how long the visit, "That's all, can't you stay longer?"

My mother and I had become such good friends. I could tell her anything. Our conversations on her porch swing are what I always go back to when I miss her the most.

Her symptoms were getting worse. She was experiencing vertigo and tremors. The doctors suspected Parkinson's disease.

Every time I saw her, and when we spoke, something new was diagnosed. They gave her more pills. She had pills for everything, and pills for the side effects of her pills. I was beginning to seriously doubt the quality of her health care.

My mother was not an educated woman and was intimidated by educated people. She would not question her doctor. I assured her there were thousands of doctors who graduated at the bottom of their class, and just because they had a license, it didn't mean they were good. Everyone with a driver's license is not a good driver. Everyone with a hairdressing license is not a great hairdresser.

I told her those doctors worked for her. She needed to ask questions and if necessary, get second opinions. I didn't like my mother pumped full of drugs, and I didn't like having so many unanswered questions. Though my stepdad did his best, I felt he didn't question enough on her behalf, and he seemed irritated when my mother's children questioned her care, as if we were accusing him of neglect.

She was afraid of losing her mind, and perhaps, with it, the opportunity to say some things she never said before. Our conversations in private were often very serious and emotional. She seemed to carry so much guilt over my childhood. She thought my drug problem was because of my childhood and that she didn't protect me enough. She asked me, "Why did you do all that to yourself, all those drugs and everything?"

I hesitated and answered as honestly as I could. "I don't really know, Ma. A lot of the times I just didn't want to feel what it feels like to be me, or think about all the things I wished were different. It worked for a while, and then, when it didn't anymore, it was too late. I was in too deep to find my way out. I'm not even sure if addiction is the same for everybody or we're all different, but I know I'm an addict and I can't change it. I've accepted it now, and I know I don't want to live that way."

We talked about my relationship. She asked me why Boone was in prison. I hesitated again before telling her the truth. I wanted her to like him, and I was afraid she wouldn't if she knew the truth about his past. When I finished, all she said was, "Are you sure this is the one you want to give up your old life for and be with?"

"Yes, Ma, I'm sure. I don't know how it will all turn out, but I have to run with it and see it through or I'll always wonder how it could have been. I love him. And sometimes I hate it that I love him so much"

She said, "Then do it. And don't let anything stop you. If you love him, then you have to go through with it. You know, honey, sometimes people do bad things and they are not bad people. Life just ain't that easy. When I was a young girl, hardly any girl I knew made it to her first period without some man pesterin' her. It's just the way men can be sometimes."

That was when she told me that her father-in-law raped her when she was pregnant. That was a hell of a thing to hear from my own mother, and it saddened me to realize there was so much about her I never knew.

Somehow that led her to the subject of Roger.

I didn't think anything needed to be said. I felt like I was over all that long ago. But I always let my mother talk freely and say what she needed to say. We had let go of those kind of boundaries in our relationship long before.

"Ernie, I'm so sorry for the way things were for you when you were a kid. I'm sorry it was so hard for you, and I didn't know how to be there for you. I just didn't know what to do. You were so different than the others. I loved you just the same, but you were so hard to handle and understand that I just gave up. Now I wish I'd somehow found a way to keep you home with me. Maybe you wouldn't have had to go through all this stuff."

Her shoulders slumped with the weight of regret and her lower lip quivered with the effort not to cry.

It was my turn to comfort her. I held her and said, "Ma, you have nothing to feel sorry about. You always did your best and you are a great mother and a great person. Why would all your kids love you so much if you were a bad mother? I have said a thousand times, everything good in me is because of you. I can only think of one thing I really regret Ma. I regret every tear you ever shed because of me. You never deserved the pain and worry I caused you. I didn't leave because you were a bad mother. I left because I didn't feel like I could be a good enough son. I would have been miserable here, trying to live up to my brothers and find a place to fit in. I had to create my own life and not let this place decide it for me. I've made some pretty grand mistakes, but so far I've had a hell of a ride and it was all my own choosing."

She laughed and said, "Boy, you sure have!"

We talked about the various relationships in our lives. She told me how she wished she had been closer to her only sister. I loved to hear her talk about her life and our family history. Her stories were treasures I stored in my heart for when I was thousands of miles away.

She had a poor but happy childhood. She had a life of struggle and heartache, but still thought it a happy one. She was seventy now. She had already outlived both her parents. She was feeling beaten by illness, and it killed me to see she was preparing us and herself for the end of her life. I was by no means prepared to consider she was nearing the end. None of us did.

I returned to California for the last time to prepare and execute the final move to South Carolina.

My coworkers and all my friends made a big deal about my leaving, and many were skeptical I was making the right choice. I was patient with their skepticism. I was making a huge decision, and their worries stemmed from love and concern for my wellbeing. Those who knew me had seen me make the wrong choices over a man before. I loved my life in California. But, after two-and-a-half decades, I was ready for a new adventure, and nothing could have swayed me from being with Boone.

His parents were still living in our house, and I could clearly see he was suffocating under the weight of it. They treated him like a child and offended his manhood. They meant well, and put their own life on hold to look after him, but he had a lot of conflicting feelings about his parents. I began to see very early on he still harbored much resentment against them, and the love-hate relationship common in severely dysfunctional families began to rear its ugly head. His mother still practiced substance abuse, with alcohol and prescription drugs, and it made

him angry and disgusted. His father's controlling personality created countless confrontations, and they butted
heads at every turn. It frustrated and depressed him that
it appeared very little had changed in the twenty years
he was gone.

I found myself playing referee or family counselor, not
just with his parents, but with everyone connected to him.
He found it difficult to assert himself or express his feelings,
and poor communication skills appeared to be a family
tradition. I seemed to be the only one he could really talk
to.

Though Maggie would continue to make efforts to
build a relationship with her father, the impenetrable wall
of silence, secrecy and isolation, built over twenty years
in prison, would prove so disappointing and frustrating,
she finally gave up.

Two years before his release, his beloved maternal
grandmother had passed away. I met her briefly on my
first visit to South Carolina, the year of my release. She
was a tiny caricature of a deep-country, chain-smoking,
gun-toting granny, living alone in near squalor. He spoke
of her often and with deep devotion. She seemed his
only source of truly happy childhood memories. She and
his mother were the only people to stand by him through
the years of incarceration, and he was devastated by
her death and remorseful that he did not get to see her
before she died.

I feel now it was a mistake to return to his home town.
Though I can't imagine what it might have been like in
California, I do know that strangers can never hurt you as
much as the people you love, and this family was a raging storm of unresolved pain and resentments.

I didn't know coming home would tear open a thousand festering old wounds for him. I thought he could
heal, the way I did with my own family. I didn't know he
had barely moved forward a single step in twenty years

toward reconciling the angers of his childhood. I didn't know a lot of things I thought I knew. And though I feel I truly had his best interests at heart in the efforts I made on his behalf, I had no idea how much I would suffer for my own ignorance. If I had, I might be writing this from my little cottage in California, or not writing it at all.

I know now that I lost myself in him. Probably from the day I met him he was more important to me than I was to myself. I thought that was how you were supposed to love. So much of who I was got wrapped up in him. I liked who I was when I loved him. In many ways he became another addiction for me.

He worried, as time passed and I did not make my exit from my old life, that I might change my mind and not make it at all. So I set a date. On February 1st of 2005, I would set out for my new life with him.

Our love affair had so much passion, I thought nothing could ever change it. I learned so much about myself while teaching him about love between men, and he unleashed a powerfully provocative sense of awareness of my own sexuality. Sex was not a tool, a weapon, or a debt to be paid. We loved each other's particularly unique image of male diversity, and our vanity enjoyed turning heads as individuals and as a couple. We were not competitive in our intimacy, as can happen between two men, and we encouraged each other to explore each other without shame or insecurity. He made me feel sexy and beautiful at a time I was struggling against the concept of being a middle-aged man. Given the nature of Boone's past, I hoped for him to enjoy and embrace sexuality within the boundaries of responsibility, respect, and dignity for our own bodies and each other's.

In many ways I'm more like a woman than most men. I know this about myself and I'm comfortable with it. I crave the emotional connection to my sexuality, but I understand that sex is not always about love, and I've lived in a man's world, by men's rules, long enough to know some men can't do both at the same time. With the absence of emotion, sex can achieve an abandon to carnal desire without responsibility that is the essence of erotica. It's a balancing act with lovers that depends on a mutual respect and understanding that most certainly is enhanced with the bonds of love and depleted without it.

We knew each other's bodies and secrets so well that a single glance made the blood rush through my body and ignited a fire. Our physical passion for each other never wavered, and sometimes was all we had as a bridge to reach one another when we found ourselves disconnected by the complications of our lives.

He threw rose petals on our bed, lit cozy fires and candles, and left little love notes about the house for me to find. He made me feel like I had never been in love before him and any other man was inconsequential by comparison. It was the real passion I dreamed of but never quite reached in the chain of selfish men who had left me bitter and nearly hopeless to love. It was not too good to be true, but it was probably too good to last.

It was Boone and Pup against the world, and we knew it. We also knew that any problems we had came from outside the sanctity of our twosome, and we unfailingly joined as a single force in the face of adversity.

Regardless of what people thought they knew about his past, or us as a couple, we held our heads high with pride and love for each other as partners and friends. When his arms were around me, nothing else mattered and all was well with my world. Once again, the nature of our attraction behind bars reinstated itself. He was the manliest of men, creating a protective barrier of muscle and fierce devotion to the outside world while dismantling his image in private to the sensitive and gentle lover and friend that was mine alone. Perhaps it was absurd to wrap oneself so completely in another. I didn't plan it and sometimes even fought it, but I couldn't stop myself from giving it all over just this one more time, with the hope I would never have to look for love again.

Letting go was harder than I thought it would be. A life is not a house or a job, or a place on a map. It's the people you shared it all with, and they were the only thing really hard to let go of. Rod and Crystal, Sue and Lilly, John, Jeff, Sharon and Kelli: this was my family for most of my life, and it was not easy to say goodbye and set out for somewhere I had only a single person who cared for me. But I had made a commitment, and I had to follow my heart and take this risk for love and a promise.

I had my important possessions shipped and the rest I gave away. I said tearful goodbyes and boarded the plane with my heart full of hope that this time everything would work out for me.

Hollow

Does your heart echo hollow
along the path you now follow
ending at my door yet again
Yet you never come in
Only stand at a distance
and whisper my name
with selfish insistence
Begging remembrance
Without solid presence
or promise.
At most just a ghost
of who you wanted to be
what you promised to me
A body without substance or soul
A smoke with no fire
consumed with desire
so childlike in rage
a man only in age
all too self-engaged
while beating my heart to submission.
Contortion, extortion,
until loves fatal abortion
you'll dance to your death
to the music you hear
in a tone deaf ear
your fists clenched with pride
as love slowly died
you murdered what was timeless and dear.

E.M.

Chapter Twelve
Gabrielle

So this was the part where I was supposed to write my happily ever after.

The next few years brought me much happiness and success. Boone's parents moved back to their home, and we filled ours with pets to love. We both found good jobs and success in our professions. We worked nonstop to give our old house a much-needed facelift, and we made some friends.

Soon after I arrived I met a lady who has become my confidante, surrogate mother and closest friend.

Growing up, Boone was not close to his Grandmother Jean. She is his father's stepmother, and his father and she do not get along. I was led to believe, by his father, that she was a wicked stepmother, but I had also come to believe his father's assessment of others was not necessarily reliable. Her husband, Boone's paternal grandfather, passed away years before, and she was alone. It behooves me not to delve too far into her turbulent relationship with her stepfamily, but suffice it to say she had successfully disengaged herself as a matter of survival and sanity since her husband's death.

Boone had not contacted his paternal grandparents in the years he was gone, but suddenly expressed a desire to contact her. I encouraged him, hoping it was an effort to heal wounds of the past and build bridges to the future. Grandmother was eighty-four when we met. She lived a somewhat solitary life. Her own small family had died off over the past decade, and she seemed to enjoy the colorful distraction we brought to her life. She and I discovered many mutual interests in entertainment, art, and conversation that solidified an unlikely but devoted friendship. She is as different from Boone's maternal grandmother as two women could be. An obviously educated and dignified woman, she was welcoming and warm. As I suspected, I found her to be anything but wicked, and we became fast friends. Though our history and lifestyle challenged her conservative views, she was never less than supportive in our friendship.

It was she who directed me to the salon where I would begin my career among the ladies of the South.

I did harbor some prejudices towards the South, some warranted, some not, and I attracted more than my share of attention until people got used to me. But it was by no means the cross-burning, redneck lynch mob my overactive imagination envisioned and feared. Small towns are similar to a prison in some ways. Very little goes unnoticed, and boredom breeds petty dramas, gossip, and speculation. Where there is less diversity, there is less tolerance. I am adaptive to my environment to a point. Beyond that point I expect others to adapt to me.

When I answered a help-wanted ad and met Grace, my future employer and friend, I was as direct and honest about my past, who I was as a person, and what I was capable of as a stylist, as I was with Sue when I applied for my first job out of prison. Grace was, and continues to be, one of the finest people I know from three corners of the country. After hiring me, she was instrumental in building my career in my new home. She and my coworkers promoted and supported me in a manner foreign to the cut-throat and competitive business practices I was accustomed to in the big city, and I quickly built a clientele and put down roots in the community that gave me a much-needed sense of security. Boone also established himself with a small local business as a talented and much sought after cabinetmaker and craftsman, building some of the most beautiful cabinetry in the county.

It was an idyllic life in many ways.

We had a modest but respectable lifestyle. The controversy over his past receded quickly. We had a nice home and good jobs. We had family ties, and my job opened doors to a social life. I have always been a social butterfly. The social life was awkward for Boone. I understood and sympathized with his feelings of inadequacy on a social level, but felt like I was constantly balancing my own gregarious nature with his reticence. Our animals and work were where he found the most comfort and pleasure and our home rapidly became a small zoo. We went with Grandmother to concerts and theatre, had dinner parties, and played at the beach. I gardened and cooked, endlessly decorated our home, and got involved in some local charities. It was all quite Middle America, and a lifestyle I thought dreary in the past, I was content with now.

As I climbed my own ladder of humble success and orchestrated our home and social life, I failed to notice my lover and best friend was not as content as I.

His communication skills with others had not improved much, but I still felt that problem didn't apply to me. I thought we told each other everything. I thought we communicated well. It seemed to me he had become suddenly secretive. There were other things I noticed but did not take too seriously, particularly his wandering eye in the presence of attractive females. It wasn't that he noticed them that bothered me. It was the secrecy in which he did it. He was furtive in his admiration. Women and beauty have been my livelihood my entire adult life, and I often admired and pointed out beautiful women and men to him no differently than I would a landscape, a full moon, or a piece of art. I saw no need to be secretive in the presence of beauty.

It was understood between us that he was bisexual. It was also understood that we were monogamous, regardless of whom we might find attractive. I was not insecure about other men. But I couldn't compete with a woman and didn't think I would ever have to.

When I spoke of my concerns, he always reassured me I was being needlessly insecure. Privately, I nursed an unshakable feeling of foreboding. I thought I sensed a yearning in him I couldn't reach or comprehend. I prayed those yearnings were not of the nature that took him to prison in his youth.

These feelings did not dominate my thoughts. They were merely fleeting, and our everyday life was one of immense satisfaction for me. For the first time in many years my life felt so normal, without the inner battles and torment of addiction, self-doubt, or unfulfilled desire.

My family members came to visit more often now that I was on the east coast. Even Ma and Everett visited several times on their way through to Florida. My family liked and accepted Boone, and it meant a lot to me and to him.

We went to Maine for another niece's wedding, and I could see Boone was a bit overwhelmed with my boisterous, overly communicative family. I always stayed close enough to rescue him in social gatherings. His anxiety wasn't visible to anyone except me. We knew each other well, and I could tell when I needed to extricate him from discomfort. I'd learned he had a habit of biting his lower lip when anxious or uncomfortable. That was my cue to rescue him.

My mother's health was still on the decline. I felt so helpless and useless. She had her good days, but they became fewer and she never got completely well. It depressed her, and me, too. The very thought of her dying reduced me to tears.

Boone finished his parole in June of 2007. The electric monitor and mandatory counseling ended after the first year, and the next two were uneventful. Other than registering for life as a sex offender, he was completely free for the first time in twenty-four years. That's when he seemed to change, or perhaps when I began to notice it. He seemed restless and discontent. Nothing seemed good enough. He was oblivious to our good fortune and his attitude was negative and resentful.

We were in our late forties. He'd missed out on his youth, and he felt like time was running out. He began to resent the power he thought I had and he lacked. In a rare argument he called our home a prison and me the warden. He accused me of being controlling. He let me carry all the responsibilities, down to the simplest decisions, and then accused me of being controlling. It made no sense to me. I was astounded and hurt as the first crack appeared in a life I thought unbreakable.

Grandmother gave him a large sum of money for his birthday. He fulfilled what he called a lifelong fantasy of owning a Harley Davidson. It was a beautiful bike, and I have to admit he looked sexy as hell on it. I hated that bike from the moment he got it. When he got on that bike the years fell away. He was young and free, and I was not a part of it. It seemed he rode away on that bike and never really came back. I felt him slipping away, and I was helpless to stop it.

While this was happening at home, I was distracted by my mother's health. She was scheduled for brain surgery. A brain scan revealed hydrocephalus, fluid on the brain, creating pressure, that I suspected was causing the

Alzheimer's and Parkinson symptoms. I never believed she had either of those diseases, and I pressured her into allowing me to speak with her doctor concerning her health care.

He was typical in his arrogant confidence that he had overlooked nothing, and said I was in denial about her condition, yet he ordered a brain scan shortly thereafter, revealing the hydrocephalus.

We all had so much hope this surgery would bring her back to us healthy and happy. It was pitiful and heart-breaking to see her suffer that way. She had lost her will to fight anymore. She felt she had no joy in her life and was a burden to her loved ones. She was afraid to be left alone, and couldn't manage the simplest tasks of cooking and housekeeping. Our conversations were short, confusing, and emotional. She had a difficult time concentrating and following a conversation. Our calls often ended with one or both of us in tears.

Other than my mother's illness and Boone's mysterious behavior, my life was going well. It all felt stable. I decided for the first time in my career to open my own salon. I felt I had come as far as I could as an employee, and stumbled on an opportunity I couldn't let pass. With Boone and my brother Norm's help, we created the salon I had kept in my imagination for many years but was never stable enough to make happen.

Trendy Salon opened April 1st 2008.

It was an immediate success for me. I was proud, and the happiest I could ever remember being. I had it all. A nice home, my own business, a man I adored and a relationship others envied. I was clean, happy, and healthy. Unfortunately, Boone was not.

As my business flourished, the bottom fell out of the building market, and his struggled. He was nearly unemployed. I was caught up in my own success and ambition, my mother's illness and all my responsibilities, and I didn't see how his ego was suffering. He felt emasculated and unnecessary. He was the man who took care of me, and now I was taking care of him and he hated it.

More than once, a well-meaning friend said to him, "You are so lucky to have Ernie, what would you do without him?"

I winced every time I heard that said, and quickly reminded them that we were a team and my success was our success. And I truly felt that way.

I knew it hurt his masculine ego for others to think he was dependent on me. I never felt that way and was careful to never use my financial superiority as a weapon. I didn't care how much money he made. He was a hard-working man and a loving, attentive friend and partner.

I enjoyed the blissful feeling of success for only six months before my world crashed and shattered into a million painful pieces.

Looking back, there were plenty of signs that only became crystal clear after it was too late. He became withdrawn, secretive, and physically distant. There were blocks of time unaccounted for, and long solitary rides on the motorcycle. He stopped bringing me lunch, calling several times a day, and stopping by the shop during my work day. He did very little around the house anymore. He spent more time away from me, and grew hostile if I questioned his whereabouts. He became belligerent, resentful, and harshly critical of me. I seemed to go from the one who could do no wrong to one who could do nothing right. I was hurt and bewildered.

This was not my Boone! My lover and best friend was becoming a stranger to me. I tried to get him to talk to me and tell me what was happening, but he just shut down more. When I grew angry with frustration and confronted him, he just got on his bike and rode away.

None of it made any sense to me, until the day I stumbled upon him sitting in a car with a friend and coworker's wife. The shock and guilt on both of their faces told me everything I needed to know. They were having an affair.

I really never knew I was capable of being so hurt. It was real physical pain, like being stabbed in the heart.

He was caught completely off guard, and didn't try to deny what was plain to see.

In seconds, all the odd behavior and suspicious incidents that worried me over the last few months flooded my head with humiliation and fury.

The woman's earring I found in the guest room he claimed was his mother's; the sand on his shoes when he was walking on the beach with her and I thought he was working; the missing hours, the waning sex life, the hostility; it was all there. All the clues were right in front of my face and I missed them. I thought myself so smart, so on top of everything, and in seconds I felt like the biggest fool on the planet.

Her husband worked with Boone in the cabinet shop. She had become a client of mine and pretended to be a friend. She and her husband sat at my dinner table and attended gatherings at our home. They had been sleeping together all along. The found earring proved they were so low they actually betrayed me in my own home, when I was working to pay the bills and he was unemployed. I wouldn't expect much more from a woman like her, but I really thought he was better than that.

She and her husband were not the kind of people I would usually befriend in a clean and sober lifestyle. They lived in a rundown trailer park, and when I felt less than charitable, I would refer to them as trailer trash. Her husband seemed a nice enough man, but an obvious alcoholic, and I found them quite insignificant and uninteresting. But he was Boone's co-worker, and when I shied away from socializing with them, he accused me of snobbery because they lived in a trailer park and were not as well off or well educated as my friends. I invited them to our home to prove him wrong.

Boone insisted she pursued him, and I didn't doubt it for a moment. She is the sort of woman that has no respect for other people's relationships because she has never had a respectable one of her own. She is the class of woman whose idea of success is a man with muscles, a Harley, and a double-wide trailer. She is the type of woman who burns her bridges wherever she goes. Catty observations perhaps, but I feel entitled considering the circumstances.

The day I caught them together I looked square into her plain, worn face, her nicotine-stained teeth, and her cheap slutty clothes from Wal-Mart, and said to him "So this trash is what you threw it all away for, Boone? You would break my heart for this dried-up hag? I gave you more credit than this."

I could tell she wanted to lash back, but the murderous look on my face kept her silent. I understand now how people kill each other in crimes of passion. I could have killed them both at that moment. In all the betrayal and pain I experienced in my life, I have never hated two people more than I did that day. I told her she better get her sorry ass home and tell her husband, so I didn't have to, and she drove away like the devil was on her tail.

I went to my knees in agony and I sobbed my heart out on the gravel drive for all I had lost in a split second. It wasn't just a man I'd lost. It was a dream I'd waited and worked for. It was a whole life he destroyed. He tried to comfort me. He tried to explain. I lashed out in rage. I slapped and kicked and screamed at him. I felt like his hands were around my throat, squeezing the life out of me.

So he was a monster after all. He hadn't changed. His ex-wife warned me he wouldn't change, and I thought she was just being bitter and vengeful. But she was right.

He was still a selfish man who took what he wanted without regard for those he hurt.

It didn't take me long to figure it all out. Of course she was exactly what I should have expected for Boone. There's not a vast pool of women willing to have an affair with a convicted rapist living in a homosexual relationship, regardless of how good looking he is.

Boone had to find someone he could feel better than to massage his fragile and bruised ego. It wasn't hard to feel better than her. He had to go that low on the food chain to feel like a man again. She cleaned toilets and sold drugs to pay for her trailer and her drug habit. She was so easy to hate. He was not.

I blamed them both, but I blamed her more.

I loved him and I looked after him, and I knew he was naive in the ways of women like her. She stroked his fragile ego and promised him sexual freedom and adventure outside the constraints of the monogamy I insisted on. She envied my life, and she thought by taking him she would get out of the trailer park. She thought our house was his. She thought our life was because of who he was. She was too stupid to see our life was because of who I was, not who he was. His life was one of prison cells, dirty secrets, and shame. He didn't have a clue how to build or maintain a life. He was only experienced at destroying one.

This was not about gender or about man versus woman. The bisexuals I've known make little distinction sexually and are equally satisfied by either gender. This fact was reinforced later when I became aware of the array of sexual encounters, with both men and women, he indulged in after I asked him to leave and while he was with her. This was about an idea of freedom, pleasure without responsibility, sex and companionship without commitment. She was willing to join him or turn a blind eye to his promiscuity rather than lose him. In my opinion there are far too many men ruining their marriages over that fantasy, but I foolishly believed it would not happen to me.

It took me a while to realize that all along I fooled myself into thinking I was having a relationship with a man, perhaps even a man my equal. He was still just a boy. He had not grown up at all since they locked him away. He was spoiled and selfish and determined to have his way.

He told me it was over with her. He said she meant nothing to him. He begged me to give him the chance to fix it, and he would do anything to make things right. I believed him.

She told him she was pregnant when he ended it. He believed her, but I knew better. That's the oldest trick in the trailer park, but not usually utilized by forty-year-old women with hysterectomies. That's when I really understood what kind of woman we were dealing with.

She cut herself with knives and had her teenage son call Boone for help. She parked near our house and stalked him. She called drunk at all hours and threatened suicide. She left notes on his car and drove by his job. She was pathetic and relentless. He was impressed by her obsession. He thought it was love. I thought it disgusting and embarrassing. It was a nonstop, white trash, Jerry Springer show, that wasn't going to end unless I ended it.

It was so hard to make him go, though he had hurt me beyond repair with his betrayals. I gave him ten years of my life. I left my friends and my job on the other side of the country. I waited over four long years and never let another man touch me. I thought he was better than that, and I knew I was.

It would have been easier if he had just left. It would have been easier if he said he didn't love me anymore, or he'd changed his mind and needed a straight life to be happy. Any of those things I could have handled and moved on. But he didn't. He wouldn't stay away and wouldn't let me go.

I vacillated from rage to despair. I embarked on a mission to find a man to replace and hurt him with. I turned up nothing meaningful, except more of the degradation and humiliation that echoed his betrayals. Only now I was doing it to myself.

I looked at myself and saw all the ugliness I felt inside, reflected in my own image.

I began to starve myself and exercise as if demons chased me. The addict in me whispered promises of relief in a bottle, a needle, a glass pipe, or a pill, anything to not face or feel the tornado of emotion consuming me. But I was too alone to give in to the addict. There was no one there to catch me when I fell.

Grandmother Jean was my only real friend, and I ran to her for comfort. She was always there for me. Her warm little house was my safe harbor from the storm that was Boone and me. Nothing bad would happen to me there, and she loved me.

I'm almost embarrassed by it now, but I slashed the tires on his Harley and dumped a half pound of sugar in the gas tank. I knew how much he loved that bike. His girlfriend loved it too. I wanted to damage something he loved, like he did to me. He took it well, better than I expected, and said he knew he had it coming. I told him it was him or the bike, and I decided one was a misdemeanor and the other a felony, I would start with the misdemeanor and see if I felt better. I did.

I'm quite sure I am the only person alive to have ever slapped his face and walked away unscathed. He said later I slapped the taste right out of his mouth and his ear rang for three days after.

He stood on the front porch of our home, looked me in the eye, and said, "Puppy, I never meant to hurt you. I love you more than anything in the world. She is nothing compared to you. You are blowing this way out of proportion." His tone was impatient and demeaning.

The absurdity of a statement like that, when I was so clearly suffering, brought back the memories of every selfish, brutal man who had shattered my heart or broken my body or spirit since I was six years old. I put every one of those men behind one roundhouse slap that rocked him back on his heels and stunned him to silence.

I knew I only had that one shot because I was sure he would kill me, and even I was surprised at the enormously satisfying power I conjured into that slap.

But I made him feel better instead of me. I gave him a reason to paint me with guilt for sinking to a level of physical violence, for losing control, for being a bad person and justifying his immorality. It was beneath me and we both knew it.

I wanted him to really understand my pain and respect it. But he was caught up in his own sense of self-importance and melodrama, and was incapable of understanding what it felt like to be one of his victims. I had been duped, betrayed, humiliated, and left to fend for myself in a strange land far away from my family and friends and the life I left behind to be with him.

But he did not retaliate when I slapped him. He seemed sad, and I knew he could see my suffering even if he couldn't feel it, but he didn't have a clue how to fix it. His only choice was to run from it. He took the easy way out.

For the second time, I went to my knees and sobbed in despair. He knelt and pulled me close to his chest, the way he always did to make me feel safe. I cried in his arms and he told me gently, "Puppy, I am so sorry. I wouldn't want you hurt for the world. It wasn't supposed to be like this. It was just supposed to be a little fun, something different, and something I didn't get to do for twenty-five years. You were never supposed to know and get hurt. But it got out of hand. Why can't you just look the other way? It's only temporary. I'll get it out of my system. She's not worth losing you. I will never leave you unless you make me do it. We could go someplace and start over. I don't want to have a life without you."

I said, "Boone, how could you do this to me? I was the only one there for you no matter what. After everything we went through to be together, this is the reward for my loyalty? What kind of person are you really? I don't know who you are anymore. You promised me the moon and the stars and undying devotion. I could not possibly have been so wrong about you. This is some horrible nightmare I'm waiting to wake from. It was always your job to keep me safe, Boone. I was willing to do everything else, the only thing you had to do was keep me from harm, and I never dreamed you would be the one to harm me the most."

I saw in his eyes he was not willing, or capable, of repairing the damage he had done, and I was not yet ready to acknowledge what I knew to be the truth, that it could never be repaired. The trust was gone. It was left up to me to decide how we went from there. He was not good at decisions. He hadn't made his own decisions in twenty-five years, and when he was finally free to, he made all the wrong ones.

My emotional and physical health was deteriorating. I worried that my business was affected. Personality is everything in my business, and clients do not want to be greeted with misery. They have their own, and they are paying me to make them happy. It's a difficult job when you're not happy and have to pretend to be. I could pull it off with all except those that surpassed mere clients, and over the years became friends. They knew when I was hurting, and many of them helped me through it.

I sought out the best plastic surgeon I could find and spent thousands of dollars and months of discomfort attempting to erase the lines of pain and betrayal from my face.

I had a hair transplant, a brow lift, my second cheek

augmentation, and countless injections to fill in lines and paralyze muscles. I lost forty pounds and did hundreds of crunches a day, until I had a twenty-eight inch waist, and not an ounce of fat remained on my forty-nine-year-old body.

Just as after my break-up with Rod many years before, I attempted to make myself someone else. Being me didn't seem to be working out that well, and I was not going to tolerate being old, balding, single and gay in Georgetown, South Carolina, on my fiftieth birthday. I couldn't imagine a worse fate. If I was going to go through hell, I was going to look good doing it!

I don't regret a single surgery I had. They helped me to feel better about myself, and gave me a sense of power over the image I wanted to show the world. I don't believe I've gone too far, and I've been careful to remain natural looking. I've been told often enough you cannot tell I've had anything done and I do intend to let myself age, I'm just not in any hurry. I needed and wanted to feel and look young and undamaged.

Being cheated on is a serious blow to one's self-esteem. You can't avoid a feeling of rejection, and I was insulted that he destroyed our life together over a person of such low moral character and limited physical allure.

In many ways I tried to hold on to Boone, as he did me. I tried to let him work his way through what I believed to be a temporary lapse of judgment and see if there was anything salvageable.

I know the tighter you hold on to something, the harder it struggles to be free, and I badly needed to salvage my own dignity. Boone wouldn't let me go, and she wouldn't let him go, so I began the process of letting myself go.

Though Boone never indicated to me he wanted the house, I intercepted a text from his girlfriend clearly showing she expected me to move out so she could move in and complete her plot to take over what was left of the life we had together. I was told she felt she had done nothing wrong and, "It's not as if they are married" was the attitude she had in breaking up our home.

Boone's father owned the mortgage on our property, and he delivered the final blow to an already fragile and mistrustful relationship with an attempt to manipulate me out of our home without compensation. His father threatened me with a lawyer. I threatened him with a better one. Both his father and his girlfriend underestimated me. I researched my legal position long before I challenged him to a fight, and I knew exactly what could or could not be done. They were both unsuccessful, and I sit in what was formerly our home writing this today. But it is simply a house now, just a roof and some walls and a place to keep the things collected during our years together. I didn't fight for the house because it mattered to me. I fought for it so no one could take it from me. I refused to suffer one more humiliation at the hands of their ugly selfishness.

Boone's daughter Maggie and I grew close over the years. Her relationship with her father was a disappointment for her, and it suffered a crushing blow when he betrayed me. This was the second time in her life she watched her father selfishly destroy a home and hurt someone she loved. I appreciated her loyalty to me, but was truly saddened he had lost the opportunity to have at least one of his daughters in his life. It seemed he was determined to destroy everything good we'd built over ten years.

He ran wild with his woman and tried to recapture his lost youth. He went to bars, drank and partied, slept around (apparently with her blessing, and sometimes her participation), worked only as much as he had to, and spent every dime he had as if there was no tomorrow. He even moved to the most appropriate of places, the former whorehouse, The Sunset Lodge.

But every time he was lonely, tired, or scared, he showed up at my door. I had every right to turn him away, but I rarely could. He seemed so lost, so unsure of himself. He said he was sorry so many times it didn't mean anything anymore. His apologies were not followed by any significant change in behavior, and he never stayed long before becoming restless.

I recently heard it said, "Everyone has two faces, and you have to love both of them to make it work."

I did not love the face he was showing me. He was not the man I loved and thought I knew. He was growing ugly in my eyes, and he was living an ugly life that was painfully familiar to me. He wanted me to party with him. He told me I was too uptight and boring. He flaunted his lifestyle in my face, and I foolishly worried for his future and safety while my own was in jeopardy. He was like an errant teen, stubborn and self-righteous, and I the frustrated and worried parent, knowing bad things were coming and helpless to stop it. He knew he was fucking up, but was too proud to admit it, and not ready to stop. He defended his right to fuck up, and his mantra was, "Nobody is ever going to tell me what to do again."

I remember his telling me wearily, "You know, Pup, maybe they shouldn't let someone out of prison after keeping them so long. Maybe it's just where I belong."

He didn't know how to live in the world comfortably and confidently. He was one of those men I sat with at a table in Soledad who didn't have a clue how hard it was to make it in the world outside. I never thought it would be easy when he got out, but I didn't think it would be this hard, or end up the way it has, or I would most certainly have made different choices for myself.

I do not regret loving him, though I know now I loved him long past when he still deserved it. He gave me love and hope when I had so little. Boone carried me through the darkest hours of my life, and I felt I owed it to him to do the same. I fulfilled my obligation to him and to my own conscience. If that is ultimately the extent of our purpose in each other's lives, then it was not a failure on my part, but his betrayals were most assuredly a failure on his. Now it was time to step away.

I had better and more important people in my life that needed and deserved my attention far more than he did.

My mother came through her brain surgery, but not without complications. I planned to be there for her recovery, but she insisted I not come home while she was hospitalized. She wanted me to wait until we could have quality time together.

She knew of my problems with Boone. She was disappointed, but not judgmental of him. She said something I doubt I'll ever forget: "Oh, Honey, men just go through things. You only have two choices – you can wait them out or you can kick them out, but you're not gonna change them."

She was a compassionate woman who knew all too well the weaknesses of men. I have often told people throughout my life I was raised around strong women and weak men. The two people I loved most, Ma and Boone, showed me that hadn't changed.

As she grew near the end of her life, she cared less what others thought and spoke her mind in delightfully colorful language. I have always found it hysterical to hear an old lady tell someone to go fuck themselves, and my mother felt quite comfortable doing so when the opportunity warranted it. But always with a smile of mischief that seemed to say, "Look what I can get away with now I'm an old lady!"

I delighted in teasing my mother and making her laugh. She made me laugh too, with her blunt personality, humor, and old country wisdom.

I remember a game of Scrabble, where she tried to make up her own words and rules. I'm a stickler for the rules. We were equally competitive and both hated to lose. My mother was not my equal in vocabulary. As I challenged and frustrated her at every turn, she pushed the entire game off the table and said, "I'm not playing with you anymore. You're an asshole and a know-it-all!"

After having a shunt installed in her brain to drain fluids, she seemed to be relieved of the Alzheimer's and Parkinson's symptoms, and we renewed our hope for her recovery. Our hope didn't last long, as she traded one set of problems for another.

Suddenly, everything I loved most was slipping away. I felt so alone in South Carolina. These were not my people, or my life. I never stopped feeling foreign here. If it were not for Grandmother Jean, I felt I might die of loneliness. She was, and continues to be, a consistent source of friendship, comfort, and acceptance through several years of personal challenges and losses. She's the one I run to now that my mother is gone. She's lived almost ninety years now, and is a fountain of wisdom and a rock of stability. I can count on her, and she can count on me.

Boone could not decide who, or where, he wanted to be, and I suffered along with his indecision with little hope we could find our way out of the mess he'd made and back to what we once were. I was growing used to being alone, and was happy to keep his never-ending drama at a distance. I didn't have any heartache left for him by the time Ma had a stroke in June of 2009.

I needed to put everything else aside and be with her. She was in a rehab facility recovering from the stroke. It was the first time I'd ever gone home and she wasn't waiting for me on the front porch.

When I entered the facility and asked a nurse where to find my mother, she smiled and said, "She's been waiting for you all morning," and directed me to the physical therapy room.

A group of old people sat in a circle of wheelchairs

doing exercises prompted by a pretty, young therapist. I spotted Ma's curly silver hair before she spotted me. For an interminable moment I watched her, and saw the end of her life. I knew I only had a short time left to tell her, and show her, how much I loved her and how important she was to me and to our family. I wanted her only to see me as strong, confident and in control of my life, even though I didn't feel any of those things at the moment, so she wouldn't feel bad or worry about the things she couldn't change.

She looked up at me from that circle of infirmities and recognition lit her face with a crooked smile. Tears slid down her beautiful wrinkled face, and she reached out to me with both arms, like a mother beckoning a small child. I was a child again in that moment, in her eyes, and in my own heart.

Her voice, compromised by the stroke, but still my mother's, cried out, "Oh, I been waitin' for ya. You look so good, Honey!"

I went to my knees to hold her in the chair. As always, we both cried at being together again.

All the other old people in the circle were lit with smiles and some cried along with us. I imagine it was a touching moment to watch, and many wished it was them receiving a loved one long missed. Grandmother Jean once told me the worst part of being old was not having anything to look forward to. I never forgot that, because I understood it. Prison is like that for people never getting out.

Ma introduced me to her fellow patients. Her manner of speaking was halting and childlike, as if she was unsure she could be understood, "This is my son, Ernie. He lives away. He came to see me."

I felt the loneliness and impending death in the air of that room, and I was embarrassed by the needy look on the old people's faces, and embarrassed by my own discomfort and desire to flee. Part of me wanted to hug each one of them and make promises I couldn't keep just to make them happy for a while. Old people as individuals do not distress me as much as in groups. In a group, I feel overwhelmed by helplessness, and that is not a feeling I am familiar or comfortable with.

I wheeled her to the colorless, sterile room she lived in, and pulled up a chair beside her. I took her hand and said, "So what do you think is going on here, Ma?"

She said, "Well, I guess I'm on my way out, Ernie. I sure am tired of being cut open and takin' pills. Seems like it's one thing after another. Life ain't very fun anymore."

It broke my heart to see and hear her resignation. I never imagined her giving up.

I said, "Ma, you're not giving up, are you? You're still young. You need to fight this thing. You can't let it end in this little room. You're supposed to be at home with your loved ones all around you. When was the last time you went outside? It's beautiful out, flowers are blooming, the sun is out, let me take you outside."

She agreed to let me take her out. I got us coffee and wheeled her out into the garden. It was a beautiful June day. I found a bench in the sun, and lit a cigarette. She looked around sneakily and said, "Gimme one of those."

"A cigarette? No way. You quit. You're not supposed to smoke, and if we get caught, I'll get the blame."

My tough, rebellious, old mother surfaced in an instant, "Who gives a shit! What are they gonna do, throw me out? How much longer do you think I'm going to live, Ernie? They fix one thing and something else goes. Ya know, I never stopped wanting to smoke. Now give me a goddamn cigarette and shut the hell up about it. I'm still your mother, and can tell you what to do. It's my right!"

How could I say no? I love my coffee and cigarettes. When my time comes, I plan on having a cigarette in one hand and a coffee in the other, if I still want them. I gave her the cigarette. We smoked and drank our coffee together in the warm Maine sun. To the best of my knowledge, it was the last one she smoked, and I am damn glad I gave her one of life's little sinful pleasures to enjoy when most all the others were taken away.

I had an idea. "Ma, why don't you come home for a day? I want to see you at home. I'll get all the kids to come over just for a few hours."

She looked worried and said, "I don't know if I can, Honey. What if something happens? I don't know if they'll let me yet."

"Let you? This isn't a friggin' prison, Ma. It's a nursing home. You can come and go as you please. Nothing is going to happen. We'll take you right in that wheelchair. Don't you want to see your dog Rosie, and see your house?" I was surprised and annoyed that she was afraid to go home. I thought she would be eager.

She said, "I'll talk to Everett about it."

It was decided she would come home the next day for a few hours, and we would all be there. I was due to leave the following day, and I needed to have all my family together in our childhood home before I left. Too much was changing too quickly, and I needed something to be the way it had always been.

We were all there, on the front porch, like old times, laughing and teasing each other and showing off. Ma sat on her porch swing with Everett beside her and Rosie, her beloved Jack Russell, on her lap. She looked happy and pretty, in a yellow and white outfit I bought for her to wear home.

Every time I went home I made everyone huddle for a group picture, boys in the back, girls in the front, Ma in the center. The boys all grumbled, and the girls fussed over their hair: some things hadn't changed. This was the last picture taken of my mother and her eight kids together. The photo was taken in Ma's living room. When I enlarged it, I noticed the camera captured my stepfather through the window, standing alone on the porch. It could not have been more telling had I planned it. He was there in the picture with us, as he had been for forty-two years, but he was apart from his wife and her children. It makes me sad to look at that photo. It reminds me I never really had a dad.

Ma was at peace with the concept of dying. Far more than any of us who loved her. I asked her if she was afraid to die. She said, "A little bit."

I asked her if she believed in God or Heaven. She said, "I just don't know, Honey. I want to believe in Heaven. I want to see Mumma and Daddy again. I've never stopped missing my mother. I hope all you kids don't miss me as much as I missed her. But I just don't know. I wish I did."

Ma was always honest. She didn't always say what you wanted to hear. She said what she thought and felt. She told me she felt like a burden and she felt useless. Her life had become doctors, pills, and surgeries. She was always in pain. If she couldn't get better, she wanted to die.

I said yet another tearful goodbye on the front porch of my childhood home, but not before I exacted a promise that she would work hard at the rehab so she could come back home.

She did exactly that and was home within a few weeks. I called nearly every day to encourage her and lift her spirits. She was afraid to be left alone, so family and friends took turns keeping her company when Everett was not home.

I came back to my empty home in South Carolina, greeted only by my pets and my now unwanted responsibilities. I owned a home and a business I couldn't walk away from, no matter how much I wanted to. I'd beaten the odds. I was clean more than eleven years. With seventy-eight percent of convicts returning to prison within a year of release, and recovery from methamphetamine addiction in the single digits, I had won the battle. So why did I feel like I was losing the war?

All I really wanted was to be back in California, to disappear among the crowds and chaos of familiar city life. It's too loud inside my head when left in the quiet. Once again I felt like I had the recipe for happiness, but none of the ingredients.

I was approaching fifty years of age. Mine is a difficult profession to grow old in. I've spent thirty years in a mirror, day after day, hour after hour, watching every wrinkle and gray hair appear, uninvited and unwelcomed, searching for that next nip or tuck that would prolong the inevitable cruelties of nature. It was coming at me like a freight train. I really hadn't thought all that much about aging. I'd lived my life at breakneck speed and never really grasped the concept of middle age. It seemed I was always young. Even when life was grueling, I felt like I had all the time in the world to reach the stars with the fire of youth fueling me. Often I was fueled by anger and rebellion against the ignorant and callous, determined to never let them see me sweat and never see me break. I don't feel all that angry anymore. Sometimes I'm scared, but I've come to believe once you survive all the worst things you thought could ever happen to you, it takes quite a lot to get you really scared. I'm a little scared of being unattractive or ignored. I'm scared of the idea of being old and infirm and having to rely on others. I saw what that did to my mother's spirit, and she had so many who loved her and were concerned for her wellbeing. But I understood she was always an independent woman, and that independence was taken away.

I'd spent so much of the past fifty years in some form of detachment from others. Through drugs or simple geographic location, I kept the people that mattered to me most at a comfortable distance. I suppose I may pay my price for that when there is no one around to mourn my passing.

At fifty, I've become envious of my siblings' children and grandchildren. Everything is always growing and changing for them. They always have something to talk about. I am often told I would have been a good parent. I'm not so sure about that. I was so troubled and self-indulgent. At least I was only responsible for screwing up one life, instead of an entire family. My kids would have thought me overbearing, neurotic and embarrassingly emotional. And I might have drowned them all the first time I had to stay home from a party for lack of a sitter, or if one dropped ice cream on my Persian rug.

I have my four-legged children that bring me comfort and the unconditional love nearly impossible to find in human beings. It's so unfair their life spans are so short, and one must suffer the pangs of grief and loss too often. I've outlived a lot of pets, and far too many peers, in my short time on this planet. I've noticed it has become easier to love and harder to lose.

After my mother's passing, Grandmother Jean repeated a quote to me, "Each death diminishes me."

I've played that quote over and over in my head in an attempt to discern its deepest meaning. I imagine it might mean something different to someone nearly ninety years old, as she is.

Perhaps I am diminished because those that are a part of my life are also a part of me, and each takes a piece of me with them. There are fewer people to share my history and my memories. Perhaps it is simply because each death reminds me of my own mortality, or my pointless search for perfection in an imperfect world.

I've had no huge intellectual or spiritual epiphanies yet. Only small ones strung together to create a chain I grip tenuously while suspended over the abyss of idiocy.

I suspect I may be more forgiving than in my youth,

with so many of my own mistakes behind me to keep me humble. I've become a bit more self-deprecating and learned to laugh at myself when I catch myself, or others, being altogether too human.

I've learned to be rigorously honest with myself and others about who I think I am, and invite them to do the same. I've learned to listen a little more and talk a little less. I was always a good talker, but not always a good listener.

I have more desire to be close to my family and the trusted friends of the past and less desire to make new ones. Besides Grandmother Jean, I have made more than a few enduring friendships since moving to South Carolina. But I know we are fortunate to find even a few that survive the test of time and troubles.

My brothers and sisters have all grown into middle age and beyond. We have all grown softer with old age staring us in the face, and it seems we all look for our mother in each other and in ourselves. Disease and disabilities have come to remind us our generation is the next to go.

We are her legacy. Eight children, and over fifty grandchildren and great-grandchildren, even a handful of great-great-grandchildren, scattering the countryside of Maine, and a few outside of it. None is rich or famous, none is a genius or philanthropist, but all are good, kind people she was proud of.

Gabrielle

I heard an angel's song today
It sang out clear and bright
It came to claim one of its own
and take her to the light
It saw our tears and heard our cries
and said kindly, "She is well."
It wrapped its wings around the child
and whispered, "Gabrielle"
It sang out, "Come and fly with me,
To a place painless and free,
open up the heavens Lord,
I bring a child to thee."
It spread its wings and leapt and soared
then disappeared from sight
Above its song I clearly heard
a child laughing with delight.

E.M.

Chapter Thirteen
Solace

I came home to South Carolina with the heaviest of hearts. I could see my mother was tired of living; Boone had gone off to find what he thought he'd lost; I was approaching fifty years of age and had not a clue what my next move was supposed to be. There must be another adventure waiting for me. There always is. I was never one to stand still for very long. There's a fire that burns in me to see, feel, be and know as much as I can before something stops me. Life still excites me. Even when it's bad, it's better than having nothing to talk about. I've crammed a lot of living into a pretty short time so far, and I have no intention of sitting still for long. My life is about as mellow as I can stand in this sleepy little southern town. It's quiet and peaceful here. It's been a perfect place to write a story. A perfect place to reflect on the past and prepare for the future, though I suspect my future will take me far from here.

Boone knew I was upset about my mother, and I knew he was trying to be a supportive friend without much commitment. Regardless of where he was or what he was doing, I knew he was only a phone call away and would rush to my side if I needed him. He loved to view himself as the hero, but he could never make it last. I chose stoicism and solitude. He destroyed my trust in him as a partner and a friend, and he could do nothing except add to my pain.

I learned much about him during this time that I hadn't known. I didn't know he was such a conflicted man. He wrestled with who he thought he was and who he wanted to be. His impulses and desires overshadowed his love and commitments. Boone felt entitled to do what he'd wanted and missed during his twenty years in prison. He seemed frustrated with his inability to convince me to see things his way.

I learned he had only two avenues to improve his self-esteem: his work and his body building. He did both with a vengeance, and what little was left was scattered on the winds of his unfulfilled desires.

I learned that he'd never forgiven himself for his past, and it stands in the way of his happiness. His sex-offender status puts limitations in his life that make it impossible to feel he has paid his debt to society, and he resents it. That resentment simmers beneath his surface. My wish for him was he that could find joy in the small pleasures in life and freedom, and accept responsibility for his conditions. He made the choices many years ago that set the future in motion; no one made them for him. I wished for him to feel as I did, that my worse days in the free world are better than my best days in prison. I don't think he felt that way. Prison doesn't just keep you away from the world; it keeps the world away from you. You can be whoever you want to be and guard your secrets from those that judge. There are no bills to pay, no families to please, no cars that break down, and time just stands still. All you have to do is survive. That's the one thing he knew how to do.

In prison he had friendships of many years with men who were not better than him. He learned how to survive in there, and command a respect his past does not allow him in the free world. I saw his struggles, and knew there was nothing I could do to help him anymore. He stepped away from me. He chose a different path, and it was time for me to find my own life without him. I did not wish him ill will, nor did I wish him happiness. I only wished him gone, and all the heartache with him.

It was only a month after my mother came home from rehab when my brother called to tell me she'd had a severe stroke and I should come right away. I'd spoken to her nearly every day. She was doing well in her recovery, and was happy to be home. I had myself convinced that she would recover completely and live a long time.

Everett woke one morning to find her unable to move or speak. She was taken to intensive care.

I flew out that night after reluctantly enlisting Boone to care for my pets and home. He offered to go with me, but I didn't want him present for my family's pain, or my own. I was very hurt by the choices he'd made that turned my happy life upside down, and I didn't have it in me to suffer for more than one person at a time.

Ma could barely speak or move when I arrived at the hospital, but she seemed to be somewhat aware of what was happening to her. The doctors said she was bleeding into her brain and they couldn't stop it. She squeezed my hand and responded to my voice. She knew I was there. She was my mother; I could tell she knew I was there.

She looked beautiful. It seemed the lines had fallen away from her face. Her hair was sparkling silver-white, and her eyes were as blue as I imagined the heavens to be. They glittered and shone like diamonds. It took me back to my first sight of Jenny in the coma. How could someone so traumatized look so beautiful? Perhaps that's what it's like to be relieved of all your cares and the worries of the world. It had been many years since her eyes were so clear and blue.

ICU allowed only three people at a time to visit, but the waiting room was full of Ma's friends and family. There was no laughter or jokes at this gathering. There was no hope in the air. Everyone knew we were there to say goodbye.

The nurses in ICU were angels of mercy. I learned it takes a very special person to do their job well. To be surrounded with pain, grief, and loss daily and to still remain compassionate and patient is a true gift. They orchestrated the patients and family with a delicacy and professionalism admirable in such an emotionally charged environment.

I spent the next three days and nights only leaving Ma's side for short intervals to feed myself, smoke furiously in the hospital parking lot, or allow others "alone time" with her. I slept on a large padded window seat that gave a fabulous third floor view of the old Maine city I knew from my youth. I was born in that very hospital my mother was dying in. I'd celebrated Jenny's birth and agonized over her tragedy on the floor below. I walked those very streets as an angry, lonely teen, looking for something that didn't have a name or address. It was only a few blocks away from The Blue Swan, my first gay bar. I gazed out that window for hours on end and remembered where my life started, in the company of the woman who gave it to me. And I knew the only thing that really connected me to it all was going to be gone, and I would no longer have a home to go back to.

I'm sure losing our mother was no less painful for my siblings, but somehow I think it was different for me. They all lived in Maine. They had lives and families that would go on as they always had. They weren't losing home. Ma was home for me. Through all my wanderings, trials and troubles, I always knew if things got too bad for me I could always go home. I never needed to, but I always knew I could. She was the main highway to my roots, and my roots were buried deep in Maine soil.

Maine people are unique in many ways, and anyone who has never been there could not possibly understand why I say this. I would challenge anyone who has been there to say there is anyone else like a Mainer. I've grown to have a great sense of pride in my people and their earthy individuality and gritty, sometimes hostile, view of the world outside theirs. In general, they view honesty, however harsh, as the greatest virtue, and phoniness as a cause for swift judgment. I come from people that believe dignity is more important than wealth, and responsibility is more important than vanity. I come from people who might wear the same pair of jeans all week but would give you the shirt off their backs if they only owned two. And I come from people who would rather be dragged through the mud than admit they are wrong if they don't believe it.

If you have only been to the tourist infested coast of Maine, perverted by the transplants drawn to its rustic beauty and charm, and distorted by their foreign wealth, then you have not seen the real Maine.

The real Maine is the families hundreds of years old, deep in the forests and dotted along the country roads, that never left the state for more than a weekend vacation to New Hampshire in between the long months of back-breaking work and bitter winters.

The real Maine is the harsh country life of denim and flannel, snow shovels and factories, where women work right alongside their men, and often in place of them.

The real Maine is the Maine of my childhood. Things have changed a bit with big box stores and the internet, but not as fast as it's changed in most other places. The true Maine people hold on stubbornly to the values and a way of life that will never be understood by someone not born there and without hundreds of years of tradition running through their veins. These are my people.

My heritage lay in a bed only a few feet from me drawing her last breaths and not at any time in my fifty years of living did where I came from mean so much to me. I was proud to be the sixth child of Lottie Jane Field. My mother left everyone better for having known her. I didn't know how to begin to say goodbye.

In this past year of writing nothing has been so painful as these last pages. I know now, to write well you can't just remember. You have to relive, and I must let her die all over again. I have put down my pen and walked away a dozen times avoiding it.

She spasmed and twitched, she babbled incoherently and every so often she focused and spoke a few words clearly. Every one of those moments of clarity was like a shower of golden hope on my breaking heart. I looked for wisdom and meaning in every word. We even had a moment of laughter together, when she looked directly at me and shouted, "This is bullshit!"

For just that precious moment she was my Ma again, and I laughed at her crooked smile of satisfaction that she had managed to communicate her feelings. "Bullshit" was one of my Ma's favorite words, and somewhere throughout the years I adopted it as my own.

Each time I squeezed her hand, she squeezed back. I didn't really know if it was voluntary, but it seemed she was only restful when someone held her hand. Otherwise, she was frightened and frustrated. She was my mother, I knew her every gesture and nuance.

I stood beside her and said, "Ma, I hate this. I hate it all so much. It feels so unfair!"

With the half of her body she could move, she shrugged. I knew that shrug. I'd seen it a thousand times before. It was a shrug of acceptance and resignation. That was the shrug she gave when she was telling you that some things in life can't be changed. It was the shrug she gave when she said, "Oh well, Honey, what can ya do? I told ya life ain't fair." It was the shrug that told me it was all over. I have seen that shrug a thousand times more in my mind since she died, and it always makes me so sad.

Mothers and their gay sons often have unique bonds. I have met few gay men in my life that were not especially close to their mothers. Perhaps it's because no other woman takes their place in our hearts. I know no other woman ever replaced my mother in mine. The closest I have come then or since is my dear Grandmother Jean. She was and is a godsend of a friend and mother figure, and I pray I will not have to say goodbye to her anytime soon.

So few words passed between us the last days of her life, but we were at peace with each other and little needed to be said.

The second night I spent in her room was more difficult than the first. Everett and my brother Bucky were there with me when she began to cry out and thrash in what appeared to be pain. I couldn't bear seeing my mother in pain. She was the one who soothed others' pain. I buried my face in a pillow and sobbed in anguish for her pain and my helplessness. I ran for a nurse. I asked her if she thought Ma was in pain, and she said there was no way of knowing what she could feel. I told her, "If there's no way of knowing, then we have to do something to be sure she is not. We can't let her suffer. Please do something."

Everett and Bucky were equally distressed at what we were witnessing and both agreed something had to be done to insure she was not in pain. The nurse quickly obtained approval to administer morphine and she quieted.

During the days I was at her side I observed the procession of sorrow that came to mourn her end. Dozens of family and friends wove in and out of that room, but the wee hours were ours alone. I was moved that she was so loved, and I respected the pain outside my own, for each one had a special relationship with her that no one else was a part of. She was one who listened closely to the lives of others and cared deeply for each one's happiness.

The morphine quieted her but she spoke very little from that point on. On that second night, a nurse came to me with hospital pants, shaving gear, soaps and towels, and said, "Honey, why don't you take a shower and shave and a little nap? I promise I will sit here with Lottie the whole time you're gone. You need to give yourself a break." When I told her a staff member told me I was not allowed to use my mother's bathroom, her eyes narrowed, and she said, "Well, I'm running this place tonight and I say you can!"

After I showered I curled up on my window seat and told my favorite nurse in the whole world the stories of my extraordinary mother and her life. I wanted her to know she was not just another person passing through this hospital. I wanted her to know she was in the presence of someone really special. I think by night's end I achieved that goal. She said to me, "Your mother is a lucky woman to be so loved. I wish I'd known her."

I blushed a bit when she told me I'd charmed every nurse on her staff. She told me they said they all hoped their own children loved them as much as I loved my mother. They brought me coffee, covered me with blankets when I dozed off, and tended to my mother with gentle affection. They were angels tending to one of their own. They were mothers caring for a queen among mothers. I will love every one of those women for the rest of my days for the way they cared for both of us.

On my last morning with her I woke with the sunrise. The old city of Lewiston, Maine, was shrouded in a light mist. In the mist, between the old church spires and massive brick factories, a dozen brightly colored hot air balloons slowly rose with the sun. The only sound in the room was the beep of monitors and Ma breathing. It was an ethereal sight and sound. I tend to associate unusual occurrences with a higher meaning. I don't think it's an uncommon thing to do. My people are inherently superstitious, and I was looking for the supernatural in my melancholy. My heavy heart wondered for a long moment if the balloons were a sign or a message from the world outside that it knew it was her time to rise from this earth too.

Ma's doctor wanted to meet with her family to explain his prognosis and allow us to make the necessary decisions as a family. Once gathered, he told us she suffered extensive brain damage, and it was doubtful she would recover any more than she was at the moment. She would not walk, talk or feed herself. She would require twenty-four hour care, and could not go home. All hope was gone.

Everett wanted her to come home at any cost, but he knew it was not what she wanted. We all knew. She said it too many times to ignore. She did not want to be kept alive in that state. She told us all at some point, "You just let me die." That was an order, not a request.

It was decided she would be moved to hospice, where she could die with dignity and comfort. She would leave late that afternoon. There was no way to know how long it would take for her to pass. I didn't know what to do. I'd only allowed myself a few days away, but had no problem staying as long as necessary. My family told me I was there when it mattered. She didn't know any different now, and I should tend to my life in the South.

I didn't want to see my mother dead. I have avoided the dead all my years of living, as I never wanted my last view of a loved one to be lifeless. I wondered if I was being selfish, leaving my siblings to deal with all the worst parts of family life while I went off to my own life away. Isn't that the way it always was with me?

I had only a few hours left in which to say goodbye. I felt too weak to stand. I pulled a chair close and lay my head next to hers on the pillow. I spoke softly, and told her how much I loved her. I told her what a good mother and friend she was to me. I told her I was going to try to be the very best person I could be so, if there is a heaven, I could go there and be with her again. I told her I was sure our lives were just a blink of an eye in the timeless expanse of heaven, and we would all be together again in the time it took to wake from a nap. I told her she was beautiful.

It wasn't just my imagination that she looked like an angel, her hair a silver cloud, her eyes glittering jewels as blue as any dream of a god's home. She smiled often in her sleep. Wherever she was, I prayed she dreamed only of beautiful things. I wouldn't have been a bit surprised had she sprouted a pair of big, white wings and flown away at any moment.

Only minutes before hospice arrived to transport her to her final destination on this earth, she squeezed my hand and managed to say the last three words I heard my mother speak. Her voice was cracked and tired, but emphatic. She said, "Ready to go!"

A dagger of pain pierced my heart with those words. I wanted to tell her, "No, Ma, don't say that. Don't quit trying. I'm not ready for you to go."

But I didn't, because I knew it wasn't the right thing to do. I had no right to make her feel bad about wanting it to be over. She had suffered enough now. I didn't want anyone to coerce her in to hanging on to a life she didn't want anymore. I kissed her soft cheeks and hands a dozen times each before they took her away. That was the last time I saw my mother. She died a week later.

I returned to South Carolina the night she moved to the hospice. She didn't know me anymore. I'm told she had moments of vague lucidity over the next week, but for the most part the morphine kept her far away.

I called every day, and every day I fought with myself not to board a plane back to Maine.

When the call came that she was gone, I felt the life go right out of me. My sweet mother was dead. I wept inconsolably, and imagined my life without her strength, humor and love.

I dreamed of her that night.

There was a field of long, green grass. The wind moved it gently. The sky was clear blue. She descended swiftly to the center of the field on white wings twice the size of her body. She wrapped her wings around me and held me to her breast. It was so vivid I felt the feathers brushing my skin. She was healthy and whole again. She glowed and smiled and stroked my hair. I felt her heart beat against my cheek.

I know it was just a dream, but it was a beautiful dream, and it made me feel better. I wished for that dream many nights after but I never had it again.

There was a viewing and a family burial service of Lottie Jane's ashes. I did not attend. I refused to see my mother's lifeless body, and I don't regret it. I remember being frightened by my Grandmother Fannie's corpse, and now my mother's remains are beside her. Everett spared no expense on the headstone that bears both their names and awaits him. He has not taken his wife's death well. I'm told he sits alone in silence in the same chair in our kitchen window he sat in for nearly forty years. I imagine he is like the rest of us and thinks of the many things he wished he'd done differently. We speak occasionally, and he never fails to remind me how much he misses her. I recall him saying once, "Ya know, Ernie, somebody ought to figure out a way for you to go together when you been with someone that long." His unending sadness makes me think he might have a good point there.

My brother Lloyd said that in her last days, the family

stood around her talking about the past and out of the blue she said, "I'd do it all again!" It made me happy to hear that. It means she loved her life, and that's all I ever wanted for her.

They said that in her final hours, a woman came to her side and played the harp. She was humming to the harp when she died. I found the image devastatingly poignant, and have carried it with me since. If there's a heaven, I know she's there. If there are angels, I know she's one. If there's a God, I know she's with my grandmother Fannie, laughing and happy and waiting for her children to be with her again. If there are no Gods, no angels, no heavens, then at least I know she is at peace. At the very least, death has to promise us that.

Boone pretended to be there for me. He was there to console me when the call came to tell me she was gone. But he was there for the wrong reasons. He was there because it would have made him look heartless if he wasn't. He was there out of some misplaced sense of duty, so it wasn't long before I sent him away again. He was never far away if I wanted him, and sometimes I did, but I resented his self-absorption at a time when I thought it should have been all about me. His girlfriend was bitterly jealous of any time he spent with me, and it seemed he was always being pulled away by some drama she conjured. The very thought of her nauseated me, and I resented them both for their intrusion on my grief. I just wanted solitude and peace. I needed to think, and breathe, and hurt. He tormented me with more promises he could not keep; not because he loved me, but because he was afraid to be without me. He played games with both my head and my heart when both were too weak to win. He continued to break every promise he made soon after he made them. He was incapable of being honest with me or himself.

Finally I came to the realization that if I could face each day without my beloved mother, I could certainly do without him.

He said he was sorry for all he had done to hurt me, but it never showed in his eyes or actions. He spoke apologies, but did nothing to correct his wrongs. I could see the man who left behind a trail of pain for nearly thirty years in the flat blue steel of his selfish eyes. The pinwheels of blue in his eyes were gone with all his promises. His self-righteous indignation at being held accountable, and his unreasonable sense of entitlement at any cost snapped the few threads of respect I had left for him. My love for him was undergoing yet another slow painful death at a time when I thought I could bear no more.

My father died just as I am finishing this book. He never did a single thing for me in his life, but I can now thank him for the generous timing of his death to close my story.

I've given his death far more than I expected to. Without the agony of loss I experienced with my mother's death, I've explored my thoughts and feelings about his passing. My mother's death required no exploration. I knew exactly how I felt, and it was predictable and appropriate for a son who lost his mother. I find I resent my father taking up undeserved space in my head. I wished him misery and suffering for much of my life. His slow death by suffocation with lung cancer granted my wish, and the scant few who mourned his passing did indeed validate my predictions of a lonely justice. In his death, new life is breathed into my anger and disappointment. His death brought me none of the satisfaction I thought I deserved. It only brought sadness with the knowledge that it is finally too late. It will never be fixed, and all that is left is to place him among the ranks of all the others I've let go. There was nothing left to say to him. He was a stranger to me. Two people could not have been more different than my parents. I surmise their warring genes may be partially responsible for the turbulent aspects of my own life and character. I'm hopeful that the quality of my mother's heart will continue to win the battle over the darkness of my father's soul for what's left of my life.

I know what real pain is. I know the anguish in a mother's eyes for her dying child. I know just how hard a heart can break when it's betrayed. I know the triumph in creating something beautiful and good, and I know the shame in destroying it. I know the humiliation of being a prisoner, and the dignity it takes to rise above it. I know the fear of aloneness and the wisdom in solitude. I know what death smells and feels like. I've been too close too many times now to forget it. And I know beauty. I know the beauty of true love and commitment. I know the beauty of freedom and independence. I know the beauty of lasting friendship and devoted family. I know the beauty of laughter. And I know that I am a survivor, and that I will never have to survive another loss as great as the loss of my mother. With all the ugly things I saw in my life, I never stopped seeing the beauty all around me, and I have never stopped laughing.

And I've learned to let go. I've learned that we spend the better part of our youth obtaining the things we think we need to be happy, and the rest of our lives learning how to let go of those things. Youth, beauty, money, love, power ... it's all only borrowed, not owned. We are all headed to the same destination, and we're not taking any of it with us. I live for today and I give it my best. I am happy. I am whole. I am evolving.

Solace

In the reaches of my craving soul
there is solace to be found
Where demons waged their lethal wars
not on air or ground
but inside me
where none can see
beneath a surface slick and proud.
Now my domain
has wrought the change
that lifts the desperate shroud
Now light and space
occupy the place
that once was a demons lair
For they cannot haunt, torment and taunt
a place of peace and prayer.

E.M.

Epilogue

The world around me has changed a lot in fifty years. Not as much as I'd hoped for my gay brothers and sisters, or for the kindness and compassion of mankind in general, but still we have come a long way from The Blue Swan of the 1970s and the hordes of beautiful dying young men of the '80s and '90s. Gays are allowed to marry in thirty-six states now, including the one I live in. Though I find it uncomfortable that my culture continues to be a subject of social debate, and there are still those that spew unreasonable hatred over the questions of equality, I am encouraged by the progress we have made in joining the rest of the world as legitimate members of society. I am always saddened by the news of young gays committing suicide as a result of bullying in our schools. I remember the torture heaped upon me and wish somehow they could know what I know now: that there is another side to it, and they can have a happy life far away from the cruelties of children and the ignorant people who bred them. The young gays should learn their history and bow their heads in respect to those who suffered to pave the way for them to an easier life we only dreamed of, and continue to fight for the freedom and happiness of those who will come after.

I am still standing behind the hairdresser's chair after thirty-four years. I still swap stories, laughter and tears with my clients and still continue to create friendships with the most unlikely of people that I know will last a lifetime. I still love what I do, and I still love my fellow humans and all their beauty and imperfections.

I have not grown used to a world without my mother, but I have learned to live in it. She still comes to me a dozen times a day in a song or a flower or a funny joke. Part of me wishes she could read this book and the rest of me is glad she didn't have to know everything about my life. It would have hurt her too much, and she would have tried to take blame that does not belong to her. I love to tell stories of her to the younger generation of our family so they can pass her on to their children someday.

My stepfather, Everett, recently died of lung cancer. I had not seen him, or returned to Maine, since the death of my mother. We were not close when my mother was alive and her death did nothing to change that. I spoke to him regularly out of obligation, but not affection. He was a difficult man to talk to and a difficult man to love. He was my stepfather for forty-seven years and I did not love him. I never believed he was good enough for my mother. I did not see the respect and affection I knew she deserved when she was alive. I only saw grief and loss when she was gone, when it was too late.

Everett knew, and resented, the obvious fact that Ma loved her children more than she loved him, and I believe he never forgave us for that. He seized his last opportunity to show us how he felt by directly betraying my mother's wishes to share all of their life's possessions equally among their eleven children and gave everything to his three daughters. I could not have cared less about the money or how he felt about me. But I care very much that he had so little respect for her wishes and the hurt he caused my younger siblings who saw him as their own father. My mother would be devastated and outraged. I am confident that wherever she may be, he is not with her and she is perfectly fine with that.

It's been several years since I last saw Boone.

I was saddened, but not shocked, when he was publicly named a person of interest in the disappearance of a young girl. It appears the police had little more than suspicion, as he is still a free man. But seeing his face and name in the papers one more time served as a not-so-gentle reminder to me that Boone will always be a suspect, and I am grateful to be free of the bondage of his past and future. My bitterness and anger is gone, and so is the passion I felt for him. I am miles away from the person that fell in love in that prison cell, and Boone is living a life that fits him. I realize that our purpose in each other's lives is fulfilled, and all is as it's meant to be.

Both of Boone's parents are dead now; his mother in an apparent overdose and his father with a self-inflicted gunshot to the head three weeks later. My heart went out to Boone for his loss, but there was really no other way for people like them to leave this world. They never were very sane to begin with, and age and mental illness won that war of weaknesses.

Grandmother Jean is in her 90's now and remains my dearest friend. She has outlived all her friends and family, and I have gladly taken on the role of primary caregiver and honorary grandson. She has not seen or spoken to Boone since we parted. She told me more than once that she has no interest in someone who would treat me so badly, and he has not made a single effort to contact her.

Just as I grew comfortable with being alone, just as I began to believe that there were no more great loves for me, and I had resigned myself to permanent bachelor status, just as I had stopped searching, hoping, needing, something or someone, to make me feel complete, I met my beautiful Argentinian lover, Steven.

I never saw it coming, but it was love at first sight, or something close.

A chance dinner with some lady friends, at a new Italian bistro in our town, brought me face to face with the handsomest man I have ever seen.

Six feet tall, slender, with lush, dark, wavy hair just beginning to gray, full, soft lips and perfect white teeth above a strong squared jaw, his lilting accent and dark, soulful eyes captivated my love of masculine beauty, and I was shameless in my pursuit of his attention.

I called two of my closest girlfriends and enlisted them to help me stalk him.

We returned to the restaurant a few days later and I boldly offered him a haircut. When he came to get his haircut, I asked him for a date.

Though I struggled to keep an air of dignity and confidence, I was terrified.

I didn't know if I could love again. I was so broken, damaged, and weary. I didn't know if I could ever trust another man after Boone's betrayal. I didn't know if I could trust myself anymore to know a good person when I met one. But I could not stop thinking about Steven. I had to try, one last time.

At the closing of our second date I was rewarded for my efforts with a kiss on a dark street, lit only by the stars, that shook me to the core of my soul and set in motion what may very well be the last time I ever fall in love. In that kiss, all the years, all the pain, all the losses and disappointments, fell away from my heavy heart and I am renewed. In that kiss I became suddenly grateful to Boone for his infidelities. Otherwise I may have not been free to meet and fall in love with the man that seems to have been made for me.

Steven's booming laugh and playfully boyish nature, his long passionate kisses and positive energy, make me young again in my heart and soul. He brings out the best in me and I am preoccupied with finding ways to make him smile. He reminds me of who I am meant to be. I am a man who loves with wild abandon and holds back nothing. I am a man determined to squeeze every drop of pleasure from this life before it is over and I am dust.

We are both excited and a little frightened of the fire ignited between us. We are both men who have walked through the fire and been burned. We are both men in our middle age who have recovered from the reckless-ness of our youth and are ready for something sweet and beautiful and forever. Steven is my reward for not break-ing. Steven is my nectar of the gods. I wake each morn-ing to gaze upon my good fortune and drink his beauty and sweet nature. He has been received with gratitude and love by all who love me, and his beautiful family has embraced me as one of their own. I am a happy man and I will forever be indebted to my beautiful Argentine for showing me that I can still love truly, madly and deep-ly, and that my struggles have not destroyed what is best in me.

I am found.

Acknowledgments

Many thanks to Kimberly Duncan for being my first reader and supporter. To Bruce and Penne Warner, Kelli and Jim Silliman, Tony and Brandy DeHaas, Pete and Veronique Stevens, Rod and David Ortiz-Laurent, and The Grahams for our wonderful friendships and making us part of your families. And so much love to my Southern sisters Kayren and Grace, who took me in their lives and hearts and taught me the Southern ways.

Thank you to Norm for being the best big brother a guy could need.

Thank you to Grandmother Jean for her unconditional love and picking up where Ma left off.

Special thanks to Mary Fitzhugh for her recommendations, Caroline Evans for her awesome editing skills, Kathi Bixler for the drawings of my tattoos, and Anne Malarich for her photographic work on the cover design.

High honors go to my darling Karen Yaniga for her praise, support and friendship, and for putting the manuscript in the right hands.

Thank you, Linda Ketron, for being "the right hands." For your love and devotion to the arts, your energy, your vision, your kind heart, and for making this all happen for me. You are a treasure to me and our community.

The highest of honors goes to my beautiful fiancee and best friend, Steven Gonzalo. Thank you for your beautiful laugh, your perfect heart, and your unconditional love. Thank you for mending my broken heart and making me whole again. Thank you for the life and love I thought I might never have. And thank you for almost always letting me have my way. Thank you Esteven for my incredible Argentinian family. Our gorgeous Mama Maria, sister Cindy and "the kids"... Devin, Amie, Jake, Jalen and our sweet little Sophie, thank you for accepting me as your Tio.

And thank you to my brothers and sisters for being part of my story. Lloyd, Rose, Norm, Bucky, Tina, Harold and Johnny, I haven't forgotten you...

CPSIA information can be obtained
at www.ICGtesting.cqm
Printed in the USA
BVHW070805020622
638503BV00016B/680

9 781941 069707